Collective Choice
in Education

STUDIES IN PUBLIC CHOICE

Gordon Tullock, *Editor*
Virginia Polytechnic Institute and State University

Other Volumes in the Series:

James M. Buchanan and Richard E. Wagner, *Fiscal Responsibility in Constitutional Democracy*, 1978
Richard B. McKenzie, *The Political Economy of the Educational Process*, 1979
Richard D. Auster and Morris Silver, *The State as a Firm*, 1979
James B. Kau and Paul H. Rubin, *Congressmen, Constituents, and Contributors: The Determinants of Roll Call Voting in the House of Representatives*, 1982

This series, like the journal *Public Choice*, is devoted to an important aspect of the interaction between the disciplines of economics and political science: the application of economic methods of analysis to matters that have traditionally been regarded as political in nature. The objective of these publications is to further the growth of knowledge in this intersection of the social sciences.

Collective Choice in Education

Edited by
Mary Jean Bowman
The University of Chicago

Kluwer·Nijhoff Publishing
BOSTON/THE HAGUE/LONDON

DISTRIBUTORS FOR NORTH AMERICA:
Kluwer Boston, Inc.
190 Old Derby Street
Hingham, Massachusetts 02043, U.S.A.

DISTRIBUTORS OUTSIDE NORTH AMERICA:
Kluwer Academic Publishers Group
Distribution Centre
P.O. Box 322
3300 AH Dordrecht, The Netherlands

Library of Congress Cataloging in Publication Data

Main entry under title:
Collective choice in education.

    (Studies in public choice;   )
    Includes index.
    1. Education–United States–Finance–Congresses.
2. Education–Great Britain–Finance–Congresses.
3. Social choice–Congresses. I. Bowman, Mary Jean.
II. Series.
LB2824.C58   379.1'2'0973   81-20777

ISBN 0–89838–091–X   AACR2

Contents

Collective Choice
in Education

Introduction

The persistently increasing scale and complexity of government, of quasi-public organizations, and of private organizations pose many problems in the economics of collective choice. Moreover, education as a quasi-public good has drawn ever more heavily on public budgets. Yet economic research into collective behavior with respect to education has been sparse (with the partial exception of recent work on teacher unions). In view of these trends, it was decided that the third conference under the Ford-sponsored U.K./U.S. Programme in the Economics of Education should make the high-risk effort of encouraging and bringing together studies relating to collective choice in education, with some emphasis on studies in educational finance. The conference exploited opportunities for an exchange of ideas between economists in the United Kingdom and in the United States; there were special gains that could come from such an interchange. British and American economists do share a common inheritance that goes back to Benthamite utilitarianism and a common training in neo-classical economic theory even when one or both of these is challenged (which happens, of course, on both sides of the Atlantic). They share also a culture of political democracy despite important dissimilarities in governmental structures and institutions. These commonalities and contrasts facilitate comparative testing of analyses developed in either setting. There also are some important differences in the aspects of collective choice that have received attention and in the leading analytical models that have been developed recently on the two sides of the Atlantic. By bringing together some of the main streams of research with applications to education, we might gain a more balanced assessment of promising approaches. The present conference volume reflects these hopes.

The term 'collective choice' is interpreted broadly in line with the criteria just outlined. Although emphasis is primarily on newer developments, older types of welfare analyses are included. The development of an important and highly technical theory of 'optimal taxation' (which has been more important in British than in American work) is applied to issues of finance in higher education. Other starting points derive from theories of decision-making in non-profit organizations and in labor-managed cooperatives. However, the literature on unions among teachers is represented only indirectly, since this has been the least neglected aspect of economic analysis of collective behavior in education.

Collective choice as a process is at the heart of the literature usually labeled 'public choice,' which is examined in an admirable survey by D. C. Mueller (*Public Choice*, Cambridge University Press, 1979). He distinguishes two main branches of this work. The 'positive' branch applies an economic analysis based on models of rational behavior to the study of collective decisions, which may be but are not necessarily public in a narrow sense. This rich and diverse literature (which has evolved primarily in the United States) usually assumes an underlying consensus with respect to the fundamental priorities and rules of the game – the 'constitutional base' of collective decision-making. The second, 'normative,' branch deals with the nature of those constitutional rules, whether in a logical-philosophical mode or (extremely rarely) as an attempt to examine how such a fundamental consensus might be brought about. Work in the logical-philosophical mode has a long history, but it has emerged recently in new formulations and with a new vitality in both Britain and the United States. Four or five of the papers in this volume either are rooted in or draw on the positive economics of public choice (as I shall point out in the comments that follow). What Mueller classifies as the normative branch emerges in these papers only indirectly, as an analysis that bridges positive and 'constitutional' aspects of public choice (primarily in the Stubblebine-Kennard and the West-Staaf papers).

The remaining pages of this introduction attempt to delineate the nature of contributions to this volume in terms of the orientations just outlined. It must be recognized, however, that no single person can give a fully balanced picture of the diverse work presented here. Nor can any summary statement begin to do justice to the richness of this material. Comments are organized in the same order, with the same clustering of papers, as that in which they appear.

I

California in the 1970s was in ferment so far as the financing of education is concerned, and more broadly for the whole question of financing state and local government (as it is still). This situation brings out more sharply than would normally be the case some of the problems in collective choice both generally and in application to education. Consequently, whether formally or not, questions in both the positive economics of public choice and what Mueller designated as 'normative theory' in public choice must be confronted.

This being the case, I have put the paper by Stubblebine and Kennard at the beginning of this book.

The Stubblebine-Kennard paper is firmly rooted in the tradition of studies in public choice. At the same time, it is built around the concept of the 'tax price' of education for families in different income brackets and resident in locations with different assessed valuations of property. With the aid of a simulation model and the tax-price concept, the authors lead us through some of the complexities of recent California history pertaining to different levels of decision-making. Disequilibria in these processes are demonstrated. Among the various agenda that have been thrown up for educational finance in the wake of the *Serrano v. Priest* decision are: (1) statewide funding in which the relevant tax price becomes the statewide income-tax-price with equal expenditures per pupil; (2) a power-equalization system that would allow for local variations in effort but with an inter-district redistribution of funds (throughout the state) that would eliminate those tax-price differences; and (3) a system of vouchers funded by the state, alone or in combination with other rearrangements. Except for (1) all the alternatives allow differences among school districts in level of public funding for education. Consistently, in cases following *Serrano v. Priest* the courts have rejected the notion that equal per pupil spending was a necessary part of compliance; 'invidious discrimination' arose from disparities in the opportunity to fund education, not from disparities in the amounts sought. The court thus upheld freedom of collective choice at local levels, but with the constraint that opportunities must be equalized among districts. This set the ground rules for voters' choices at both state and local levels.

Between 1972 and 1978 the State was accumulating a 'Serrano war chest' preparatory to compliance with the order of the court. Stubblebine and Kennard suggest that as part of the overall state surplus this informal war chest contributed to the sense of taxpayer outrage that was expressed in the two-to-one vote in favor of 'Proposition 13,' a constitutional amendment setting a maximum on property tax rates (the main source of local revenues) and specifying responsibility of the State legislature for apportionment of revenue from this tax. The inability of the legislature to achieve earlier compliance with *Serrano v. Priest* is traced to the determination of local voters to be masters of their own fiscal fate, but with Proposition 13 the voters surrendered that independence – an ironic outcome.

Discussion at the conference was extremely interesting despite the fact that the paper did not reach us ahead of time. In fact Werner Hirsch, one of the formally assigned discussants, simply presented his own analysis of events in California, a revised version of which appears as Chapter 2 in this volume. Richard Zeckhauser, the other formally designated discussant, responded in the context of public choice theory with some tightly reasoned queries and suggestions for the promised final section of the Stubblebine-Kennard paper, which was to incorporate applications of the analysis projected into the 1980s. Unfortunately, Stubblebine still is postponing that undertaking. We must all hope that he will go on to carry it out, even though it will not be ready for this publication. Fortunately, even a quick scanning and brief oral presentation of the Stubblebine-Kennard paper was sufficient to alert participants to the utility and flexibility as an analytical tool of the concept of tax price. Though that concept is not new, the demonstration of its application in a simulation model gave rise to observations concerning its much wider relevance in diverse institutional settings. This analysis cuts across otherwise markedly differing approaches, positive or normative, and whether in the tradition of recent economic analyses of processes and criteria of collective choice or in the much older sort of welfare analysis.

Hirsch's delineation of the post-Proposition 13 scene demonstrates at least four points of general importance. First, while it was easy in the environment of 1978 to secure a large majority in favor of a state constitutional amendment that would reduce property taxes, there was no parallel readiness to cut back on the services provided by those taxes. In terms of 'public choice,' the California action can be seen as a confounding of the constitutional-normative and the legislative aspects of collective choice. Second, some unanticipated distortions are likely to persist despite ingenuity in finding detours around constitutional and legislative roadblocks; the combination of *Serrano v. Priest* and Proposition 13 are likely to have such lasting effects for the public funding of primary and secondary education in California. Third, voters on a popular, seemingly simple issue, as cutting property taxes, cannot be expected to think through the ramifications of such actions. This is a well-recognized problem in representative democracy; logrolling does not resolve it. Fourth, as Stubblebine and Kennard also pointed out, collective choices can have interactive effects that are unambiguously perverse relative to the long-term preferences of most voters; in this case the drift to more centralized control of schools appears to be such a contradiction.

Jackman and Papadachi, like Stubblebine and Kennard, examine variations across local districts (in this case, British 'Local Authorities') in educational inputs per pupil year. However, they deal only with the positive economics of collective choice; their model (like Inman's) is one of representative, not direct, democracy. No question is raised concerning the underlying rules for collective decision. Moreover, the starting point is the reverse of that in the Stubblebine-Kennard paper, asking the question: Why, when the 'major objective of education policy in Britain since the war has been to achieve an approximate uniformity in the standards of educational provision across local authorities', do we find persisting substantial inequalities? The authors concluded that over half of the variation could be attributed to cost factors and hence did not entail differences in standards of provision. However, preferences and financial factors accounted for substantial variations, and it is concluded that 'central government grants appear to do little to offset variations resulting from differences in household incomes.' The institutional setting is carefully specified and a regression model is set up to explain expenditures, distinguishing three types of factors: (1) those affecting committed expenditures on the service; (2) those indicating preferences (measured by use of a variable for political affiliation of councillors); and (3) budgetary factors. The concept of 'maximum acceptable rate bill' as a rising function of income partially takes the place in this analysis of 'tax price' as a rising cost of given services for those in higher tax brackets, but with quite different interpretations. Unfortunately, as Windham pointed out in a generally supportive commentary, the data base for the income measure is extremely weak. Nevertheless, the findings suggest that there is little or no 'fiscal illusion' in responses to central government grants. This paper, and the insightful discussion of it by Donald Verry, mark an important step in the international flow of ideas and the spread of applications of positive economics to the analysis of collective decisions on particular issues – in this case in education.

II

Whether the focus of analysis is on collective decision-making as a process or on its substantive results in public policy, the reconciliation of distributive and allocative goals emerges as a recurrent problem. The three papers in Part II are focused on one or another aspect of this problem in the determination of policies for the financing of education: What, ideally, should policy be, given goals of Pareto optimization and redistribution toward more equal opportunities or outcomes?

Inman's paper on identification of preferences in a representative democracy asks in effect: can (or how can) practicing economic advisers identify operational preference functions that can help them lay out the implications of alternative strategies in ways that will be meaningful to the political agents of a society. The paper reports on some experimental research in this sphere. Such an effort is intrinsically vulnerable from the perspective of a sophisticated normative economic theory, as is exemplified in Mirrlees' comments (which refer also to debates in this area some of which we were unable to represent in this volume or conference). Inman is less vulnerable from a positive public choice perspective, primarily because he made no attempt to analyze the decision-making process or structure as a subject for the application of positive economic theory. McFadden approached this paper essentially in the spirit of its author, but he would like to see a distinction between the type of advisory role on which Inman focused his attention and the roles of economic advisers to particular parties or interest groups within the political structure – roles he regards as perhaps more important than those on which Inman concentrated. His comments constitute a creative and challenging contribution in their own right.

Both venerable and relatively new issues are imbedded in this work and in reactions to it. If the paper stimulates some of its readers to tackle the problems with which Inman was concerned or, more fundamentally, to redefine those problems and proceed with questions restructured accordingly, it will have served us well.

Very different in purpose and method is the paper by Hare and Ulph. They combine optimal tax theory with an analysis embodying recent developments in the economics of the household to set up an intergenerational model of wealth distribution. This model serves as the basis for an analysis of grants and loans to students in higher education. (They give no explicit attention to the opportunity cost of education in foregone earnings, but this could be incorporated in the model without major alterations.) Parents endow their children with education and/or a cash bequest; the child's earned income and the cash bequest can be taxed. There is no capital market for the funding of education. Under plausible assumptions, they prove the existence and uniqueness of a stable long-run distribution of wealth as the limiting distribution for any given initial distributions of wealth and of ability. They then assume that the government can tax an individual's income and the bequest he receives either separately or together, imposing on the choice of tax functions the constraint that they should be such as to guarantee the existence of a unique and stable distribution of wealth. The optimal tax scheme is required to be purely redistributional within each period, so that the gross wealth available for redistribution equals the total net wealth after redistribution. It is shown that with the optimal tax scheme the marginal rate on income will be positive virtually everywhere, and that on bequests must be strictly smaller than on earned income. The question is then raised: if the government has all the tax powers attributed to it in the model, is there any place for educational policy as an additional instrument of redistribution? Since transfers of income can be handled by the tax system, the question then takes the form, should lower bounds be set on the amount of education a parent can choose to buy for his children? Despite the fact that in a first-best world such constraints would be undesirable, Hare and Ulph conclude that they become desirable in the second-best world that lacks capital markets for investment in education – in order to overcome the tendency to underinvestment in education in such a world. They find further that grants in support of such a policy are justified and that 'even in a model in which one source of inequality arises from the unequal dispersion of abilities, there is still a case for giving educational grants on the basis of parental wealth.' A model is then explored in which, with optimal taxation, there are educational loans combined with the lower-bound constraint on educational investments and the requirement that the loans be used for education. Some awkward problems arise with this model, which must be modified before firmer results can be established. The authors conclude, however, that within the limits of their model loans appear to be superior to grants in their affects on resource allocation.

Starting from different orientations, Pissarides and Mirrlees provide very different sorts of comments on this paper, though not with any direct conflict of views. Pissarides puts greater emphasis on a more immediate or direct treatment of substantive policy questions, challenging the authors to analyze ways of overcoming capital market imperfections instead of elaborating second- or third-best solutions under those constraints. Mirrlees, on the other hand, applauds this work as a step forward in the development and specification of normative analysis in the framework of optimal tax theory.

The paper by Nelson and Breneman contrasts sharply with that by Hare and Ulph in its comparative simplicity methodologically and in its empirical character. Nelson and Breneman assess the results and interpretations of empirical studies of the distributive effects of public subsidies of higher education, giving special attention to the facts and controversies with respect to disparities in treatment of students at junior colleges and in four-year institutions. They lay bare a number of defects in previous work, both empirically and logically, concluding that allegations of discrimination in financing against students of junior colleges finds little support in the facts. (This is a conclusion cited by James and Neuberger also.) It is argued that a policy of high tuition with need-based grants can reconcile the seemingly conflicting goals of optimality in resource allocation and equalization of opportunity; unfortunately, however, that position can be sustained only in a constrained second-best world that they do not specify. The limitations of their work are evident if one views it in the terms set by Hare and Ulph, but the purpose of the endeavor by Nelson and Breneman was in fact very different. As a challenge to those who have been debating issues and facts in the arenas in which collective decisions in fact are made, the analysis by Nelson and Breneman constitutes a real step forward. It is of course much closer in nature to the papers on recurrent education than to that by Hare and Ulph.

III

The papers on recurrent education differ from others in that they are focused on a particular service and explicitly in favor of government support for it. Peston took the strongest position, presenting his theoretical arguments in polemical style, as he did in comments on other papers as well. Glennerster built up a complex picture of the nature and extent of recurrent education in

Europe. Extended comments on both of these papers by Blaug and on Glennerster's paper by E. G. West add other perspectives on a subject that is receiving more attention each year.

Reacting to Peston from the perspective of a devotee of the positive theory of public choice, West said: 'I have already observed that the central issue for collective choice is to resolve the question: How are differing individual preferences to be reconciled in reaching results that must, by definition, be shared jointly by all members of a community?... In his paper, and much more in the subsequent discussion, Maurice Peston declares himself to be an unabashed paternalist. This being so, no questions of collective choice arise.' Peston presumably would assert that he is concerned about collective choice, but primarily in its substance than its processes. Hia paper is less a theory of collective choice than an affirmation by a participant in the process, who seeks to influence decisions by persuasion. In that sense Peston's arguments, both written and oral, might best be viewed by a public choice economist as part of the subject matter of a positive analysis of processes of collective decision. The contrast between Peston's political position and that exemplified by Milton Friedman cuts deeper, however. It cuts into problems of what Mueller classified as normative theories of collective choice; how, if at all, can consensus be reached on the underlying rules within which collective choices are made? All participants shared a commitment to political democracy, but it is not entirely clear how easily we might have arrived at a unanimous agreement on ground rules and priorities for the exercise of collective choice – the crucial question of a normative approach to public choice.

IV

The two papers in Part IV have very little in common except that the collectives on which attention is focused could be viewed as 'clubs' or 'quasi-clubs' (as that term is used in the public choice theory) and both papers draw in greater or lesser degree on such theory.

The first of these papers, on university departments, has two main components – treatment of the department as a multi-product non-profit labor collective, and application of some elements of the positive economics of public choice to analysis of departmental decision-making. The former is the more fully developed component in their work. Given that the department is a labor-managed collective, its objective function – initially assumed to reflect full agreement on a 'team' utility function – includes opportunities for on-the-job consumption (in this case primarily in research and teaching small classes of advanced or graduate students, as against the 'production' activity of teaching large classes of undergraduates). Following prior trials of alternative formulations, an objective function is specified and characteristics of optimizing behavior derived from it are applied, successfully, to explaining commonly observed characteristics of universities.

The second part of the study focuses directly on the decision process, requiring that the assumption of an unambiguous, unanimous 'team' utility function be dropped to allow for the fact that a non-profit collective 'faces the need to aggregate over many preference functions, each having several arguments.' Different strategies for resolving indeterminancy in decisions and for controlling the costs of decision-making are noted, including reversion to dictatorial procedures when democratic strategies fail. Any member of an academic community who has watched the processes James and Neuberger suggest will find their observations all too familiar. Since this part of the paper is approached in a relatively non-rigorous manner, much room remains for future work to explore the full applicability public choice theories to the analysis of university behavior.

The James-Neuberger paper is an exploration in positive analysis that could have practical value for understanding feasible and unpromising incentive strategies in university administration. However, such applications would have to reassess the validity of some of the simplifications for a particular institutional setting, whatever the seeming predictive success of the model may be. Just such questions are among those raised by Laurie Hunter in his appreciative commentary.

West and Staaf have given us what might be viewed as an exercise in the applied normative economics of collective choice. This may seem to be almost a contradiction in terms if one takes as models the writings Mueller grouped under 'normative public choice,' which were highly abstract and logical-philosophical (as exemplified in particular by A. K. Sen and by Rawls, though also in part by Tullock and others in the 'public choice' literature). However, West and Staaf are dealing with issues that could be regarded as at the 'constitutional' level, in much more than the incidental sense that the focus of the study is on a decision by the U.S. Supreme Court. On the other hand, this is also an exercise in positive economics applied to the analysis of alternative institutional arrangements for the negotiation of labor contracts and the implications of those alternatives – implications not only for the arguments that have characterized disputes over union powers in the courts (in particular, in this case, negotiation costs, 'labor stability,' 'free riders') but for other allocative and distributive effects as well. Furthermore, this essay includes a number of elements closely associated with the positive economics of public choice. Most interesting perhaps, from this point of view, are the discussions of revealed and unrevealed preferences as related to 'free riders' and 'forced riders,' and of lobbying activities of agents of public employees (and the power of an aggressively represented interest group of teachers under exclusive-agency arrangements relative to the unrepresented children or parents) as factors in collective decisions relating to education in a representative democracy. The mixture of positive economics and of normative analysis at a fundamental ('constitutional') level rounds out the final section of this paper.

It should hardly be surprising, given these levels of analysis and the preoccupation with perennially debated issues, that the West and Staaf paper evoked strong reactions among those committed to a different view. Fortunately the discussion displayed a high level of intellectual competence and of etiquette in debate, as the formal comments and the rejoinder attest.

Mary Jean Bowman
Editor

PART I

Central and local roles in educational provision

California school finance: The 1970s decade

WM. CRAIG STUBBLEBINE and DAVID N. KENNARD*

Claremont Men's College

The decade of the 1970s opened and closed with *Serrano v. Priest* before the California courts. The decade was opened by a rejection of property tax reductions for Californians and closed by an acceptance of both constitutional limits on property tax rates and on government spending. In between much and little changed. The substantial equilibrium with which the decade began has given way; the decade ends in substantial disequilibrium.

Two histories have been written in the period from 1970 through 1979: the legal-judicial history of *Serrano v. Priest* and the law-legislative history of California school finance. Three distinct periods may be distinguished: 'Pre-Serrano' (through 1972), 'Post-Serrano/Pre-Proposition 13' (1973-1978), and 'Post-Proposition 13' (1978 to the present). These separate, if not clearly converging, histories and their periods occupy Section II of this paper. To provide a simple structure in which to develop these histories, Section I outlines a simple simulation model. Finally, Section III undertakes the beginnings of a collective choice analysis for the 1980s.

I

The basic decision unit with respect to primary and secondary (K-12) education in California is the school district: elementary, high school or unified district. As its name suggests, a unified school district is responsible for both elementary and high school education. Each district has its own elected board. By type, 680 elementary school districts were responsible for educating twenty

* Stubblebine is the Von Tobel Professor of Political Economy at the Claremont Men's College and Claremont Graduate School and Director of the Center for the Study of Law Structures at the Claremont Men's College. Kennard is a Ph.D. candidate at the Claremont Graduate School and a graduate Research Assistant at the Center for the Study of Law Structures at Claremont Men's College.

percent of total pupils statewide, 115 high school districts for twelve percent, and 250 unified school districts for sixty-five percent. Over time, elementary and high school districts have shown a marked tendency to consolidate into unified districts (due in part to pressure by the state). For present purposes, all districts may be treated as if they were unified.

Funding for districts is a mixture of local, state, and Federal revenues. Local revenues, for practical purposes, represent the proceeds of a uniform proportional property tax. State revenues represent a mixture of general aid and categorical grants. Federal aid has been predominately categorical.

From the standpoint of local fiscal effort, the two primary determinants are district family income and district assessed valuation per family. In essence, the higher the family income and the higher the assessed valuation per family, the lower the fiscal effort required to support educational services for district pupils.

As suggested by Figure 1, formulation of a simulation model begins with these variables. Assuming a high-average-low categorization of the variables,

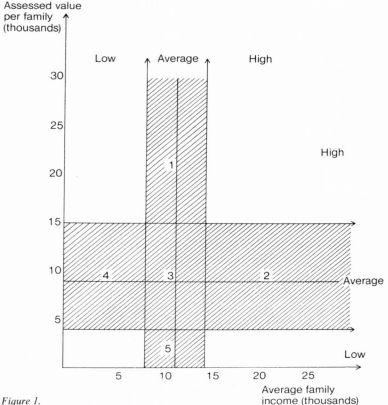

Figure 1.

each school district must fit into one of nine cells. Based on work by A. J. Alexander (1975), a scatter diagram of California suggests that the bulk of school districts lies in one of the five shaded cells. Few districts are to be found at the extremes represented by the four 'corner' cells. Accordingly, the model focuses on five types of districts which may be designated as HA, AH, AA, AL, and LA where H is high, A is average, and L is low, and where the first letter refers to assessed valuation per family and the second to average family income.

Within any district, family income may be high, average, or low. For modeling purposes, high is taken as $ 25,000 per year, average as $ 10,000 and low as $ 5,000. High income families are assumed to occupy housing equivalent to 1.6 times income, or $ 40,000, and average and low income families equivalent to 2 times income, or $ 20,000 and $ 10,000 respectively. With a ratio of 4 to 1, market value to assessed value, assessed residential property value is given as $ 10,000, $ 5,000, and $ 2,500, respectively.

Some families have children in or approaching school age, some do not. Accordingly, the model assigns to each income class a range of children, as well as the number of families so characterized. For simplicity, district types other than AA are assumed to contain ten percent of all households, with the 'center cell' district type (AA) containing sixty percent.

These parameters are summarized in Table 1 where f_i^k represents a family residing in the kth school district and having the ith income level: $k = 1, 2, 3, 4, 5$ with $1 = $ HA, $2 = $ AH, $3 = $ AA, $4 = $ AL, $5 = $ LA and $i = 1, 2, 3$ with $1 = $ $ 25,000, $2 = $ $ 10,000 and $3 = $ $ 5,000.

Within these parameters, the aggregate district characteristics may be computed. Relative to assessed valuation, a high district ($k = 1$) has an assessed value per family of $ 16,000 and per pupil of $ 18,700, an average district ($k = 2, 3, 4$) has $ 9,000 per family and $ 12,600 per pupil, and a low district ($k = 5$) has $ 5,000 per family and $ 8,800 per pupil. Statewide, assessed value per family is $ 9,300 and per pupil is $ 13,000.[1] Relative to income, a high district ($k = 2$) has a per family income of $ 17,800, an average district ($k = 1, 3, 5$) has $ 10,700, and a low district ($k = 4$) has $ 6,400. Statewide, income per family is $ 11,000.[2] The State has a total family component of 7 million, 3.8 million of which have no school children and 3.2 million of which do have school children. The total component of school children is 5 million.

Tax-prices and opportunity sets

The simple simulation model permits computation of various tax-prices implied by various institutional settings. Thus, for example, if $ 100 per pupil provided to each school is financed by a proportional statewide income tax, the (marginal) tax rate is .00649 (5 × 100/77,000). High income families would pay $ 162, average income families would pay $ 65, and low income families would pay $ 32 (.00649 × 5,000).

Table 1.

School district	Class	Income (taxable)	Residential property	Children W/o	Children W/	Families (000,000)		Income (000,000,000)	Property Residential (000,000,000)	Property C-I-A (000,000,000)	Property Total (000,000,000)	Number of children (000,000)	Number of families (000,000)
	High	25000	10000	0	1	.0	.1	2.5	1.0	—	—	.1	.1
	Average	10000	5000	0	2	.2	.2	4.0	2.0	—	—	.4	.4
$k=1$	Low	5000	2500	0	1	.1	.1	1.0	.5	—	—	.1	.2
	Total	—	—	—	—	.3	.4	7.5	3.5	7.7	11.2	.6	.7
	Average	—	—	—	—			10700	5000	11000	16000	18700	—
	High	25000	10000	0	1	.1	.3	10.0	4.0	—	—	.3	.1
	Average	10000	5000	0	2	.1	.1	2.0	1.0	—	—	.2	.4
$k=2$	Low	5000	2500	0	0	.1	0	.5	.25	—	—	0	.2
	Total	—	—	—	—	.3	.4	12.5	5.25	1.05	6.3	.5	.7
	Average	—	—	—	—			17800	7500	15000	9000	12600	—
	High	25000	10000	0	1	.4	.2	15.0	6.0	—	—	.2	.6
	Average	10000	5000	0	2	1.2	1.2	24.0	12.0	—	—	2.4	2.4
$k=3$	Low	5000	2500	0	1	.8	.4	6.0	3.0	—	—	.4	1.2
	Total	—	—	—	—	2.4	1.8	45.0	21.0	16.8	37.8	3.0	4.2
	Average	—	—	—	—			10700	5000	4000	9000	12600	—
	High	25000	10000	0	0	0	0	0	0	—	—	0	0
	Average	10000	5000	0	1	.1	.1	2.0	1.0	—	—	.1	.2
$k=4$	Low	5000	2500	0	2	.3	.2	2.5	1.25	—	—	.4	.5
	Total	—	—	—	—	.4	.3	4.5	2.25	4.05	6.3	.5	.7
	Average	—	—	—	—			6400	3200	5800	9000	12600	—
	High	25000	10000	0	0	.1	0	2.5	1.0	—	—	0	.1
	Average	10000	5000	0	1	.2	.2	4.0	2.0	—	—	.2	.4
$k=5$	Low	5000	2500	0	2	.1	.1	1.0	.5	—	—	.2	.2
	Total	—	—	—	—	.4	.3	7.5	3.5	0	3.5	.4	.7
	Average	—	—	—	—			10700	5000	0	5000	8800	—
	High	25000	10000	—	—	.6	.6	30.0	12.0	—	—	.6	.9
	Average	10000	5000	—	—	1.8	1.8	36.0	18.0	—	—	3.3	3.8
State	Low	5000	2500	—	—	1.4	.8	11.0	5.5	—	—	1.1	2.3
	Total	—	—	—	—	3.8	3.2	77.0	35.5	29.6	65.1	5.0	7.0
	Average	—	—	—	—	.54	.46	11000	5100	4200	9300	13000	—

In the same way, $100 per pupil in the AA school district ($k = 3$) financed by a local proportional property tax would require a tax rate of .00794 ($3 \times 100/37,800$). High income families would pay $79, average income families $40, and low income families $20 (.00794 × $2500). Implicit in these computations is the notion that the family treats as *de minimus* the burden of taxes levied on commercial, industrial, and agricultural property. This view can be justified on the basis that such taxes are shifted statewide and ultimately borne by families in proportion to their incomes. For the individual school district, its 'C-I-A' property will represent but a small part of the state total. The implied burden of changes in its own tax rate, therefore, will tend toward zero.[3]

Were all districts to levy taxes on commercial-industrial-agricultural property, the total burden shifted to families would be significant. For example, $100 per pupil derived from local property taxes would imply $215 million statewide in C-I-A property taxes, an implicit proportional income 'adjustment' rate of .00279 (215/77,000), and a C-I-A property tax burden of $70 for high income families, $28 for average income families, and $14 for low income families. As borne, however, they reduce the family's 'real' disposable income. In technical terms, the burden has an income effect, but no relative price effect in the trade-off between education and other goods.[4]

Tax-prices, in turn, may be used in conjunction with demand curves and to delineate the individual family's choice or opportunity set, as depicted in Figure 3, for example. Changing institutional settings change tax-prices faced by individuals, the opportunity set, and hence behavior with respect to the chosen bundle of consumption goods. These choices, expressed through some process such as referenda, permit insights to develop through collective choice analysis.

Homeowners' exemption

Tax-price analysis may be applied to the California "homeowners' exemption," which has played a role in school finance during the 1970s. The exemption is fairly standard: each owner-occupied residence pays property taxes levied on an assessed value reduced by H dollars. The taxing jurisdiction's property tax rate is established inclusive of the homeowners' exemption with any reduction in property tax revenues replaced by state funds.

For any pre-existing pattern of property tax rates in the state, increases in the homeowners' exemption leads to a substitution of state funding for local funding. If the property tax levied throughout the state were one percent, an increase in the homeowners' exemption of $1,000 would require an additional $70 million in state tax revenues. At the implied proportional income tax rate of .00091, high income families would pay an additional $23, average income families $9.10, and low income families $5.

Since each family finds its local property tax payment reduced by $ 10, high income families would tend to oppose increases in the homeowners' exemption which average and low income families would tend to approve. Taken in isolation, one would expect the homeowners' exemption to be set at $ 5000, such that no average or low income family would pay local property taxes. This follows from the substantial majority of voters among average and low income families.[5]

The homeowners' exemption also adjusts local property tax-prices. Whereas an increase in the exemption has significant state income tax implications, adjustment of the local property tax rate implies *de minimus* repercussions on local taxpayers. For families in the AH school district ($k = 1$), the tax-price per $ 100 of revenue generated per pupil declines $ 5 for each $ 1,000 of exemption; in districts $k = 2, 3, 4$, the decline is $ 8 (.00794 × 1000) and in the AL district ($k = 5$), the decline is $ 11. Assuming normal downward-sloping demand curves for public goods, the reduced tax-prices should lead to a larger local public sector. In turn, the higher property tax rates generated will necessitate increases in the state income tax rate.

With allowance for the tax-price repercussions of the homeowners' exemption, any given family of any income class or taxing jurisdiction may find itself benefitted or harmed by an increase in the homeowners' exemption. The family depicted in Figure 2 is indifferent between its position with and without a given exemption level. One may easily depict families who would prefer one situation or the other.

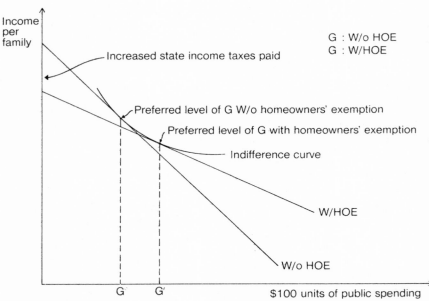

Figure 2.

In consequence, the collective choice implications of proposals to alter the homeowners' exemption are indeterminate without additional assumptions specifying the community within which choice is made. Majorities may or may not emerge to revise any existing situation.

II

Table 2 provides a brief summary of the legal and legislative history of California school finance during the decade from 1970 through 1979. Three

Table 2.

Law-legislative		Legal-judicial
Senate Bill 1: Basic Aid of $125 per pupil; Foundation Program of $355 per elementary pupil and of $488 per high school pupil with an equalization tax rate of $1.00 for elementary pupils and $0.30 for high school pupils. Maximum property tax rates and voter overrides for school districts. (Homeowners' exemption set at $750 of assessed value.)		
	1969	*Serrano v. Priest:* Initiated in Superior Court. Defendants demurred. Trial court sustained demurrers. Case appealed.
	1970	
	1971	California Supreme Court reverses *Serrano v. Priest* judgment and remands case to Superior Court for trial.
Senate Bill 90: Basic Aid of $125 per pupil; Foundation Program increased to $765 per elementary pupil and to $950 per high school pupil with an equalization tax rate of $2.23 for elementary pupils and $1.64 for high school pupils. Maximum property tax rate determination formulae (partially) 'Serranoized'; voter overrides continued. Homeowners' exemption increased to $1,750 of assessed value.	1972	
	1973	
	1974	*Serrano v. Priest* retried in Superior Court incorporating SB 90 (1972) school finance system. System declared unconstitutional. Judgment appealed.
	1975	
	1976	

20

Table 2 (continued).

Law-legislative		Legal-judicial
Assembly Bill 65: Basic Aid of $ 120 per pupil; Foundation Program inflation adjustment factor increased; Districts proposing to spend in excess of foundation levels must surrender portion of excess for redistribution to low spending districts. Maximum property tax rate and overrides continued. Homeowners' exemption continued at $ 1750 of assessed value.	1977	California Supreme Court affirms trial court judgment in *Serrano v. Priest.*
Article XIIIA (Proposition 13) introduced into California constitution providing for maximum property tax rate of 1% of market value; property tax revenues to be apportioned 'according to law.'	1978	
Senate Bills 154 and 2212 provide funding for school districts as percentage of prior year's spending for one year.		
Assembly Bill 8 provides formulae for eventual 'Serrano-ization' of school funding.		
Article XIIIB (Proposition 4) introduced into California Constitution providing spending limits for state and local governments controlled by respective electorates.	1979	*Serrano v. Priest* plaintiffs challenge post-Proposition 13 school financing system.

periods may be distinguished: Pre-Serrano, Post-Serrano/Pre-Proposition 13 and Post-Proposition 13.

Pre-Serrano (through 1972)

In the years prior to *Serrano v. Priest*, California had developed a complex set of school finance relationships. Some 4.5 million pupils were served by some 1000 school districts: elementary, high school, and unified. An additional .5 million pupils were enrolled in private schools. In size, districts ranged from the small one-room school to the 650,000 a.d.a. Los Angeles Unified School District.

Local revenue sources accounted for some sixty percent of total district revenues, State sources some thirty-four percent, and Federal sources the balance. Local revenues are based almost exclusively on the property tax, the rates of which were set by elected school boards within maximum rates established by a combination of State statute and the district electorates. General obligation bonds were subject to approval by a two-thirds majority of those voting on the issue in a district-wide referendum.

Eighty percent of State aid to districts represented apportionments from the State school fund created annually by constitutional mandate from State general revenues. The grants were broken down into:

> Basic Aid of $ 125 per a.d.a., of which $ 120 was constitutionally guaranteed.
>
> Equalization Aid established a 'foundation level' of $ 355 per elementary student and $ 488 per high school student, with aid based on a computational property tax of 1% for elementary schools and 0.8% for high schools. The difference between the foundation level and Basic Aid *plus* computed property tax revenues per a.d.a. defined a district's equalization aid.[6]
>
> Equalization Aid Cost Adjustment provided for a scaling up of Equalization Aid in response to inflation.
>
> Supplemental Aid provided additional grants to districts with assessed property valuations per student below specified limits.

For 1970-71, Basic Aid amounted to $ 580 million, Equalization Aid to $ 439 million, Equalization Aid Cost Adjustment to $ 79 million, and Supplemental Aid to $ 39 million. Total School Fund Apportionments were $ 1.4 billion. An additional $ 219 million in State funds was made available under various categorical grant programs.

The State also conditions local choice by:

> Monitoring property assessments to achieve relative parity among county assessment practices against a target of twenty-five percent of market value.
>
> Providing senior citizen property exemptions as a function of income and assessed valuation.
>
> Providing homeowners' exemptions in the amount of $ 750 of assessed valuation.
>
> Mandating a host of rules and regulations.

Table 3 provides the tax-prices relevant to modeling this set of relationships. The accompanying Figure 3 depicts the derived opportunity set for each district based on Column 5 of Table 3.[7]

Basic aid, provided per pupil from state revenues, carries a tax-price (Column 2) greater than the independent district tax-price (Column 4) for families at every income level and every district. One wonders, therefore, why any basic aid is provided.

Part of the answer may lie in the tax-prices computed on the basis that every

22

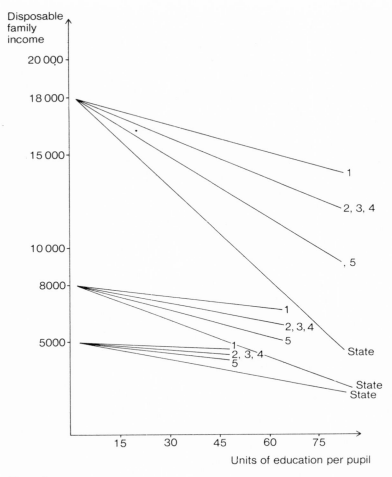

Figure 3.

district would provide at least one $100 of education per pupil even without state aid (Column 3). Voters may reason that this minimum will translate into a proportionate share of the property tax burden shifted from commercial-industrial-agricultural property. All voters in AL districts ($k = 5$) and average and low income voters in average assessed valuation districts ($k = 2, 3, 4$) will find the basic aid state income tax-price (Column 2) lower than the implicit property tax-price (Column 3). Since these represent a statewide majority, one would expect at least some minimal level of state funding to emerge from the political process.

One might also wonder why a state majority does not impose a maximum level of locally determined educational units. Such limits would constrain the C-I-A property tax burden visited upon families as consumers, wage earners,

Table 3.

| Tax | District (1) | State basic aid (2) | Tax-price of providing | | | | | |
| | | | $100 per pupil in every district (3) | District property tax | | | Average cost per $100 per pupil of education with equalization aid | |
				W/O HOE (4)	$750 HOE (5)	$1750 HOE (6)	Pre-Serrano (7)	Post-Serrano (8)
Rate					(.0054)			
Price i=1	1		127	54	50	44	142	131
2	(AH)		56	27	23	17	62	57
3			28	13	9	4	31	29
Rate								
Price i=1	2							
2	(HA)							
3								
Rate		(.0065)			(.0079)			
Price i=1	3	162	153	79	73	65	154	152
2	(AA)	65	69	40	34	26	68	67
3		32	35	20	14	6	34	34
Rate								
Price i=1	4							
2	(LA)							
3								
Rate					(.0114)			
Price i=1	5		188	114	106	94		
2	(AL)		87	57	49	37		
3			43	29	20	9		

Computations based on the simulation model presented in Table 1.

and investors in property. In part, the answer here may lie in the notion that each district would be benefitted from limits imposed on all other districts, but not on its own. Since this cannot be achieved, each electorate accepts the total burden, even if perceived 'excessive,' in exchange for the opportunity to adjust the level of education provided pupils within the district.[8]

The homeowners' exemption has been discussed in Section I, above. For the present, one need note only the reduction in tax-prices recorded in Column 5 of Table 3 as compared with Column 4.

Equalization aid redistributes income from families residing in districts with relatively high assessed valuations per pupil to families residing in districts with relatively low assessed valuations per pupil. Initially, assume the computational tax rate is zero. Increasing the foundation level by $ 100 per pupil generates additional state aid of $ 100 per pupil throughout the State. In effect, it is identical to an increase in basic aid by $ 100 per pupil. These tax-price consequences have been shown in Table 3 (Column 2) and the collective choice aspects discussed above.

Increasing the computational tax rate from zero progressively reduces the number of districts receiving equalization aid. This is shown in Figure 4 where basic aid of $ 125 per pupil is assumed. At a foundation level of $ 400 per student and computational tax rate of 1.8%,[9] all districts with assessed valuations per a.d.a. below $ 15,275 receive at least some equalization aid. With a computational rate of 3.8%, only districts below an assessed valuation per a.d.a. of $ 7,100 would receive equalization aid.

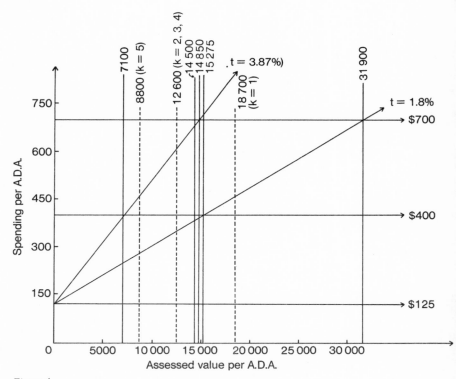

Figure 4.

From the electorate's standpoint, an increase in the computational tax rate substitutes explicit state aid with its implications for state income tax payments for their implicit shares of the C-I-A property tax burden imposed by districts exercising independent choice. As with basic aid, if the electorate predicts that each district will fund at least $ 400 (275 + 125) of education per pupil, some families will benefit from a substitution of state equalization aid for local funding. In Table 3, comparing Column 7 with Column 3 suggests average and low income families in average assessed valuation per a.d.a. districts ($k = 2, 3, 4$) and all families in low assessed value districts ($k = 5$) will find the per $ 100 cost less with equalization aid. Since they constitute a majority, some move to state funding is to be expected.

The anomaly presented by the tax-price comparisons (Columns 2 and 7) is why the electorate simply does not set basic aid at $ 400 per pupil statewide. The explanation for reliance on equalization may be twofold. First, the tax-price differentials for the majority of families are relatively small, permitting other factors to hold sway in their decisions. Second, increases in basic aid also generate state revenues for relatively wealthy districts. To the extent voters find this objectionable on equity grounds, they will tend to feel more at ease with equalization aid.

As with basic aid, equalization aid comes to the district as a lump-sum grant. As such, it has an income effect on district decision-making, but no relative tax-price effect. Varying the foundation level and/or the computational tax rate shifts the opportunity sets of Figure 3 up or down parallel to the opportunity sets derived from the tax-prices in Column 5 of Table 3.

What Table 3 and Figure 3 make clear is the issue on which *Serrano v. Priest* turned.

Post Serrano/Pre-Proposition 13 (1972-1978)

Serrano v. Priest[10] was initiated in the Los Angeles County Superior Court as a class action on behalf of pupils and parents residing in school districts offering inferior education opportunities. Defendants to the case argued, and the Court concurred, that the plaintiffs claims were insufficient to constitute a cause for action. That decision was sustained by the Court of Appeals, then reversed and remanded by the California Supreme Court to the trial court 'with direction to overrule the demurers.'

In rendering its decision, the Supreme Court established no specific conditions for constitutionality. It argued merely that, as a result of the (tax-price) disparities observable in Column 5 of Table 3 and its accompanying Figure 3, 'wide differentials remain in the revenue available to individual districts and, consequently, in the level of educational expenditures'.[11]

Inasmuch as assessments reflect wealth *and* wealth is judicially recognized as an 'inherently suspect classification which may be justified only on the basis of a compelling state interest'[12] *and* education is a 'fundamental interest' *and* the instant funding system is 'not necessary' to accomplishing this interest, it follows that the system 'denies to the plaintiffs and others similarly situated the equal protection of the laws.'[13]

The Court voided only the present *system* of educational financing. It did not declare that property taxation is an unconstitutional source of school funds. Neither did the Court establish a constitutional standard of equal expenditure per pupil.[14]

Perhaps lacking the analytical apparatus of tax-price, the Court expressed 'individuous discrimination' in terms of the more readily observable tax rates:

But, say defendants, the expenditure per child does not accurately reflect a district's wealth because that expenditure is partly determined by the district's tax rate. Thus, a district with a high total assessed valuation might levy a low school tax, and end up spending the same amount per pupil as a poorer district whose residents opt to pay higher taxes. This argument is also meritless. Obviously, the richer district is favored when it can provide the same educational quality for its children with less tax effort. Furthermore, as a statistical matter, the poorer districts are financially unable to raise their taxes high enough to match the educational offerings of wealthier districts (Legislative Analyst, Part V, supra, pp. 8-9). Thus, affluent districts can have their cake and eat it too: they can provide a high quality education for their children while paying lower taxes. Poor districts, by contrast, have no cake at all (pp. 611-612).

More basically, however, we reject defendants' underlying thesis that classification by wealth is constitutional so long as the wealth is that of the district, not the individual. We think that discrimination on the basis of district wealth is equally invalid. The commercial and industrial property which augments a district's tax base is distributed unevenly throughout the state. To allot more educational dollars to the children of one district than to those of another merely because of the fortuitous presence of such property is to make the quality of a child's education dependent upon the location of private commercial and industrial establishments. Surely, this is to rely on the most irrelevant of factors as the basis for educational financing (pp. 612-613).

In summary, so long as the assessed valuation within a district's boundaries is a major determinant of how much it can spend for its schools, only a district with a large tax base will be truly able to decide how much it really cares about education. The poor district cannot freely choose to tax itself into an excellence which its tax rolls cannot provide. Far from being necessary to promote local fiscal choice, the present financing system actually deprives the less wealthy districts of that option (pp. 620).

It is worth noting, perhaps, that rejection of the Pre-Serrano financing system has its counterpart in statute and judicial treatment of the private sector. Different prices charged to different customers by the same firm at the same point in time are inherently suspect unless there be a showing of differences in costs of serving the customers. With respect to education, differences in tax-prices for families of similar income are not traceable to differences among districts in the cost of providing education. By analogy with treatment of private exchange, the pattern of tax-prices would impart suspicion to the system of financing under review.

Attention also may be directed to the Court's treatment of basic aid which it found to widen 'the gap between rich and poor districts.'[15]

Furthermore, basic aid, which constitutes about half of the state educational funds (Legislative Analyst, Public School Finance, Part II, The State School Fund: Its Derivation, Distribution and Apportionment, 1970, p. 9), actually widens the gap between rich and poor districts (see Cal. Senate Fact Finding Committee on Revenue and Taxation, State and Local Fiscal Relationships in Public Education in California, 1965, p. 19). Such aid is distributed on a uniform per pupil basis to all districts, irrespective of a district's wealth. Beverly Hills, as well as Baldwin Park, receives $ 125 from the state for each of its students.

For Baldwin Park the basic grant is essentially meaningless. Under the foundation program the state must make up the difference between $ 355 per elementary child and $ 47.91, the amount of revenue per child which Baldwin Park could raise by levying a tax of $ 1 per $ 100 of assessed valuation. Although under present law, that difference is composed partly of basic aid and partly of equalization aid, if the basic aid grant did not exist, the district would still receive the same amount of state aid – all in equalizing funds.

For Beverly Hills, however, the $ 125 flat grant has real financial significance. Since a tax rate of $ 1 per $ 100 there would produce $ 870 per elementary student, Beverly Hills is far too rich to qualify for equalizing aid. Nevertheless, it still receives $ 125 per child from the state, thus enlarging the economic chasm between it and Baldwin Park (p. 608).

If district $k = 5$ may be taken as a representative '(relatively) poor district,' basic aid is preferable to exclusive reliance on the local tax base (Column 2 vs. Column 3 of Table 3).

Contrary to the Court's understanding, basic aid would tend to narrow the gap with respect to relative funding levels. If at first the result seems counter-intuitive, a lump-sum grant to a low income area is likely to have a greater impact on choice than the same sum received by an upper income area. This will be reinforced further by the fact that the increases in state taxes necessary to fund the basic aid will have a greater *income* effect on the upper income families who differentially tend to populate upper income areas.

It is only in the context of a choice between basic aid and equalization aid that basic aid widens the gap. From the Court's standpoint, basic aid should be eliminated from a program which also includes equalization aid. However, no significant constitutional issue arises here within California since its constitution specifies a minimum of $ 120 in basic aid.

The initial legislative response was embodied in Senate Bill 90 signed into law in December 1972, slightly one year after the Supreme Court had re-manded *Serrano v. Priest* to the trial court. Equalization foundation levels were increased to $ 765 for elementary school students and to $ 950 for high school students together with provision for (partial) inflation adjustment. The corresponding computational tax rates also were increased to 2.23% and 1.64% respectively. The homeowners' exemption was increased to $ 1,750 of assessed value.

By itself, the increase in foundation levels would be fully equivalent to an increase in basic aid for districts previously receiving equalization aid. Districts with higher assessed valuations per a.d.a. now also would qualify for equalization aid, up to $ 31,900 in Figure 4. Coupled with the increase in the computational tax rates, the effect was to hold substantially constant the assessed valuation level below which districts qualified for aid. Districts previously qualifying for aid now qualified for more aid, with districts at low levels (below $ 7,100 in assessed valuation per a.d.a. in Figure 4) receiving an increase equivalent to an increase in basic aid.[16]

Comparing Columns 3, 7, and 8 in Table 3 suggests the new equalization aid formulae resulted in some reshuffling of the educational burden among taxpayers, especially away from taxpayers residing in relatively low assessed valuation per a.d.a. districts ($k = 5$) onto taxpayers in relatively high assessed valuation districts ($k = 1$).

The increase in the homeowners' exemption, in addition to its (negative) income effects on taxpayers generally, also further reduced the tax-prices of education (Column 6 of Table 3) and other publicly funded services. This (positive) relative price effect was independent of fiscal jurisdiction, rich or poor. Whether truly helpful to a majority of the statewide electorate, the added homeowners' exemptions clearly tended to benefit lower income homeowners.

It should be noted that the real purchasing power of the basic aid grant had been declining in the face of the post-1967 inflation. By not increasing or indexing the basic aid level, the legislature effectively contributed to its diminishing importance in the school financing equation. This is shown in Figure 5, along with average total expenditures per a.d.a. and foundation levels.

From the standpoint of *Serrano v. Priest*, the 1972 legislative action did nothing to remove the basis on which the system initially had been challenged. Increases in the foundation level, computational tax rate, and homeowners' exemption do nothing to reduce the tax-price disparities which had drawn fire from the Court. At the margin of choice, a margin albeit higher in consequence of the new funding, well-situated districts still were faced with lower tax-prices.

Not surprisingly, the trial court determined the California school finance system was not in constitutional compliance. This decision, rendered in 1974, incorporated the 1972 financing changes. This judgment was affirmed by the Supreme Court in early 1977:

Substantial disparities in expenditures per pupil among school districts cause and perpetuate substantial disparities in the quality and extent of availability of educational opportunities. For this reason the school financing system before the fails to provide equality of treatment to all the pupils in the state. Although an equal expenditure level per pupil in every district is not educationally sound or desireable because of differing educational needs, equality of educational opportunity requires that all school districts possess an equal ability in terms of revenue to provide students with substantially equal opportunities for learning. The system before the court fails in this respect, for it gives high-wealth districts a substantial advantage in obtaining higher quality staff, program expansion and variety, beneficial teacher-pupil ratios and class sizes, modern equipment and materials, and high-quality buildings (Sup., 135, Cal. Rptr. 345; p. 355).

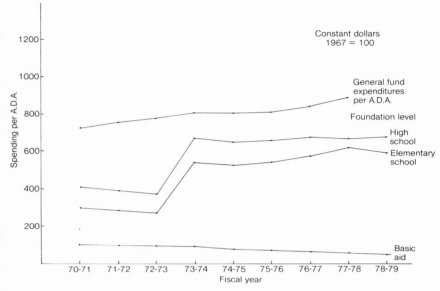

Figure 5.

Legislative response to the Court's affirmation of the trial court's decision took the form of Assembly Bill 65 which reduced basic aid by five dollar to its constitutional minimum of $ 120, increased the inflation adjustment factor for equalization aid, and imposed a penalty on districts proposing to spend in excess of the foundation level. For high assessed valuation per a.d.a. districts funding education in excess of foundation levels, the penalty would have the effect of increasing their tax-prices relative to those of low assessed valuation districts. This change in relative tax-prices among districts moves toward compliance with *Serrano v. Priest*.

Before AB 65 could be implemented, the electorate approved Proposition 13. With that approval, California government finance entered a new era.

Post Proposition 13

In addition to setting a maximum property tax rate of one percent of market value, hence reducing property tax revenues statewide by an estimated $ 7 billion, Proposition 13 also provided that the property tax revenues raised would be apportioned among local fiscal jurisdictions 'according to law.' Since local governments are creatures of the State, the revenue apportionment law became the responsibility of the State legislature. Local governments, including school districts, were faced with a substantial loss of own revenues on the one hand and with a significant loss of fiscal autonomy. Local tax-prices became virtually non-existent in that Proposition 13 made no provision for changes in the maximum one percent tax rate either by elected officials or voter approved overrides.

For fiscal year 1978-79, the Legislature adopted Senate Bills 154/2212 which substantially provided that individual school districts receive from the remaining one-percent property tax revenues the same proportion of pre-Proposition 13 property tax revenues. Approximately 85 percent of any revenues lost relatively to fiscal year 1977-78 would be made up from State funds. This initial response, therefore, left in place in the pattern of revenue disparities among districts which previously characterized school funding.

For fiscal year 1979-80 and beyond, the Legislature adopted Assembly Bill 8 which revised the method of computing school district revenue limits. Under the new legislation, relatively high spending school districts would have their limits adjusted more slowly than relatively low spending districts. State funds would supply the difference between the district's property tax revenues derived under the apportionment law and the district's revenue limit. Over time, the revenue limits per a.d.a. of all school districts would converge. This convergence, the State claims, serves to comply with *Serrano v. Priest.*

There is a certain irony in Proposition 13. Prior to 1978, the State had been accumulating a 'Serrano war-chest' with which to move to compliance with the order of the court, whatever form that order eventually might take. As part of the overall State surplus, this informal war chest contributed to the sense of taxpayer outrage expressed in the two-to-one vote in favor of Proposition 13. In the process of responding to the resulting loss of local property tax revenues and to demands for further tax relief, the Legislature has been forced to deplete the surplus.

The Legislature's impotence to achieve early and full compliance with *Serrano v. Priest* is traceable to the determination of local voters to be masters of their own fiscal fate. In Proposition 13, the voters surrendered this independence to the Legislature. Henceforth, the relevant tax-prices are those calculable statewide.

With respect to tax-price disparities, Proposition 13 would seem to have vitiated the basis on which *Serrano v. Priest* was affirmed. However, under the legislation adopted, the distribution of school district revenues begins with the pattern of differences generated under the system ruled unconstitutional. Until convergence everywhere occurs, the system will fail to comply.[17]

In its 1977 decision, the California Supreme Court stated that:

There exist several alternative potential methods of financing the public school system of this state which would not produce wealth-related spending disparities. These alternative methods which are 'workable, practical and feasible,' include: '(1) full state funding with the imposition of a statewide property tax; (2) consolidation of the present 1,067 school districts into about five hundred districts, with boundary realignments to equalize assessed valuations of real property among all school districts; (3) retention of the present school district boundaries but the removal of commercial and industrial property from local taxation for school purposes and taxation of such property at the state level; (4) school district power equalizing[,] which has as its essential ingredient the concept that school districts could choose to spend at different levels but for each level of expenditure chosen the tax effort would be the same for each school district choosing such level whether it be a high-wealth or a low wealth district; (5) vouchers; and (6) some combination of two or more of the above' (pp. 354-355).

If convergence is achieved under present or future legislation, one effect of Proposition 13 will have been to convert the system for financing education to 'full state funding,' the first of the Courts alternatives. It will be of no consequence to school districts whether or not some portion of the one-percent property tax revenues is earmarked for school finance. As noted, the relevant tax-price becomes the statewide income tax-price (Column 2 of Table 3).

The second Court alternative, consolidation, clearly would have equalized tax-prices among school districts. It suffers from the attribute that district boundaries would have to be changed with reasonable frequency to keep pace with changes in the relative rates of growth of the pupil population and assessed valuations.

To re-introduce district tax-prices, consolidation also would require either a major revision of Proposition 13 to permit voter approved property tax overrides or a major revision of district tax base. The obvious alternative here would be the personal income tax.[18]

Exclusion of commercial and industrial (and agricultural) property from a district's tax base is something of an anomaly in the Court's list of alternatives. There surely would be no presumption that assessed values of residential property per pupil are uniform among districts. In the simulation model, residential property values per pupil range from $4,500 to $10,500, with corresponding differences in tax-prices.

As with consolidation of districts, power equalizing would remove any tax-price differences among districts. It also would require the same revision of financing arrangements. The simplest scheme would be one in which each district was entitled to retain the same revenues per pupil that the tax-rate adopted by the district would produce per pupil statewide. Any revenues generated in excess of the statewide average would be surrendered to the State while any deficiency of revenues would be made up by the State. In such a system, the State would need perform at most a computational-disbursing-collection role.[19]

Vouchers, the fifth alternative, could be funded by the State, with equal vouchers per pupil statewide, or by individual school districts reformed either by consolidation or by power equalizing. In either instance, families seeking education in excess of that available at the level approved by the entity's electorate majority would add to the voucher whatever funds were necessary. The tax-price of vouchers would be uniform among districts, as would the private price of additional educational units. Such a plan would have the advantage, or disadvantage, of permitting parents the widest possible independence in securing the education of their children.

Comparing a statewide state-funded program of tuition vouchers, permitting use in private schools or add-ons by district public schools, with full state funding of public schools and privately-funded private schools, work by Stubblebine and Teeples (1974) suggests that vouchers would lead to lower per pupil spending on average and to greater differentials among pupils. Although they did not simulate the comparison, presumably this differential would be closed by a system of district funded vouchers. [20]

The noteworthy characteristics of the alternatives cited by the Court, save for statewide funding, is that they permit variations among school districts in the level of publicly funded education. The Court consistently has rejected the notion that equal spending was a necessary part of compliance. 'Individious discrimination' arose from disparities in the opportunity to fund education, not from disparities in the funding itself.

Confusion on this point, among commentators generally and among legislators particularly, may flow from a failure to appreciate the narrow confines within which the Court worked. The Court dealt with a funding system it found, on essentially tax-price grounds, to be unconstitutional. [21]

It invited the legislature to adopt a constitutional funding system. When the legislature failed to do so, the Court responded by saying, in essence, 'if you would continue with the system as we find it, you must reduce spending differences below $ 100 per pupil *within that funding system*. There are, however, other systems of funding which would satisfy us on equal opportunity grounds. Should one of these systems be adopted and should it produce spending disparities, we also might find it unconstitutional but the instant case of *Serrano* would not serve as precedent.'

An equal opportunity system which permitted districts the freedom to determine funding levels surely would result in substantial differences in the level of (public) funding per pupil among districts. Higher income districts would seem likely to fund higher levels of publicly financed education than would lower income districts. The Court may find challenging the issue of whether high income people prefer more education for their children because they have more income or because the same characteristics which lead them to prefer more education also lead them to generate more income.

The issue would be substantial. To find unconstitutional more spending per pupil in high income districts would call into question a host of parent regulated adtivities which serve to educate their children: religious school, museum visits, opera and concert attendance, Disneyland, and participate in the family's home life. More income permits the choice of more consumption. The issue of whether the rich can consume more than the poor strikes to the very heart of the economic system supported by the U.S. Constitution for some two hundred years.

It is, perhaps, the final irony of Proposition 13 that the body politic seems likely to find itself saddled with the very system of financing resisted for so many years: statewide funding of education with equal spending per pupil.

NOTES

1. For 1970, reported data shows 5 million California households and pupils with statewide assessed valuation of $ 55.3 billion, or $ 11,100 per household and per pupil. The data also suggest a much wider range of assessed valuations per pupil, reflecting observations in the corner cells ommitted from the simulation model. Cf., U.S. Bureau of the Census (1978: 47) and California State Department of Education (1972-73).
2. For 1970, reported data show California personal income of $ 88.6 billion, or $ 17,800 per household.
3. The smaller the district's state share, the closer to zero; the larger the share, the less appropriate the *de minimus* argument.
4. This would not be true of a statewide property tax to fund education. Here, the jointness of the funding decision would translate the C-I-A property taxes paid into a component of the individual's implicit tax price.
5. In practice, of course, things are never so clear cut: renters may perceive no advantages in this exemption. If sufficient in number, potentially they could form a majority with high income families to defeat increases in the exemption.
6. If the computational result is negative, the district is not required to surrender funds to the State.
7. The y-axis intercepts for each income class have been reduced to reflect the income effect of taxes imposed to support public services provided by fiscal jurisdictions at all levels of government-Federal, State, and local. The 'budget line' origins are shifted to the right, away from the y-axis, to reflect the basic aid of $ 125 per pupil.
8. Electorates in average and below average districts may be tempted to impose such limits on above average districts. However, the smaller the number of affected pupils, the less the potential gain from the units restriction.
9. $ 400 per student represents the weighted average of $ 355 per elementary a.d.a. and $ 488 per high school a.d.a. The 1.8% computational rate represents the sum of 1% for elementary school districts and 0.8% foe high school districts, since every family must reside in one and only one elementary and high school district.
10. Cf. Sup. 96 Cal. Rptr. 601 (20 September 1971).
11. Sup. 96, p. 607.
12. Ibid., p. 624.
13. Ibid., p. 623.
14. Ibid., p. 609: 'Consequently, we must reject plaintiffs' argument that the provision in section 5 for a "system of common schools" requires uniform educational expenditures.'

The Court also did not foreclose the possibility that an equal expenditure case could be brought under equal protection. However, the instant case could not serve as precedent:

> The other asserted policy interest is that of allowing a local district to choose how much it wishes to spend on the education of its children. Defendants argue: [I]f one district raises a lesser amount per pupil than another district, this is a matter of choice and preference of the individual desire for lower taxes rather than an expanded educational program, or may reflect a greater interest within that district in such other services that

are supported by local property taxes as, for example, police and fire protection or hospital services.

We need not decide whether such decentralized financial decision-making is a compelling state interest, since under the present financing system, such fiscal freewill is a cruel illusion for the poor school districts (p. 620).

15. Cf. ibid., p. 608.
16. A word of explanation with respect to the data is in order. The new foundation levels of $765 and $970 produce a weighted state average of $825 per pupil. When adjusted for inflation, between 1970 and 1973, this mean foundation level translates as $700 per pupil. This adjustment is necessary to maintain parity with the 1970 data, particularly with assessed values.

    Average total expenditures per a.d.a. were $861 in 1970 and $1,133 in 1973. Adjusted for inflation, average total expenditures were substantially the same in the two years, $861 and $858 respectively.
17. The trial court ordered compliance by 1980. Since the adjustment provided by AB 82 will not produce convergence for some years beyond 1980, a case can be made that the State continues to be in violation of the trial court order.
18. The corporate income tax should be retained by the state to avoid either potentially complex tax determination problems for corporations doing business in two or more school districts or conditioning corporate location on the basis of anticipated school district (and other fiscal jurisdiction) tax rates.
19. This scheme previously was developed as 'coordinated tax base sharing' in a paper by Stubblebine and Teeples (1974).
20. The Stubblebine-Teeples simulations also suggested that 'coordinated tax base sharing' would lead to average per pupil spending statewide comparable to that realized under the Pre-Serrano foundation-equalization-aid program, but with substantially reduced spending differentials among school districts.
21. The trial court may have added to the confusion by utilizing the phrase 'equal treatment' in various places, a terminology not incorporated into eithet of the Supreme Court's decisions.

REFERENCES

Alexander, A. J. (1975). *Inequality in California school finance: Dimensions, sources, remedies.* Santa Monica: The Rand Corporation, R-1440-FF, March.

Bureau of the Census, U.S. Department of Commerce (1978). *Statistical abstract of the United States: 1978.* Washington, D.C.: U.S. Government Printing Office.

California Reporter. *Serrano v. Priest* (1971). Sup. 96 Cal Rptr 601.

California Reporter. *Serrano v. Priest* (1977). Sup. 135 Cal Rptr 345.

California State Department of Education (1974). *California public schools selected statistics, 1972-73.* Sacramento.

Stubblebine, W. C., and Teeples, R. K. (1974). Abridged versions published as: California and the finance of education: Alternatives in the wake of Serrano v. Priest, in *Property taxation and the finance of education,* R. W. Lindholm, Editor (Madison: University of Wisconsin Press), 163-178. Original available from the authors as Paper Number 44, Claremont Economic Papers, Claremont Colleges, Claremont, California.

The post-Proposition 13 environment in California and its consequences for education

WERNER Z. HIRSCH*

University of California, Los Angeles

Any analysis of California's Revenue Limitation movement must consider not merely Proposition 13 but also its various legislative responses. In this spirit, I will briefly review Proposition 13 passed in June 1978 and key legislative responses that followed. Next, I will analyze direct effects of these constitutional and statutory steps, particularly on public education in California; finally secondary effects resulting from private and public responses to the new environment which, in turn, affect public education will be assessed.

I

On June 6, 1978 the electorate of California, by a large majority, passed a constitutional amendment – Proposition 13. It rolled back property tax assessments to their 1975 levels and restricted increases in assessments to 2% per year for as long as the property is retained by the same owner. Property taxes are prohibited from exceeding 1% of the property's full value; increases in state taxes are permitted only if approved by a $\frac{2}{3}$ majority of both houses of the state legislature; and local taxes must be approved by a $\frac{2}{3}$ majority of jurisdiction's voters.

What led to this collective action by California voters is not entirely clear. Various causes have been held responsible among them the following – unreasonably high and rapidly increasing property taxes, a large and continuously rising surplus of state funds, alleged flabby and inefficient local government, resentment against redistribution of monies to low income groups in general and minorities in particular, and the belief that the price at which government was providing services was too high. Which of these or any other factors prompted California voters to approve as extreme a revenue limitation measure as Proposition 13 so far has not been determined.

* Helpful assistance by David Mengle is gratefully acknowledged.

No less interesting than the collective choice that produced Proposition 13 are the decisions made by the California Legislature in response. Thus, shortly after the passage of Proposition 13, the State Legislature passed a one-year bail-out bill, which as of July 1, 1979 was superceded by a long-term program to shift state funds to California's local governments and provide new local revenue sources. Actually two alternative proposals were offered as a long-term solution.

The Brown Administration proposed on March 6, 1979, a program of providing local government with state funds on a permanent basis to make up local property tax losses. Under the Governor's proposal schools, while retaining their current share of property taxes, were to receive the counties' portion of local property taxes (based on *situs*) on a county-wide basis, together with some additional state funds for further equalization. The funding of counties, cities, and special districts was to be shifted from property to sales taxes. Specifically, these governments would give up their property tax base and in return receive a portion – $2\frac{1}{2}\cent$ – of state salex tax. Counties could levy a $1\cent$ sales tax to finance essentially health and welfare programs, and a further $1\frac{1}{2}\cent$ sales tax would be shared by counties, special districts and cities. In this manner, in the first year $ 4.8 billion would be transferred from state to local governments.

This proposal did not make any headway in the Legislature, and on April 2, 1979, Speaker Leo McCarthy sketched out his plan to finance local government on a permanent basis. His ideas were incorporated later into Assembly Bill 8 to provide school districts with substantial new annual funds from the State's General Fund. According to Assembly Bill 8, as passed by the California Legislature and signed by the Governor in mid-July, 1979, the state assumed most costs earlier incurred by counties in performing welfare program. Parts of the property taxes earlier levied by school districts were transferred to counties, cities, and special districts. As a consequence, special districts and counties rely almost exclusively on property taxes, whereas cities, while retaining their share of the sales tax, somewhat increase their reliance on the property tax. Slightly less than $ 5 billion – $ 4.84 billion – were transferred from the state to local governments for the fiscal year 1979-80.

A second important step was taken by the Legislature to help local governments deal with Proposition 13. Specifically, the Legislature passed Assembly Bill 549 permitting special districts to levy assessments for road maintenance, lighting, flood control, etc. Counties were authorized to fix and collect charges for such services in any zone in a county service area and to impose such charges on the basis of the estimated benefit to each parcel. In the first year the County Board of Supervisors can impose these benefit assessments without a vote of the people, although for subsequent years approval by a majority of those voting in a popular referendum is required. Furthermore, Assembly Bill 618 was passed and signed by the Governor, permitting special fees for police and fire protection to be assessed against property owners. Thus, cities, counties and other local agencies can levy an assessment for fire and police proyection if two-thirds of those voting on such a proposition approve it. The fees are to be based on benefits to the property owner.

In summary, the collective choices in the form of legislative action have greatly modified the Proposition 13 environment. Up to now, the state government in California has picked up much of the revenue loss incurred by local governments under Proposition 13. Moreover, the State of California has also enacted legislation which under specified conditions permits authorization of new revenue sources in the form of benefit assessments. But AB549 and AB618 not only fail to help public education, they also will tend to undermine the financing of public education by favoring the support of non-educational services. We will next consider major direct effects of the new constitutional and statutory enactments following Proposition 13 which are having a profound effect.

II

The passage of Proposition 13 and the subsequent state legislation have created a new politico-economic environment in California. I shall discuss a number of the major components and their efficiency and equity implications.

Increasingly centralized government

Public schools in California have always been subject to many state regulations. Now, however, as the state under AB8 has increased its annual aid to local governments by about $5 billion in real terms, additional power and control has shifted from local school boards to the state. Moreover, as school districts face fiscal difficulties, more federal subvention will be sought and most likely granted; thus some of the control will also shift to Washington. The ultimate results of these developments will be a general decline in home rule and local control in the presence of more and more intervention by centralized governments in Sacramento and Washington.

The efficiency implications of increased control over education by the state (and federal) governments are, by and large, negative. It can be demonstrated that, in the absence of economies of scale due to centralization and of spillover effects between localities, decentralized provision of a public good is more efficient than centralized provision (Oates, 1972: 54-59). To begin with, assume a two-person, two-good economy, represented by the Edgeworth Box in Figure 1. Assume initially that both goods A and B are private goods. The locus of all possible tangency (i.e., Pareto optimal) points for individual 1's indifference curve (U_1) with that of individual 2 (U_2) is given by $0_1 0_2$. Suppose

38

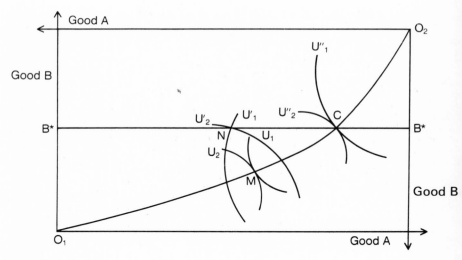

Figure 1.

1 and 2 reach a tangency at point M. If, suddenly, a uniform quantity B^* is imposed on both individuals, the outcome will no longer be Pareto-efficient. This outcome is shown by the new position at point N, at which the individuals are no longer on their efficiency locus. The outcome would be efficient only if both 1 and 2 would have chosen the imposed level anyway, a choice they *could* have made, but obviously did not. In short, imposing a specific quantity constrains the range of choice and is inefficient. (By the way, Point C in Figure 1, in which equal quantities of the public good are consumed, is also Pareto-optimal. However, in the absence of a specific social welfare function that can justify massive redistributions there is no a priori reason for preferring C to M.)

This argument can be generalized to groups making collective choices. If communities arrive at different choices concerning how much of a publicly provided good to consume, it may be assumed that their decisions reflect the divergent tastes of each community. To the extent that members of a community 'vote with their feet,' particularly small communities would tend to be composed of members with roughly similar preferences regarding major public goods, e.g., education (Tiebout, 1956). Centralization can take into account few of these differences among communities and would probably result in imposing a uniform quantity of a good. Again, each community *could* have chosen this level under decentralization, but not all did. As in the case of two individuals, the uniform quantity is inefficient.

Of course, in any real-life situation inefficiencies of centralization must be balanced against gains due to economies of scale and internalization of spillover effects. For some services gains from centralization will tend to outweigh losses due to centralization; in the case of education, however, this does not seem likely. There is no reason to expect large economies of scale to result from more centralized decision making about education since production will continue in the same units. The issue of spillovers, however, is less clear. There are spillover effects in the sense that other communities benefit from one locality's provision of education when an individual moves to one of those other areas. However, if these effects were very significant, one would expect to see high-expenditure communities reducing the amounts they spend because they do not fully receive the benefits of the education they provide. The final result would be a more or less uniformly low level of educational expenditure across communities. In fact, this is not observed, and before the passage of Proposition 13 there were large differences among localities in the resources they devoted to education. Since neither economies of scale nor spillover effects appear to be significant in the case of education, centralized financing and decision making in the post-Proposition 13 era is likely to result in inefficiencies.

Disproportionate tax burdens on residential property owners

The fiscal implications of Proposition 13 are several. Some arise from the fact that, whenever real property is sold, Proposition 13 requires that the purchase price become the new tax base. In the presence of rapidly increasing real estate prices (for example, in Southern California prices of residential property increased by about 20% during 1979 alone), real estate taxes are much higher if the property changed hands since 1975 then if it did not. As long as a property is not sold, the tax base increases by only 2% per year (or slightly higher if bonded debt must be serviced). These aspects of Proposition 13 in conjunction with the fact that not all classes of property change hands equally often within a given period, imply that the shares of taxes paid by residential and non-residential property owners will show some predictable divergencies over time.

Residential property turns over much more rapidly than does commercial and industrial property. Consequently, the assessed value of residential property can be expected to grow relative to that of commercial and industrial property until the entire stock of both types of property has turned over. Once this has occurred, the growth rates of assessed value will be the same for both classes. However, before this point is reached, given equal values of assessed property of the two classes in the initial period and equal appreciation rates, the ratio of assessed value of residential to commercial/industrial property will in all subsequent periods be greater than one. Therefore, the total taxes paid by residential property owners will be disproportionality greater than those paid by business property owners. (Moreover, since certain industrial property, i.e., large specialized factories, are never sold, the growth rates of assessed residential values will always exceed those of industrial values.)

The growth of assessed values before both stocks have turned over completely may be illustrated in the following formulae:

$$A_t^h = A_0^h(1 + \bar{p}_t + (t - 1)a)$$

$$A_t^c = A_t^c(1 + \pi\bar{p}_t + (1 - \pi)(t - 1)a)$$

where:

> A is assessed value of real property
> t is number of years greater than zero but less than the time in which all properties have turned over at least once
> h is residential land use
> c is commercial/industrial land use
> π is the probability of commercial/industrial property changing owners during the t-year period
> $\bar{p}_t = \dfrac{1}{t}\sum_{i=1}^{t} p_i$ = average appreciation rate of property values over the t-year period
> a is allowable growth rate of assessed values under Proposition 13.

Since π is a probability and therefore must satisfy $0 \le \pi \le 1$, the growth rate of assessed values for commercial/industrial properties will never be greater than that of residential properties during the t-year period. Once the growth rates have equalized, taxes paid will remain relatively higher for the residential sector. This already is happening. Thus, while in 1978 the assessed value of residential properties accounted for 64% of total real property value in Los Angeles County, within one year the share had increased to 72%.

Disproportionate tax burden on younger property owners

Another fiscal implication of Proposition 13 is that the share of property taxes paid by younger families will grow faster over time than will that paid by older families. This is so because many young families seek their own homes and purchase larger ones as their families grow; thus they make more frequent purchases than do middle aged and older persons. In a manner similar to the preceding analysis regarding residential versus commercial properties, it can be shown that the growth multiplier of assessed valuation of property held by younger families is higher than that for older ones, and that the same holds for the growth multiplier of property taxes. In other words, the share of taxes paid by young families will increase over time.

Those who would want to apply the benefit principle of taxation can argue that to the extent that young people use more public schooling than do older people, there could result an improved matching between benefits and taxes.

However, with the tax burden on young people increasing while that on older people is falling, underinvestment in such a merit good as education is likely to result. Thus, the ability-to-pay principle that should be applied to a merit good is violated.

Discriminatory treatment of tenants

Proposition 13 was written in a manner that resulted in major tax benefits to home owners and businesses, and particularly those engaged in farming; no comparable aid was awarded to tenants whose relative tax burden increased accordingly. Yet, one of the points used to sell Proposition 13 had been the promise that landlords would pass tax savings on to tenants in the form of lower rents. This promise was totally fallacious, particularly in the short run, as can be shown in Figure 2. A rent reduction pass-through is most unlikely, so that all tax benefits will tend to accrue to property owners.

Assume that the supply of rental housing units, i.e., apartments, is fixed at amount X_0 in the short run (see Figure 2). Tenants pay P_0 in rent and landlords receive P_1 after taxes, and the market clears. Now assume that, for simplicity, the property tax be abolished altogether. The result is a transfer of wealth to landlords from previous recipients of property tax proceeds. This is shown by the shaded area in the diagram. Even if landlords attempt to pass on their savings as lower rents, they will not be able to maintain these lower levels because excess demand (distance $X_0 X_1$) will arise. Competition among tenants and prospective tenants in bidding for the fixed supply will force rents back up to about their original level. The tax benefits, then, turn out to be one-sided indeed.

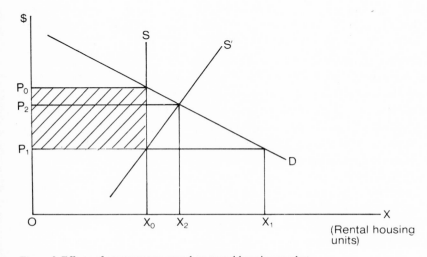

Figure 2. Effects of property tax repeal on rental housing market

What of the longer-term response? As supply becomes more elastic over time so that the supply curve becomes S', tenants could benefit from increased supply (X_2) and lower rents (P_2). However, the actual outcome has been that tenants, angry over the lack of any immediate benefits, have begun to organize throughout California. This has led to rent control measures in a number of jurisdictions such as the County of Los Angeles and the cities of Los Angeles and Santa Monica. Despite the fact that rent control laws tend to be counter-productive in that they dry up supplies of rental housing (this process is not shown in the diagram), their enactment as a means for tenants to capture a share of available benefits is clearly a result of Proposition 13.

The fact that Proposition 13 treats tenants unfairly and is resulting in selective rent control, also has efficiency implications. If rents are rolled back to reflect tax savings, i.e., to P_1 in Figure 2, excess demand will be X_0X_1 in the 'immediate' run. Since only QX_0 units of housing will be rented out, and since there is no guarantee that all those who succeed in finding housing are those whose demand price is equal to or greater than P_0, all the housing units might not go to the highest-valuing users. Families with school aged children who seek rental housing will therefore encounter additional difficulties locating in places they find suitable.

Increased tax burdens on low income groups

While many low income groups are renters and according to the argument presented in the earlier section face disproportionate tax burdens because of Proposition 13, there exist additional reasons for this tendency. Thus passage of Proposition 13 has led many local governments to increase their reliance on user fees, while some have sought benefit assessments authorized under AB549. The shift away from reliance on property taxes to more fees (and assessments) has a bearing on whether local taxation in California is becoming more or less progressive.

While there is no universal agreement about the progressivity or regressivity of the property tax, R. Musgrave and P. Musgrave (1976: 355) have argued that under certain circumstances the tax is progressive. This position is supported by a number of empirical studies which have been summarized as concluding that 'the income elasticity of the property tax... is slightly higher than one, i.e., between 1 and 1.3' (Hirsch, 1970: 110). Since taxes which are income elastic are progressive, we can conclude that the property tax is slightly progressive.

On the other hand, many fee-financed local services are income inelastic, and they are widely considered to be by and large regressive. Thus, as the percentage change of income increases that of spending for fee-financed services (e.g., court proceedings, water and electricity) increases also, but at a lower rate. In short, replacing property taxes with user fees (and assessments) tends to provide gains to middle- and high-income households at the expense of lower income households, though efficiency may increase.

III

A number of secondary effects result when private and public decisions are made in the post-Proposition 13 politico-economic environment.

Wholesale deterioration of the social infrastructure

As local governments find themselves short of funds, one of the less painful decisions is to defer repair and maintenance. Yet, as upkeep of buildings, roads, bridges, sewer systems, and buses is underfinanced year after year, large losses are likely to occur. These losses, in both monetary and human terms, are compounded by the fact that the eventual cost of restoring these facilities tends to be substantially higher than the savings from deferred maintenance. This is simply the well-known principle that preventive maintenance is less costly over the long run than corrective maintenance. Possible human losses could result not only from school buildings collapsing but also from school bus accidents due to washed out roads and bridges and lack of mechanical maintenance of buses.

Politically rather than economically motivated service level reduction

In the post-Proposition 13 era, school budgets will decline in real terms. Since productivity increases will be difficult to attain, the level of services will have to be reduced. However, cutbacks are unlikely to be guided mainly by efficiency considerations. For political reasons, a meat-axe approach in which all departments are cut back by roughly the same percentage, is politically least damaging. The only modification might be disproportionate budget cuts of departments with relatively weak constituents. Examples in post-Proposition 13 California are libraries and museums which in 1978-79 incurred much larger relative budget cuts than departments which could elicit the support of powerful interest groups, e.g., police and fire protection.

Deteriorating and more militant public school labor force

Schools are labor intensive; therefore, as budgets shrink in real terms, the labor force will also decline. In the abstract, such a decline can be looked upon as a positive development. However, the shrinkage is unlikely to result in the firing of workers with the poorest performance; many such workers are protected by seniority rules. Thus, assured of continued employment, these public employees have little incentive to exert themselves in an effort to increase productivity. Moreover, to the extent that public school employees, faced with adversity in the post-Proposition 13 environment, turn more and more to unions who tend to vigorously protect and enforce seniority rules, productivity declines should become more and more severe.

As budgets tighten, school superintendents will be forced to institute cutbacks or wage freezes which unions can be expected to oppose adamantly. Moreover, efforts to economize through contracting out services to the private sector will also be the object of union opposition. The result may be more disputes between public employee representatives and managers, as well as a higher probability of strikes.

Finally, as schools retrench, fewer employment opportunities will open up for minorities who long have looked upon public employment in schools as a means to enter the mainstream of America. Black and brown children will continue to be taught mainly by white teachers, hampering school desegregation.
also to a redistribution of the geographic demand for public education.

Retarded growth

Efficient land use requires that issuance of planning, zoning and building permits by local governments be based on whether a particular land use fits into the community and has a comparative advantage there. However, since in the post-Proposition 13 era cities and counties must mainly fund their activities from property taxes whose rates are limited to a low 1% of market value, they will often fear that new land uses will cost them more in services than will be covered by prospective tax receipts. Consequently, building permits will tend to be denied regardless of how efficient a land use would actually result. The effects on income and tax base can be chilling, and lead also to a redistribution of the geographic demand for public education.

IV

In conclusion, passage of Proposition 13 has generated a sustained chain reaction of collective and private steps. Together, they have produced outcomes which may be very different from those intended by the sponsors of the proposition and those who voted for it.

Most observers agree that one major objective or Proposition 13 was to increase the efficiency of government in general and of public schools in particular. Yet, various aspects of Proposition 13 and the ensuing state legislation are likely to have the opposite effect. As local responsibility and discretion is reduced, and as financial survival requires living with complicated state laws and outguessing and outmaneuvering state and (to a lesser extent) Federal government, more and more inefficiencies are likely to emerge in the operations of local school districts. Moreover, the continued discrepancy between revenue raising and control, together with potentially distorted land use decisions, declining quality of public school personnel, politically rather than economically motivated reductions in service levels and deterioration of the social infrastructure all can add up to lower productivity in the public schools.

Likewise, many observers agree that Proposition 13 was to eliminate the huge state's tax surplus. But instead of reforming the state's tax system or at least assigning parts of one of its major tax bases to local governments, the legislature voted to distribute annually additional money from the state's General Fund. Specifically, the annual transfer of money from the General Fund to school districts was increased. The continued *de facto* existence of large state surpluses helped those who would seek to pass Howard Jarvis' new constitutional amendment which would have cut state income tax rates by half. This amendment was defeated in 1980. Had it passed, AB8's deflator mechanism would have placed annual appropriations from the General Fund in serious jeopardy. The reduction in state subventions to school districts in 1980-81 – the first year of the amendment's effect – could have amounted to $ 2.6 billion.

REFERENCES

Hirsch, W. Z. (1970). *The economics of state and local government.* New York: McGraw-Hill.
Musgrave, R. A., and Musgrave, P. B. (1971). *Public finance in theory and practice,* 2nd ed. New York: McGraw-Hill.
Oates, W. E. (1971). *Fiscal federalism.* New York: Harcourt, Brace, Javanovich.
Tiebout, C. T. (1956). A pure theory of local expenditures. *Journal of Political Economy* 64: 416-424.

Local authority education expenditure in England and Wales: Why standards differ and the impact of government grants

RICHARD JACKMAN   and   JOHN PAPADACHI

London School of Economics   *Centre for Environmental Studies, London*

1. Introduction

A major objective of education policy in Britain since the war has been to achieve an approximate uniformity in the standards of educational provision across local authorities. Such an objective can be defined in a number of ways: in this paper we adopt what might be described as a 'minimal' definition, namely the equalisation of educational inputs per pupil year.[1] While there is no doubt that the gross inequalities of the past have been reduced, substantial variations in expenditure (per pupil year) remain.[2] The purpose of this paper is to explore the causes of these variations and to draw some rather tentative implications for policy.

The main results are that just over half of the existing variation in expenditure in both primary and secondary education can be attributed to cost factors, and hence does not imply differences in standards of provision. However, preference and financial factors, which we would associate with differences in standards, do appear to account for a significant part of the variation (about one-third for primary and one-quarter for secondary, the remainder of the variation being accounted for by the interaction between the two sets of factors). Within the sphere of financially induced variations in expenditure, central government grants appear to do little to offset variations resulting from differences in household incomes, and, indeed, in the case of primary education appear to add to, rather than offset this source of variation. This suggests that central government grants are not fulfilling their equalisation objective (see Layfield, 1976, particularly Annex 28).

The plan of the paper is as follows. Section 2 describes the budget constraint facing local authorities, taking into account the existing (as of 1978/79) system of central government grants. Local authorities are subject to an array of statutory (and semi-statutory) obligations, and we assume these 'committed' expenditures have first claim on their budget. Any remaining funds can be allocated between services, or used to reduce local taxes, according to the local authority's preferences. The linear expenditure system provides an analytically convenient framework for distinguishing 'committed' from 'discretionary' elements in expenditure (Stone, 1954, and for an application to local government expenditure, Inman, 1971).

This procedure generates a system of equations relating expenditure to the various budgetary factors, committed expenditures and the local authority's preferences. We have no explicit model of the factors likely to cause differences in local authorities' committed expenditures, or in their preferences. Our procedure, therefore, is to estimate, by regression analysis, equations relating expenditure to the factors thought likely to affect either costs or preferences, together with variables generated from the budget constraint. The use of regression analysis in this way provides information on the correlation between the different variables, but cannot be regarded as a test of the linear expenditure model specification. The regression results are presented in Section 3, and very briefly compared with estimates from other studies.

From the regression estimates it is possible to compute the contributions of the various factors to the observed variation in expenditure, both individually and in combination. In Section 4 we discuss some of the more interesting of these estimates.

2. The budget constraint

For the purposes of the present analysis, the local authority's budget is its general or 'rate fund' account. This incorporates all local authority expenditure net of incomes from rents, fees and charges, and net of specific and supplementary grants (which are central government contributions towards the finance of particular services, especially public housing). Rate fund expenditure is financed from the taxes local authorities levy (rates) and from the Rate Support Grant (RSG) which is a general grant from central government not tied to the provision of particular services.

Per capita rate fund revenue in a local authority is given by

$$r(t - d) + st + g_n + (\bar{v} - r - s)t + rd$$
$$= g_n + \bar{v}t$$

where:

  r is per-capita domestic (household) rateable value.
  s is per-capita non-domestic (commercial and industrial) rateable value.
  t is the rate poundage levied on commerce and industry.

g_n is the 'needs element' of RSG, which is a lump sum grant designed to compensate authorities for differences in their spending 'needs'.

$\bar{v}$ is the national standard rateable value per head. $(\bar{v} - r - s)$ is therefore the local authority's deficiency of rateable value per head. Central government pays grant, known as 'resources element' to local authorities which is equal to the product of their rate poundage and their rateable value deficiency.

d is the domestic rate poundage reduction arising from the 'domestic element' of RSG.

Local authorities are required to levy a lower rate poundage on domestic ratepayers than on non-domestic (the difference being prescribed by central government), and central government refunds the revenue the local authority would lose as a result through the 'domestic element'.

In the case of a few authorities $r + s > \bar{v}$, that is the per capita rateable value of property within the local authority is greater than the national standard rateable value per head. Such authorities receive no resources element grant, either positive or negative. Per capita rate fund revenue for these authorities is thus

$$r(t - d) + st + g_n + rd = g_n + (r + s)t$$

It is convenient to define v, the 'inclusive rateable value', as equal to $\bar{v}$ for authorities in receipt of resources element, and as $(r + s)$ for authorities whose rateable value per head is in excess of the national standard. Per capita fund revenue can then generally be written

$$g_n + vt$$

We assume there are **J** different local authority services. Most local authority services, including education, are provided only to a subset of the population. We write per capita expenditure on service j as $n_j p_j q_j$ where:

n_j is the proportion of the population in receipt of the service
p_j is the cost per unit of service provision
q_j is the quantity or standard of service provision

It follows that the local authority budget constraint can be written

$$\sum_{j=1}^{J} n_j p_j q_j = g_n + vt$$

Likewise if there are K private goods in the economy, the budget constraint for private goods for the average man in the local authority is given by

$$\sum_{k=1}^{K} p_k q_k = y - r(t - d)$$

where p_k and q_k are respectively the prices and quantities of each of the private goods, and y is average per capita income net of central government taxes.

Combining the budget constraints gives

$$\frac{r}{v} \sum_{j=1}^{J} n_j p_j q_j + \sum_{k=1}^{K} p_k q_k = y + \frac{r}{v} g_n + rd$$

Expenditure on each service depends on the budget constraint and on preferences, which raises the question of whose preferences are held to determine the allocation of resources. At one extreme, the 'median voter' model (Downs, 1957; Bergstrom and Goodman, 1973) assumes that, in their competition for votes, political parties allocate resources in the local government sector in accordance with the preferences of the median voter. Within the framework of a linear expenditure system, one would then assume the median voter had a Stone-Geary utility function of the form

$$u = \sum_{j=1}^{J} B_j \log(q_j - c_j) + \sum_{k=1}^{K} B_k \log(q_k - c_k)$$

and expenditure on a particular local authority service (say service 1) would be given by

$$p_1 q_1 = p_1 c_1 + \frac{b_1}{n_1} \cdot \frac{v}{r} \left[y + \frac{r}{v} g_n + rd - \frac{r}{v} \sum_{j=1}^{J} n_j p_j c_j - \sum_{k=1}^{K} p_k c_k \right]$$

It is well-known that the median voter model requires a number of very restrictive assumptions (Bergstrom and Goodman, 1973). Additionally, it carries with it the implication – widely regarded as implausible – that the payment of additional (lump sum) grants to local authorities has no effect on their expenditure. Local authorities are perceived as 'transparent' so that people simply lump together local authority grants with their own incomes and then allocate the total between private goods and local government services. If central government levies higher taxes to finance additional local authority grants, the total of resources available is unaffected, and so there should be no effect on local government expenditure.[3]

In this paper we adopt a more general formulation. Expenditure decisions are made by the local authority – that is by elected members and officials who are assumed to want to promote the welfare of the community and who are under continual political pressure of many forms (including electoral) to do so. That is, decision-makers within the local authority behave as if they were maximising a utility function in which the standards of the services they provide and the rate bills they levy are important arguments. This more general specification does not require that the local authority's preferences are the same as those of its average citizen, and allows the possibility of 'fiscal illusion' in the sense that local taxpayers are not assumed to know how much grant the local authority is receiving and hence are unaware of the opportunity cost to them of grant-financed local services.[4]

Again, consistent with a linear expenditure system, we might assume the local authority's utility function Stone-Geary of the form

$$u = \sum_{j=1}^{J} B_j \log(q_j - c_j) + B_x \log(x_0 - x)$$

where x is the actual average rate bill levied, and x_0 some 'maximum acceptable rate bill'.

Then $x = r(t - d)$ and the local authority budget constraint can be written

$$\sum_{j=1}^{J} n_j p_j q_j = g_n + dv + \frac{v}{r} x$$

giving an expenditure function for service 1

$$p_1 q_1 = p_1 c_1 + \frac{b_1}{n_1} \left[g_n + dv + \frac{v}{r} x_0 - \sum_{j=1}^{J} n_j p_j c_j \right]$$

Expenditure on a service, in this formulation, depends on three types of factors:

i) those affecting 'committed' expenditure on the service ($p_1 c_1$). We would expect that statutory obligations etc. set the minimum standards uniform across authorities (that is a common value for c_1 across authorities), but that the cost of meeting those standards would vary across authorities. We therefore attribute differences in committed expenditures to 'cost factors', for example differences in the need for school transport, or differences in average wage rates, between areas. (We set out the cost factors that appear relevant in Section 3.)

ii) those affecting 'preferences'. In the linear expenditure system, b_1 is the marginal budget share – that is the proportion of discretionary funds spent on service 1. Since, in this formulation, the preferences are those of local councillors, one might in general assume that their political ideology would provide a good indication of where their preferences lay. While Labour is the party of higher public spending in general, there is less reason to expect a strong effect of political ideology on education expenditure. The benefits of public education – particularly at the secondary stage – accrue as much, if not more, to children from better-off families than to those from poorer families. Labour councils may well wish to concentrate their higher spending on services with a greater redistributive effect. We nonetheless incorporate a political variable as a possible indication of differences in preferences.

iii) budgetary factors. There are two terms which cannot be measured directly: the maximum acceptable rate bill (x_0), and committed expenditure on all local government services $(\sum n_j p_j c_j)$.

The maximum acceptable rate bill is simply a linearisation of the increasing disutility of paying rates because of the consumption of private goods and services foregone. It follows that the maximum acceptable rate bill will normally be higher for people with higher incomes.

One approach to attempting to measure committed expenditure on all local authority services would be to carry out a regression analysis on total local authority expenditure. But in England and Wales the needs grant paid to local authorities has itself been based on such a regression analysis since 1974. It follows that, if the government's regression analysis is doing its job, variations in authorities in $\sum n_j p_j c_j$ will be measured by differences in needs grant receipts. It follows that the payment of needs grant will appear both positively as a component of lump sum grants, and negatively as a measure of committed expenditures and hence drop out of the equation. Total expenditure per head of population of a local authority on the J services it provides is given by

$$\sum_{j=1}^{J} n_j p_j q_j = \sum_{j=1}^{J} n_j p_j c_j + \sum_{j=1}^{J} b_j \left(g_n + dv + \frac{v}{r} x_0 - \sum_{j=1}^{J} n_j p_j c_j \right)$$

In the government's regression regression analysis, the independent variables tested are confined to 'need' and 'cost' factors, that is to n_j and p_j terms in the present notation. A regression based on actual expenditure will give an unbiased estimate of $\sum_{j=1}^{J} n_j p_j c_j$ only if variations in the second term in the above expression are uncorrelated with those in the first. While this appears to have been the government's assumption in operating this technique, it is clearly vulnerable to criticism (on the grounds, for example that political preferences or financial factors may be correlated with the various needs factors and hence bias their estimates (Jackman and Sellars, 1978)). Insofar as payments of needs grant are influenced by preference and financial factors, the estimated coefficients on these variables will be upward biased because they will include induced needs grant effects.

The regression exercise provides a measure of the assessed spending need of each authority. The per capita needs grant actually paid equals the assessed spending need per head less a constant term. The constant term is the same for all local authorities outside London, but for London authorities it is increased (so their grant is reduced) by a mechanism known as 'clawback', designed to counteract the effect of higher rateable values in London.[5] We have (arbitrarily) set the difference between needs grant and committed expenditure on all services for non-London authorities as equal to zero: hence the 'clawback' appears as a negative lump sum grant for the London authorities. The other component of the lump sum grant term, inclusive rateable value per head multiplied by the domestic element rate poundage reduction, varies between authorities (a) because the domestic rate poundage reduction is higher in Wales than in England, and (b) because the inclusive rateable value per head of some authorities, especially in London, is higher than the national standard rateable value per head.

Taking these factors into account, we may write the expenditure equation in the form

$$p_1 q_1 = p_1 c_1 + b_1 \left[\frac{dv - g_k}{n_1} + \frac{v}{r} \frac{x_0}{n_1} \right]$$

where g_k is the needs grant 'clawback'.

Finally, we have assumed that local authorities are concerned about the rate bills they levy on households but not about the rate bills levied on firms. Our reason for this is not that we think local authorities are always indifferent to the level of non-domestic rates. Rather it is that their concern is likely to be indirect – for example they may be concerned with the possible effects of non-domestic rates on business investment and hence on local employment opportunities. What would matter is the level of rate bills on a particular type of a firm in one locality as against another. But the yield of non-domestic rates per head of population depends mainly on the number and type of firms in the area rather than on differences in the rate bill levied on firms of a given type. Non-domestic rate yield per head of population gives a very misleading indication of rate bills on any particular type of firm. Indeed, we would argue that *domestic* rate bills per head may give a better indication, because domestic and non-domestic property values tend to move together, as do domestic and non-domestic rate poundages.

3. Regression estimates

The independent variables we consider are, as argued in Section 2, of three types:

i) *Cost factors*

a) Sparsity: in areas of sparse population either the average size of schools must be smaller, entailing higher average costs, or else more school transport must be provided as children will, on average, have to travel longer distances.

b) Population density: in areas of high population density, factor costs tend to be higher, and other aspects of urban conditions (e.g. higher labour turnover) may add to school costs.

c) Labour costs: teachers are paid on a national scale so that labour costs, in principle, are the same for all authorities (apart from the London weighting). In practice labour market conditions do differ, and one would expect this to affect labour costs despite the national scales. The variable is measured as an index of comparable private sector wage rates. Unfortunately this index is available only for authorities in London and the South East, but this does cover the main area of variation.

d) Total pupil numbers: this is intended to take account of economies or diseconomies of scale associated with the size of the education authority. (We do not examine the effect of average school size on expenditure because the number of schools in an authority, and hence their average size is a policy decision of the education authority.)

ii) *Preference factor*

e) Politics, measured by the percentage of councillors who are members of the Labour party, or of parties to the left of it.

iii) *Budgetary factors*

f) Proportion of domestic to inclusive rateable value (r/v), which measures the share of local government expenditure (net of lump sum grants) financed by local residents, which will be termed the 'tax share'.

g) Lump sum grants, net of committed expenditure, per schoolchild. This is the term $(dv - g_k)/n_1$ as described in Section 2.

h) Personal incomes per schoolchild. This variable is related to maximum acceptable rate bills (x_0/n_1). There is, however, no data on household incomes at a local authority level in Britain. We have therefore used regional income data.

Precise definitions of the data are given in the Appendix.

Adjustment for sixth-formers

Costs of education for sixth-formers (16-18 year olds) are substantially higher per pupil than those for 11-16 year olds, and the proportion of sixth-form pupils differs considerably across authorities. It follows that a large part of the variation in secondary school expenditure per pupil results from differences in the proportions of sixth-formers rather than from differences in educational resources per pupil at any given stage.

The expenditure data for individual local authorities does not distinguish between expenditure on sixth-formers, and expenditure on 11-16 year olds. We have therefore weighted sixth-formers by their national average cost relative to 11-16 year olds (1.5536) and the variables in the secondary education equations have been redefined in terms of numbers of weighted schoolchildren where appropriate. Thus the dependent variable becomes estimated expenditure on education for 11-16 year olds per 11-16 year old.

Results

The regression estimates for the expenditure, net of debt charges, for the 104 education authorities in England and Wales for 1978/79, for primary and secondary education are set out in Table 1.

The estimates for primary education are reasonably satisfactory: six of the eight variables are statistically significant at the 5% level, and have the 'correct' sign. The two variables that are not statistically significant are labour costs (which does, though, have the expected sign), and total numbers of pupils (which has a positive coefficient which would imply diseconomies of scale were it significant).

The equation for secondary education is less satisfactory in that it accounts for a smaller proportion of the variation in expenditure and fewer of the variables are statistically significant at the 5% level. Nonetheless all the variables have the same sign and are of around the same order of magnitude as in the primary education equation.

We have examined the rubustness of these equations, first by the exclusion of the Inner London Education Authority (ILEA) and second by running separate regressions for different types of authority. For many of the variables, ILEA is an 'outlier' – its expenditure is very high, as is its population density and its inclusive rateable value per head, its 'tax share' is low and it alone of the education authorities is significantly affected by clawback. However, the exclusion of ILEA did not materially affect the regression results. Likewise the results for the different types of authority (shire counties, metropolitan districts, London boroughs) were basically similar to the results for all authorities combined.

From the regression results it is possible to derive estimates of the effects of income and relative prices on education expenditure. The elasticities with

Table 1. Regression estimates

	Primary	Secondary
Cost factors		
(a) Sparsity	17.57	8.83
	(5.52)	(2.52)
(b) Density	5.15	3.52
	(5.66)	(3.53)
(c) Labour costs	2.72	3.71
	(1.58)	(1.92)
(d) Total pupils	0.221	0.186
	(1.57)	(1.15)
Preference factor		
(e) Politics	0.865	0.319
	(3.20)	(1.07)
Budgetary factors		
(f) Tax share	−267.06	−138.02
	(−4.24)	(1.92)
(g) Lump sum grant (per schoolchild)	0.074	0.025
	(2.25)	(0.68)
(h) Household income (per schoolchild)	0.101	0.134
	(4.49)	(4.65)
R^2	0.74	0.60
$\bar{R}^2$	0.72	0.57
F	33.86	18.00

(Figures in parentheses are t-statistics.)

respect to household incomes, measured at the sample mean, are 0.19 for primary education and 0.23 for secondary education. The relative price (or tax share) elasticities are −0.19 for primary and −0.08 for secondary education. Finally, the expenditure elasticity with respect to lump sum grants is 0.10 for primary and 0.03 for secondary education.

While it is not our purpose here to provide a detailed comparison with studies on U.S. data, it appears that our estimates for England and Wales are within the range of published U.S. estimates, but close to the lower end of that range. In his recent survey, Inman (1979) summarizes the results of twelve recent U.S. studies on educational expenditure. The estimated income elasticities range from 0.24 to 1.35, tax share elasticities range from −0.07 to −0.70 and lump sum grant elasticities from 0.03 to 0.71.

Studies of educational expenditure have also been carried out for England and Wales, but they have typically not been based on the type of theoretical model used in the U.S. studies and in this paper. However, in one study, Boaden (1971) did examine the impact of domestic to inclusive rateable value (our 'tax share' variable) and found it negatively, but insignificantly, correlated with expenditure. Because he calculated only correlation coefficients it is impossible to derive an estimate of the price elasticity from his study.

It is interesting to note that the coefficient on household incomes in Table 1 is higher than that on lump sum grants. One must adjust for the fact that the former is measured per household and the latter per capita, but even so the coefficients are of the same order of magnitude. This suggests that a given sum of money has the same impact on education expenditure whether it appears in the form of private household income or in local government lump sum grants.[6] That is, there appears to be no 'fiscal illusion'. The belief that an increase in grants will increase local government spending to a greater extent than an equivalent increase in private incomes may be based on a misplaced assumption as to the exogeneity of central government grants. Local authorities typically receive higher grants because their expenditure commitments (and hence their expenditures) rise, but it is misleading to view this association between grants and expenditure as an 'income effect' of higher grants causing higher expenditure. The measure of this income effect adopted in this paper is grant net of committed expenditure, which should, in principle, avoid spurious correlation.

4. Components of expenditure variation

In general, if a variable Y is regressed against N variables X_i ($i = 1, \ldots, N$), the 'explained' variance in Y is given by

$$\text{var}(\hat{Y}) = \text{var}(\sum_{i=1}^{N} b_i X_i)$$

$$= \sum_{i=1}^{N} b_i^2 \, \text{var}(X_i) + \sum_{i=1}^{N} \sum_{j=1}^{N} b_i b_j \, \text{covar}(X_i, X_j) \quad (j \neq i)$$

where b_i are the estimated regression coefficients on X_i.

From this formula, we can construct a form of variance/covariance matrix, the diagonal elements of which are the terms in $b_i^2 \, \text{var}(X_i)/\text{var}(\hat{Y})$ and the off-diagonal terms $b_i b_j \, \text{covar}(X_i, X_j)/\text{var}(\hat{Y})$. Thus calculated the terms in the matrix all added together will sum to unity, and to find the proportion of the total variation attributable to any variable, or group of variables, all that is required is to sum together the variance and covariance terms associated with that variable, or group of variables.[7]

These estimates are set out in Table 2 (for primary education) and Table 3 (for secondary). The numbers in Tables 2 and 3 have been multiplied by 100 (and thus measure the percentage of the explained variance associated with each variable or pair of variables) and the (symmetrical) off-diagonal terms have been added together to reduce clutter.

The figures in Tables 2 and 3 can be used to decompose the explained variation in expenditure into a part attributable to variation in costs, a part

Table 2. Components of variation: Primary education

	a	b	c	d	e	f	g	h
a) Sparsity	20.80	–	–	–	–	–	–	–
b) Density	−25.42	44.17	–	–	–	–	–	–
c) Labour costs	−4.04	17.00	3.27	–	–	–	–	–
d) Total pupils	−0.24	−3.92	−0.72	1.52	–	–	–	–
e) Politics	12.44	26.78	3.62	−2.86	13.01	–	–	–
f) Tax share	14.28	−29.14	−11.86	2.00	6.20	25.27	–	–
g) Lump sum grant	4.98	−5.80	−0.42	−2.02	−1.56	−2.36	3.50	–
h) Income	−3.26	20.86	8.04	−1.30	−2.68	−23.06	2.92	14.92

Table 3. Components of variation: Secondary education

	a	b	c	d	e	f	g	h
a) Sparsity	8.02	–	–	–	–	–	–	–
b) Density	−13.33	31.50	–	–	–	–	–	–
c) Labour costs	−4.22	24.19	9.28	–	–	–	–	–
d) Total pupils	−0.12	−2.74	−0.98	1.53	–	–	–	–
e) Politics	−3.52	10.31	2.78	−1.23	2.70	–	–	–
f) Tax share	5.66	−15.71	−12.77	1.42	1.81	10.30	–	–
g) Lump sum grant	1.14	−2.21	−0.33	−0.78	−0.28	−0.54	0.57	–
h) Income	−4.98	23.58	20.59	−0.47	−2.16	−23.79	1.67	32.90

attributable to variation in preferences and finances, and a part due to the interaction between the two sets of factors. The variation attributable to cost factors alone is the sum of the variation attributable to each of the cost factors individually and of that due to the covariance between them – that is, it is the sum of the numbers in the top left hand quadrant of Tables 2 and 3. In each case cost factors appear to account for just over half of the observed variation in expenditure (52% for primary and 53% for secondary).

Similarly the variation attributable to preference and financial factors can be calculated from the numbers in the bottom right hand quadrant of Tables 2 and 3. It amounts to 36% for primary and 23% for secondary education expenditure. The remaining variation (12% for primary and 24% for secondary) results from the interaction between the two sets of factors (the bottom left hand quadrant of the Tables).

If the objective of policy is to equalise standards, defined in terms of putting all authorities on an equivalent budget line, a policy should be judged not by its effect on the total variation in expenditure but by its effect on the variation attributable to financial factors alone. One such policy concerns the equalisation of fiscal capacity – defined in terms of rateable value per head – embodied in the Rate Support Grant mechanism.

To the extent that domestic rateable values are related to income, the lower are incomes the lower will be the tax share and hence the higher the matching grant the local authority will receive. Low income areas can thus purchase local authority services at a lower relative price. If the objective is equal standards, as Feldstein (1975) has shown, the grant must be structured to affect prices in such a way that the income and price effects cancel out.

In primary education the variation in expenditure resulting from differences in income and differences in tax shares combined $(25.27 + 14.92 - 23.06 = 17.13)$ is greater than that which would result from differences in income alone (14.92), as shown in Table 2. In secondary education, however, the reverse appears to hold in that the variation from the two factors combined $(10.30 + 32.90 - 23.79 = 19.41)$ is less than that which would result from income alone (32.90).

Feldstein argued on the basis of his results that in Massachusetts the resource equalising component of the grant tended to 'over-equalise', that is set up relative price differences more than sufficient to offset the income effects. It would be difficult to draw similar conclusions about over or under equalisation in England and Wales, however, in part because of the weak relationship between incomes and rateable values and in part because our income data is only regional rather than based on local authority areas.

The removal of the residual lump sum elements in the grant (the higher domestic element in Wales and the clawback effect in London) would appear to have the effect of reducing that part of the variation in expenditure due to preferences and finance, but by relatively small amounts. The variation due to financial factors would be reduced from 21% to 17% for primary education and from 21% to $19\frac{1}{2}\%$ for secondary. The effect of both removing the lump sum grants and equalising tax shares would be to reduce the financial component of variation from 21% to 15% for primary, but increase it from 21% to 33% for secondary. We can put this point another way around by saying that the resources element, domestic element and London clawback of the RSG succeed in reducing income-induced variations in standards in secondary education by about one-third, while in primary education these components of the grant appear actually to increase financial-induced variations in expenditure.

Appendix

Definitions and sources of data

The dependent variables are primary school expenditure per primary schoolchild aged 5 years or over, and secondary school expenditure per secondary school pupil up to age 16. (Miscellaneous education expenditure is allocated as a percentage overhead.) The figures are for estimated expenditure at estimated outturn prices for 1978/79, and derived from CIPFA *Education Statistics* for 1978/79.

The cost variables are defined as follows:

Sparsity is acres per head of population, with both acreage and population derived from local authorities' own estimates, in the case of population the figures being for June 1978. Figures are published in CIPFA *Financial, General and Rating Statistics*, 1978/79.

Density is the reciprocal of sparsity.

Labour costs are based on an index constructed by the Department of the Environment which applies a profile of local authority employees to earnings data from the *New Earnings Survey* (published by the Department of Employment) for 1977 and 1978. It is calculated only for Inner London, the Outer London boroughs (taken as a group) and counties in South East England. All other authorities are assigned a value of 100.

Proportion of sixth-formers is derived from CIPFA *Education Statistics*.

The financial factors are:

Household income is the mean regional weekly income of households derived from the Department of Employment's *Family Expenditure Survey* for 1976 and 1977.

The tax share is the ratio of domestic rateable value per head, taken from *Rates and Rateable Values* (Department of the Environment), to inclusive rateable value derived from CIPFA *Financial, General and Rating Statistics* 1978/79.

The London grant 'clawback' is derived from Department of the Environment figures. The domestic element term from CIPFA *Financial, General and Rating Statistics* 1978/79.

The political variable is the proportion of Labour, Independent Labour and Communist councillors after the elections of May 5, 1977, reported in the 1978 and 1979 *Municipal Yearbook*.

The figure for the adjustment for sixth-formers was calculated from the local authority associations publication *Rate Support Grant*, Seventh Period, 1976.

NOTES

1. Other definitions might attempt to include the effects of a pupil's home background ('positive discrimination') or to allow for the differences in the number of years pupils spend at school.
2. In primary education, expenditure per primary schoolchild in 1978/79 varied from £331 per year (in Dudley) to £669 per year (Inner London) with a mean of £438 and a coefficient of variation of 14.9%. In secondary education, after adjustment for differences in the proportion of sixth-formers (by the method described on p. 433 of this paper), the comparable figures are a range of £439 per year (in Dudley) to £782 (Haringey) with a mean of £565 and a coefficient of variation of 10.4%.
3. There could be distributional effects, however, if the government were to tax more heavily in one area and distribute more in grant to another. Local government expenditure in the first area would fall and in the second rise. Grants to local authorities on this interpretation are simply an indirect form of income redistribution between people – with the same effect on desired expenditures.
4. A similar argument was used by Gramlich and Galper (1973) which they termed the 'flypaper theory' of local finance – that 'money sticks where it hits'.
5. For a description of the workings of the London clawback, see Department of the Environment (1977) especially Annex E, or Jackman (1979).
6. We are grateful to Robert Inman for pointing out this result.
7. For a fuller discussion of this approach see Layard and Zabalza (1979).

REFERENCES

Bergstrom, T. C., and Goodman, R. P. (1973). Private demand for public goods. *American Economic Review* 63: 280-296.

Boaden, N. (1971). *Urban policy making.* Cambridge: Cambridge University Press.

Department of the Environment. (1977). *Report on the rate support grant order.* November.

Downs, A. (1957). *An economic theory of democracy.* New York: Harper and Row.

Feldstein, M. S. (1975). Wealth neutrality and local choice in public education. *American Economic Review* 65: 75-89.

Gramlich, E., and Galper, H. (1973). State and local fiscal behaviour and federal grant policy. *Brookings Papers on Economic Activity* 3: 15-58.

Inman, R. P. (1971). Towards an econometric model of local budgeting. *Proceedings of the 64th Annual Conference of Taxation.* National Tax Association. 699-719.

Inman, R. P. (1979). The fiscal performance of local governments: An interpretive review. In P. Mieszkowski and M. Straszheim (Eds.), *Current issues in urban economics.* 270-321.

Jackman, R. A. (1979). London's needs grant. *Centre for Environmental Studies Review* 5: 28-34.

Jackman, R. A., and Sellars, M. (1978). Local expenditure and local discretion. *Centre for Environmental Studies Review* 3: 63-73.

Layard, P. R. G., and Zabalza, A. (1979). Family income distribution: Explanation and policy evaluation. *Journal of Political Economy* 87: S 133-161.

Layfield, F. (1976). (Chairman). *Report of the Committee of Inquiry into Local Government Finance,* Cmnd 6453.

Stone, J. R. N. (1954). Linear expenditure systems and demand analysis: An application to the pattern of British demand. *Economic Journal* 64: 511-527.

Comments on R. Jackman and J. Papadachi

DOUGLAS M. WINDHAM

State University of New York, Albany

This interesting and valuable paper is in the tradition of the large number of efforts in the United States to divide the variations in local expenditures on education between those caused by differences in locational cost factors and those caused by differences in the local standards of educational provision. This division of causality is politically important in the United Kingdom as in the United States.

Data are rarely what we might wish, and rather obvious specification problems arise in this study with three of the variables: labour costs, total number of pupils, and personal incomes, each of which is assigned an important role in the analysis. Labour costs are defined according to an index of 'comparable' private sector wages – the index being available only for London and the South East. Total pupil numbers are offered as a proxy for diseconomies and yet these should be primarily school effects (except for diseconomies of local central administration). Finally, the income data are regional and not tied to local authority boundaries.

Concern over the suspected specification difficulty with these factors is reinforced when one notes the insignificant regression coefficients for labour costs and total pupil numbers. The regression estimates for income are significant and of the expected sign. What is disturbing here is that when one moves to the covariance analysis the association between income and the central government grant is positive (though weakly so). As the authors point out, it is difficult to draw conclusions about equalizing (or disequalizing) effects given the weak relationships between rateable values and incomes and the lack of locally-specific income indicators. It would be useful, first, to improve the income variable by deriving a proxy that would conform more to local district boundaries; second, if the grant is still a source of inequality it would be important to determine just why this result obtains.

Three general issues should be clarified if one is to appreciate the value of this paper. First, the use of compensatory formulas is a much more difficult task than most advocates originally assumed. The data requirements and the potential for anomalous effects are such that one must wonder at the formulas' continued political popularity.

63

Second, if one is truly interested in the equalization of resource flows to individual students of different social and economic groups then the present methodology of both policymaking and economic analysis is inadequate. Variabilities within local authorities, within schools, and even within classrooms are such that the effect of central government compensatory efforts is indeterminate.

Finally, the analysis of effects of aid formulas requires consideration of the possibilities for adaptive local responses, which can result in a flow of central government funds that deviates substantially from plans and expectations. An aid formula is simultaneously an incentive configuration to which local officials will react in an attempt to shift local government costs to the central government.

The authors are undoubtedly aware of many of these problems, which confront scholars and policymakers alike. The candor and excellence of presentation in this paper sets a standard and style of exposition that all in the economics of education could well emulate.

Comments on R. Jackman and J. Papadachi

DONALD W. VERRY

University College, London

The real virtue of this paper, in my opinion, is its careful modelling of the U.K. institutional structure, in particular as this relates to the local authority budget constraint. This has not been done before in U.K. studies to the best of my knowledge. I was particularly pleased to see the authors take explicit account of the fact that the central government itself uses regression analysis as a basis for allocating grants to local authorities. There is a real danger that the unwary economist, while claiming to have unearthed a behavioural relationship applying to decentralised decision makers, will in his regression simply be replicating the rule used by the central authorities in allocating funds to state or local authorities. Jackman and Papadachi have not fallen into this trap.

The main problem with the paper, it seems to me, is that the lack of a fully developed theoretical model makes the estimated educational expenditure regressions difficult to interpret. Are they the electorate's demand functions, the local authority bureaucrats' supply function, or (more likely) some combination of the two? Although the authors disavow any explicit model in their paper, two types of model of local authority behaviour are in fact considered. The first is the median-voter model, which the authors rapidly reject; correctly so in my opinion. One of the assumptions required for local authority expenditure to reflect the preferences of the median voter is that preferences (among the electorate) are 'single peaked', an assumption which is not easy to defend in the sphere of education – especially where public and private provision co-exist. The second implicit model (which the authors call 'a more general formulation') is more realistic. This model envisages councillors and bureaucrats exercising their own preferences but in a constrained fashion; discretionary expenditure is limited by voters' educational preferences and their unwillingness to accept rate bills above some maximum amount (the determination of this maximum is only modelled in a rather *ad hoc* fashion, and measured even more loosely). Expenditure by local government is also of course constrained by statutory obligations imposed by central government, but this constraint is captured in the committed expenditures term in the linear expenditure function. While I think that this second (implicit) model is a move in the right direction, it is here so generally specified that there really is no reason for believing that it implies linear expenditure function in local authority goods and services of the form arrived at by the authors.

Turning to the empirical section of the paper, while the estimating equations are intuitively plausible and the variables carefully defined, it cannot really be claimed that the estimated regressions of Section 3 correspond in any direct sense to the 'general formulation' of Section 2. If the local authority Stone-Geary utility function is to be taken seriously then surely the resulting linear expenditure system should be estimated as such – i.e., simultaneous estimation of a *system* of equations (one for each major type of local authority expenditure), paying heed to cross-equation restrictions. At least the conditions under which it would be legitimate to extract two equations from such a system and estimate them individually by OLS could have been discussed. Similarly there are problems with some of the individual variables. For example regional income averages would seem a poor proxy for the maximum acceptable rate bill, and their statistical significance in the estimated regressions is open to alternative explanations (e.g., as a proxy for residents' preferences for education). The political preference variable would of course have no place in a median-voter model. In the more general model politics could indeed affect the utility function, but whether political influences would show up as a simply shift variable in the expenditure function is not clear. The authors earlier imply that preferences might affect the marginal budget share but this does not seem to be the way preferences enter into the estimated equation.

These points notwithstanding the estimation is successful both in terms of variance explained and the significance of individual coefficients. I would draw attention in particular to the potentially important implication of absence of fiscal illusion. The broad conformity of the results with those of U.S. studies is also noteworthy, although of course there is no presumption that the expenditure elasticities should be identical or even similar.

The variance/covariance analysis is also interesting but I think great care is needed in attaching any welfare significance to these results. For example while the results imply that the included elements of the central government Rate Support Grant increase the variation in local authorities' primary school expenditures, the welfare interpretation of this result would require careful specification of central government objectives with respect to matching grants. For example increased variance could be consistent with the poor getting better education, and this may outweigh the disadvantages (if any) of increased variance. Also the effect of these grants on non-educational local authority services would have to be considered, i.e., the effects on educational expenditure alone would probably not enable us to draw any policy implications; the total effects of matching grants would have to be considered.

To sum up I think the Jackman-Papadachi paper performs an extremely useful service by its careful specification of the budget constraint faced by local authorities in the U.K. and by successfully estimating the quantitative effects of some of the major factors associated with variations in local authorities' per capita educational expenditures.

The approach could be extended relatively easily by using data from additional years (this may be a better way of picking up political preference effects) and by applying the technique to non-educational as well as educational expenditures, preferably using simultaneous equations to estimate a genuine linear expenditure system. In the longer run we will all need to consider more carefully how best to model local government provision of services and the effects of central government financial support of such provision.

PART II

Financing formal education:
Equity, efficiency and the institutional context

On setting the agenda for Pennsylvania school finance reform: An exercise in giving policy advice*

ROBERT P. INMAN

University of Pennsylvania

1. Introduction

School finance reform has emerged as one of this decade's most widely debated policy issues. Prompted initially by court decisions in California and New Jersey demanding a more equitable school finance structure,[1] most state legislatures in the U.S. have passed or are now considering significant changes in the way local elementary and secondary education is to be financed.[2] Yet in most instances, those who frame and decide the reform measures are travelling through virgin territory. New aid formulaes are being written and new taxes are being proposed. We are not simply making small changes in old programs to keep up with the changing times. The programs being proposed (or required by the courts) are likely to have short- and long-run implications which families, school officials, and legislators cannot easily anticipate. Exposing these unanticipated consequences of reform may be crucial to the choice of a preferred policy. Recent research has examined the likely implications of a broad range of reform proposals. The literature is long and thoughtful.[3] This essay examines the question of what one might usefully do with all of this good research. Simply put, how should economists transmit their growing knowledge about an issue as complicated as school finance reform to the busy and, for the most part, technically unsophisticated elected representatives who must select new policies?

The problem of giving economic advice to assist decision-making obviously extends beyond the school finance reform issue; indeed, one might reasonably

* This paper is a preliminary report of work in progress for the Governor's Tax Commission of Pennsylvania. The paper has not been reviewed by the Commission: neither the approach to reform policy nor the specific conclusions presented have the formal endorsement of the Commission. The comments of Daniel McFadden, James Mirrlees, and other participants of the U.K.-U.S. Conference on School Finance are appreciated, as are the comments of friends at Penn and Princeton who heard a preliminary version of this paper.

argue that the problem is central to economics itself as an applied science. In many instances it is easily solved. When choices are to be made by a single decision-maker with known and well-defined preferences and outcomes can be predicted with certainty, advice is simply given as a utility maximizing or profit maximizing recommendation. When preferences are known but outcomes are uncertain, we again have a compelling, generally accepted, procedure for giving advice; we recommend that one proposal which maximizes expected utility or, for a risk neutral firm, expected profit.

Yet in certain situations, the usual advice-giving strategy of recommending a single utility maximizing policy may not be appropriate; such is the situation where decision-maker preferences are themselves unknown to the economist at the time the recommendation must be made. Faced with unknown preferences economists have adopted eitheir of two strategies, neither of which has proven uniformily helpful to busy decision-makers. The first is to describe the pareto frontier, i.e., the full set of undominated policies for all conceivable preference functions. Then the decision-makers are left alone to choose. While certainly the preferred strategy when decision-making is a costless activity, in most instances decision-makers have only a finite and usually very limited capacity for making choices. The second strategy conserves on scarce decision-making capacities, but bears high risks of having the subsequent recommendation simply ignored. This is the social welfare maximizing strategy in which the economist selects a preference function, calculates the policy which maximizes the chosen objective function, and then recommends this one 'optimal' policy to the decision-makers. Unless the selected preference function upon which the recommendation is based is the decision-makers' own, there is no reason to believe that the decision-makers will have been helped in their search for a preferred reform by such advice. Indeed, the chances are very high that under both strategies the useful things that economists do have to say about complicated policy problems will be ignored. A compromise advice-giving strategy for the case when decision-maker preferences are unknown is offered here and is applied to the policy problem of school finance reform. The compromise is to set an *agenda* for reform, an agenda which is smaller than the full set of pareto-improving policies yet offers more choice than the single recommendation generated by the welfare maximization approach.

Section 2 argues that agenda-setting is generally the preferred strategy for giving advice and outlines one approach to setting an optimal agenda. Sections 3 and 4 apply the agenda-setting approach for giving advice to the issue of school finance reform in Pennsylvania. Section 5 summarizes our results.

2. Giving advice when preferences are unknown: The advantage of agenda-setting

The problem of giving economic advice when decision-makers preferences are unknown is hardly a new one, and some research in the past has made an effort to deal with it. For example, Marglin (1967) in his short treatise on benefit-cost analysis for developing economies devotes one chapter to the problem of eliciting planners' preferences.[4] Eckstein (1961), Mera (1969), and Weisbrod (1968) have attempted, each in his own way, to fill the gap in our knowledge about public decision-makers' distributional preferences from statistical analyses of past public decisions. Johansen (1974) reviews and comments upon Frisch's earlier efforts to describe planner preferences for macro-policy making, while Friedlander (1973) follows the Eckstein lead and attempts to infer preferences over alternative macro targets from past macro policy decisions. While useful, neither approach to actually measuring preferences quite solves our problems. The eliciting of individual decision-maker preferences over policy outcomes is important (as we shall see below), but by itself it is not sufficient to tell us what a group of such decision-makers is likely to prefer. We can, of course, look at past choices of the group as Eckstein and others have done.[5] But in the public sector, at least, where decision-making groups change continually or groups which decide one policy (e.g., tax) do not necessarily decide another (e.g., expenditure), such econometric inferences of group preferences as a basis for current recommendations is suspect; it is too easy to extrapolate outside the legitimate sample. Even when used carefully, the econometric procedures still leave us with less than certain knowledge of the group's preference function. The fact remains that decision-makers' preferences are often unknown and the need to offer good recommendations in the face of this uncertainty continues despite these recent efforts to measure preferences. What to do now?

Here, previous work is less clear on a solution, but two papers stand out. Zellner (1974) has examined the sensitivity of 'true' social welfare to policy errors based on misspecifications of the societal welfare function. He is particularly interested in how the planner's guesses as to the parameter values of a social welfare function can be offsetting or re-inforcing in the sense of leading us towards the one best policy based on true societial preferences. The research of Burmeister, Jackson, and Ross (1977) on growth planning with misspecified welfare functions also examines the sensitivity of optimal policies to errors in the specification of the societal preference function. Errors are measured by how much additional initial capital an economy would require to exactly compensate for the fact that the planner offered a recommendation based on an incorrect specification of the societal preference function; the required compensation so calculated can be significant. More importantly, Burmeister et al. suggest that when preferences are unknown but the planner can specify a subjective probability distribution over alternative social preference functions, then a maximize-expected-utility criterion becomes a possible candidate upon which to base recommendations for policy consideration. If $U(x, \alpha)$ is the preference relationship over policy x given the unknown preference parameters represented by the vector α and $f(\alpha)$ is the economist-planner's subjective probability distribution over α, then the Burmeister et al. suggestion is to recommend that one policy x which maximizes $\int U(x, \alpha)f(\alpha)d\alpha$. As we shall see below, this criterion has some appeal.[6] It requires a willingness, however, to accept the normalization $U(x, \alpha)$ as a basis for policy.

The search for a preferred agenda begins here. In the analysis which follows I assume that the decision-making group's preferences can be represented by a continuous, twice differentiable preference function and that a normalization of group preferences to the form $U(x, \alpha)$ can be agreed upon, where x in the vector of policy variables to be chosen (e.g., a school aid formula) and α is a vector of preference parameters which define U – e.g., the relative weights on education and on income or the weights on rich and poor families.[7] Given particular values for $\alpha = \alpha^i$, we can specify $U^i = U(X, \alpha^i)$ and select that vector of policy variables which is optimal for α^i. We shall denote this optimal policy vector as x^i; x^i is obviously a function of $\alpha^i - x^i = \chi(\alpha^i)$. Our problem is that the true α is unknown and a single policy is unlikely to be optimal for all possible values of α. Recommendations based on the wrong α can be seriously misleading as Burmeister et al. have shown, yet to totally retreat from the task of offering economic advice can be equally harmful. The trick is to offer a set of recommendations that fully utilizes the economist's knowledge of the consequences of any policy x without, at the same time, leading the policy process to a bad choice because of the economist's lack of precise knowledge about α.[8]

As a general matter, we do know something about the parameter values α which define $U(\cdot)$. Observations of the policy choice process will suggest that some values of α are more likely to be true than others. Personal observation and interviews with political experts may allow us in fact to specify a prior distribution on the likelihood that any α will be the correct α. Denote this prior distribution on α as $f(\alpha)$. More important – indeed, the crucial point for agenda-setting as an advice-giving strategy – is that additional information about the correct α is generally revealed as the policy process moves towards a decision. Speaking loosely, at that final moment before group choice the actual α is agreed upon. It is desirable to make maximum use of such preference information when recommending policies.

The following two theorems, due to Mangasarian (1964), on optimization with stochastic objective functions outlines how we might best use available information about the k-dimensional vector of preference parameters, α.

Theorem 1: Let $U(x, \alpha)$ be a convex function of α in a closed convex region R of the k-dimensional Euclidean space for every value of x satisfying $g(x) \geq 0$.

Then the function,

$$V(\alpha) = \max_x \{U(x, \alpha) \mid g(x) \geq 0\}$$

is a convex and continuous function of α in the interior of R (*Proof*: Mangasarian, 1964: Theorem 1).

The function $V(\alpha)$ is simply $U(x, \alpha)$ when x assumes its maximal value for each value of $\alpha - V(\alpha) = U(x(\alpha), \alpha)$. The convexity of $V(\alpha)$ allows us to establish, in part, the results in Theorem 2:

Theorem 2: If α takes on values only in some (finite or infinite) convex region R of the k-dimensional Euclidean space and if $U(x, \alpha)$ is a convex and continuous function of α in R for every x satisfying $g(x) \geq 0$, then,

$$EV(\alpha) \geq \max_x \{EU(x, \alpha) \mid g(x) \geq 0\} \geq \max_x \{U(x, E\alpha) \mid g(x) \geq 0\},$$

where E denotes the expectation with respect to the distribution of α (*Proof*: Mangasarian, 1964: Theorem 3).

Theorem 2 establishes the following important conclusions. First, in the choice of a single policy recommendation when preferences are unknown, selecting a policy which maximizes the expected utility over alternative values of α (the problem, $\max_x \{EU(x, \alpha) \mid g(x) \geq 0\}$) will generally be preferable to simply maximizing $U(\cdot)$ evaluated at the most likely value of α (the problem, $\max_x \{U(x, E\alpha) \mid g(x) \geq 0\}$).[9] This result supports the conjecture of Burmeister et al. as to the most effective way to use our preference information when making a single policy recommendation.

The second result in Theorem 2, which establishes that $EV(\alpha)$ is at least as great as the utility available from any single recommendation strategy, is equally important, however. $EV(\alpha)$ is the expected value to the decision-makers of being able to 'wait and see' what value of α actually emerges from the decision process and to then select a preferred x, given the actual value of α. When the decision-making process produces a group consensus on α (that is, an agreement on how alternatives should be ordered) and that consensus is achieved before a final policy choice is made, then Theorem 2 says the group should prefer to 'wait and see' before acting upon the recommendation of the policy analyst. The best recommendation to offer in this case is a wide range of choice so that the advantages of the 'wait and see' approach can be realized. If the costs of considering each single policy are very small, then the range of choice should encompass the preferred policies for all possible α values – that is, the set of pareto optimal policies. As the costs of evaluating alternatives increases, then the set of policies recommended for consideration may shrink. The basic point of Theorem 2, however, is to establish the general desirability of a range of recommendations – an 'agenda' – as the preferred means for giving policy advice.

Unfortunately, Theorem 2 does not tell us what the preferred agenda should be, or even how to find it. A strategy for agenda-setting is required. One approach is outlined here, and developed in greated detail in a companion piece (Inman, 1980). In setting the preferred agenda we should add policies to the agenda as long as those additions offer a potential gain in decision-makers' welfare which more than compensates them for the costs incurred in considering the added policies. To make such a principal operational we must specify more carefully the gains and costs of expanding agendas.[10]

To understand the gains from expanding the agenda, assume that policy $\hat{x}$ is the status quo and consideration is being given to consider an agenda of policies one of which will be $\hat{x}$. What is the value to the group of adding one item to the agenda, say x_i, for consideration? The group is free to choose either x_i or $\hat{x}$. The value to the group of admitting a given policy x_i to the agenda will be the additional utility derived from being able to choose x_i over $\hat{x}$, given that the group's correct α has been revealed before selection. Formally, the value of adding policy x_i is specified as

$$v(x_i, \alpha; \hat{x}) = \max\{U(x_i, \alpha) - U(\hat{x}, \alpha), 0\}.$$

The item x_i has value in the agenda only when x_i is preferred to x for at least one value of α. Since the agenda must be set (by the policy analyst) before α is known with certainty, it is the expected value of adding x_i to the agenda which is of central interest, where $Ev(x_i, \alpha; \hat{x}) = \int v(x_i, \alpha; \hat{x})f(\alpha)d\alpha$ and where $f(\alpha)$ is the analyst's prior probability distribution over alternative values of α. As $v(x_i, \alpha; \hat{x}) \geq 0$, the expected value of adding any x_i to the agenda with x must be non-negative.

In a fully analogous way, the value of an agenda of 'n' items can be defined. Let $\Delta U(x_i, \alpha; \hat{x})$ denote the utility gain of policy x_i over $\hat{x}$ for a given α: $\Delta U(x_i, \alpha; \hat{x}) = U(x_i, \alpha) - U(\hat{x}, \alpha)$. Then the value for a given α of adding any ($n - 1$) new policies for consideration along with $\hat{x}$ will be:

$$v(\langle x \rangle^{n-1}, \alpha; \hat{x}) = \max\{\Delta U(x_1, \alpha; \hat{x}), \cdots, \Delta U(x_{n-1}, \alpha; \hat{x}), 0\},$$

Where the ($n - 1$) new policies are denoted $x_1 \cdots x_{n-1}$. As the agenda must be chosen before the true α value has been revealed, the relevant criterion for selecting the best n item agenda is to maximize the expected value of $\langle x \rangle^{n-1}$ over all possible combinations of ($n - 1$) policies. Formally, we maximize:

$$Ev(\langle x \rangle^{n-1}, \alpha; \hat{x}) = \int v(\langle x \rangle^{n-1}, \alpha; \hat{x}) f(\alpha) d\alpha$$

over the $_pC_{n-1} = p!/(n-1)!(p-n+1)!$ possible combinations of p new policies taken $(n-1)$ at a time. The computational task of this maximization is formidable, but hardly impossible with high speed computers.[11]

Within this framework, it is straightforward to show that increasing the size of the agenda while also being allowed to alter the agenda's composition will always increase or leave unchanged the agenda's expected value to the decision-makers. Furthermore, the expected value of the best, single policy recommendation ($EU(\tilde{x}, \alpha)$) and the expected value of an agenda containing all pareto policies, $EV(\alpha)$, bound the expected gains from the agenda-setting process – that is, $EU(\tilde{x}, \alpha) \leq Ev(x_i, \alpha; \hat{x}) \leq Ev(\langle x \rangle^2, \alpha; \hat{x}) \cdots \leq Ev(\langle x \rangle^{p-1}, \alpha; \hat{x})$ $\leq Ev(\langle x \rangle^p, \alpha; \hat{x}) = EV(\alpha)$.[12]

The question of whether a larger agenda is in fact preferred depends of course upon the costs of selecting a preferred policy from each agenda. Specifying the costs of considering additional agenda items is far from easy, however. Additional staff resources and decision-makers' time will of course be needed to consider a new policy with the same care as that given to each item in a smaller agenda, and one might reasonably try to evaluate these marginal resource costs. However, *resource* costs might seriously underestimate the *opportunity* costs of expanding the agenda within any single policy arena. For most political decision-making bodies during any legislative session, the number of legislators, their staffs, and the other resources available for policy analysis are fixed. If the marginal value of aggregate agenda expansion over all possible policy areas (school finance, tax reform, business regulation, etc.) at this constraint exceeds the marginal resource costs of such expansion, then we will have a less than optimal level of total agenda 'spots' available for legislative consideration. If so, and if this aggregate constraint remains binding, then the relevant marginal cost of agenda expansion *within* a given policy area will not be the observed marginal resource costs of adding a new agenda spot, but rather the opportunity costs of reduced decision-maker utility from taking an agenda spot from another policy area. Setting the optimal agenda within any policy area therefore requires us to allocate a fixed total number of agenda spots across all policy areas until the marginal gains on decision-makers' welfare from expanding each policy area's agenda have been equalized. Making this principle operational is hardly a trivial matter, but under certain circumstances which insure additive separable group utility functions across policy areas, optimal agenda-setting becomes manageable.[13]

As a practical matter, however, the economist as advisor is generally not free to set the optimal agenda for each policy area. A maximal number of agenda items is exogenously given in most instances. If so, our job then is *simply* to find that one agenda which is optimal against the constraint.

Sections 3 and 4 apply this logic of agenda-setting to the issue of school finance reform.

3. Reforming Pennsylvania school finance: Issues and analytics

One of the first orders of the new Governor of Pennsylvania following his election in 1978 was to establish a blue ribbon Tax Commission to evaluate the state's tax structure. One of the commission's charges was to propose possible new methods for financing educational services within the state's major metropolitan areas – Pittsburgh and Philadelphia. An emphasis was to be given to policies that might replace, or at least significantly reduce, the role of local-based property taxation in the financing of elementary and secondary education. The Governor felt, and the evidence supports his impressions, that property tax financing of local education is regressive in its effects on the distribution of family income and on the distribution of school resources across children.[14] He wants an agenda of reform proposals to present to the state legislature to improve the allocation of resources in the financing of local schools. As an example of how such an agenda might be constructed following the agenda-setting logic presented in Section 2 above, I have developed preferred agenda of property tax credits for the Philadelphia metropolitan school economy. The results provide insight into the feasibility and usefulness of the agenda approach to policy advice as well as clarifying the precise consequences of such property tax reform for the Philadelphia public school economy.

To establish the preferred agenda of reform, however, it is first necessary to develop a behavioral model of the local school economy within a metropolitan area so that the consequences of any policy can be predicted. Two outcome variables are of central interest to us here: education per child and family after-education income following the taxation for, and any private purchase of, such education.[15] The behavioral model of the local economy outlined below is directed towards predicting effects of each reform on education and on after-education income across all families in the region.

To predict the equilibrium impacts of fiscal reform policies on education and incomes in a regional economy of local governments, descriptive models of the costs and provision of local public education, household location, residential housing and land value determinations, firm location and investment decisions, and school district fiscal behavior are required.[16]

3.1 *Local public education and taxation*

Education per child (denoted hereafter by E) is a function of the level of school facilities provided by a local government and the number of children who use the facilities. The total cost to the district of school services will depend on the level of E and the number of children who receive E. An increase in education per child or in the number of children will increase total costs.

It is necessary to make two assumptions about the costliness of providing education. First, we assume that for each district the cost per child of providing a given level of E is fixed and equal to $k(E)$ dollars per child. Over a sample range, as districts grow in size there are no significant economies or diseconomies in the provision of education (see Wales, 1973). The second assumption is more suspect. We shall assume all districts are equally efficient in the production of education: two districts providing similar levels of E can provide that level at the same cost per child.

To pay the costs of education the school district taxes the market value of residential and commercial/industrial property. This effective tax rate (r) is assumed to be a proportional rate against all property. The tax rate is set to cover educational costs per child less any matching aid (at the percentage rate m) or lump sum aid (at z dollars per child) received by the district. If B is the market value of the local tax base then:

$$r = \frac{k(E)(1 - m) - z}{B}.$$

3.2 Household location and community land values

The cornerstone of this fiscal model is the fact that families are sensitive to the levels of local education and taxes when choosing a place to live. This search for the 'best fiscal package' may have important implications for the value of residential land, and consequentially the tax base, in local communities.

When choosing a residential location, families are assumed to maximize their well-being by finding that community which offers the most attractive available package of private goods (Y) and local public education (E). The family's consumption of E is of course defined by the town in which the family resides, but the family's level of private goods is also specific to each location. Y is defined by the family's before-local-tax income (I) minus the annual net costs of owning a piece of residential land. The annual net costs of owning a residential site in a given town will equal the annual mortgage payment plus the local tax costs of the site. Clearly, the lower the price of residential land in a town and/or the lower the local tax rate, the higher will be the family's disposable private income, Y. Fiscally attractive communities are towns which offer high levels of E and Y. The price of land in those communities will be higher than the price of residential land elsewhere. It is important to stress that the fiscal attractiveness of any community also depends on what fiscal advantages neighboring towns can offer. It is this competitive process which defines each town's land price. Fiscal factors which increase the relative attractiveness of a community – that is, raise services or lower tax rates relative to neighboring towns – will increase the price of land in the favored town and reduce the prices of residential land elsewhere (see Inman, 1978a, for details).

3.3 Household demand for housing

Once families have chosen a community, they will spend some portion of their disposable income to buy a stock of housing capital. A family's purchase of housing (H) is positively related to disposable income (Y) and negatively related to the annual net price of housing (p_H). The annual net price of a unit of housing equals the annual mortgage costs per unit of house built plus the net property tax costs on each unit. An increase in Y or a fall in p_H increases H, while a fall in Y or a rise in p_H decreases H (through deterioration). Thus, an increase in local tax rates reduces Y and increases p_H leading to a fall in housing, while a fall in the local property tax rate will increase Y and reduce p_H which acts to increase housing.

3.4 Firm location and investment decisions

In addition to households and governments, the other major actor in the regional public economy is private business. Firms must choose a location, and once located, they must invest. The value of their land and capital property are often important components of the property tax base of local communities, and the model must specify any feedbacks of local fiscal choices on the value of this commercial-industrial property.

The role of firms in our regional political economy is defined by two facts. First, recent evidence from a variety of regions indicates that the *location decisions of firms* are largely insensitive to changes in the level of local education and the level of local tax rates.[17] Second, and more importantly, the *value of the business capital stock* of existing firms (plant and equipment, denoted hereafter as K) is negatively related to the local property tax rate. Increases in local taxation do reduce firm investment.[18]

3.5 Local politics and the demand for local education

A model of a regional school economy also requires a description of how the local level of education (E), and thus the local property tax rate, is decided. We shall assume that the political process of local fiscal decision-making produces a consensus on E and r which reflects the well-defined preferences of some 'decisive' subset of community voters. In the empirical work which operationalizes this model, we have estimated this decisive voter in each district as the family with approximately the median income (see Inman, 1978b).[19]

This decisive voter has a typical downward sloping demand schedule with respect to the marginal 'tax price' of local education (τ), with the schedule positively related to before tax income (I) and exogenous grants in aid (z): $E = g(\tau, z, I)$. The marginal tax costs of E are the change in the decisive voter's taxes as we change E. This decisive voter is assumed to deduct local taxes from federal and state income taxes at their marginal tax rates (whose weighted average is ω) and, when available, receives tax credits at a rate $\lambda (0 \leq \lambda \leq 1)$ per dollar of local taxes. The combined effects of deductions and credits is to reduce the final out-of-pocket costs of local taxes to $\pi = 1 - \omega - \lambda$. If b is the decisive voter's own tax base (home value plus land value) and r the local tax rate, then the marginal tax cost schedule will be:[20]

$$\tau = d(\pi rb)/dE \simeq \pi b(dr/dE) \simeq \pi(1 - m)b/B,$$

using (6) and the normalization $k/E = k' \equiv 1$. Note that even though the marginal cost of producing education is constant, both b and B can depend on E through the capitalization and investment effects of tax financed changes in E, and thus $\tau = \tau(E)$. The equilibrium level of E is therefore given implicitly by $E^* = g(\tau(E^*), z, I)$. Given E the local tax rate follows.

3.6 Local education and exit to private schools

An alternative for families living within any community following the adjustments to a school finance reform is to exit to a private school system if they find the new-post reform educational options in the public sector unacceptable. An initial major exodus to private schools following reform can have a considerable subsequent negative impact on local school spending (the coalition of low-spending votes has now increased) perhaps leading to additional departures and a spiral towards a two-class system: a rich and middle class private school system and a poor and lower middle class public school system. It is important therefore that we be able to predict the likely effects of any reform on the potential demand for private schools.

The simulation model developed here does so in a simple way. Using estimates of household demand for education, we compare the consumer surplus received from education by each family in each district under the post-reform equilibrium to the consumer surplus if that family were to exit to a private school and buy their preferred level of school spending at full marginal cost ($k' \equiv 1$). If the family's private school consumer surplus exceeds their public school surplus then exit occurs. In making the private school surplus calculation we assume families do not relocate in 'private school enclaves' but must continue to pay school taxes in their town even though they no longer use the public schools. In the long run, however, we might well expect such enclaves to form, particularly if the initial exit (calculated under the pay-local-taxes assumption) is large. Our results of exit are therefore to be interpreted as the *impact* effects of reform on private school enrollment. If the initial exit is 'small' (say 15% or less), it seems reasonable to assume enclaves will not form and the impact estimate provided here will be reasonably close to the long-run effects of reform on exit.

3.7 *Financing fiscal reform*

As any fiscal reform proposal will move resources from one community to another, the state government must have a taxing mechanism to facilitate such transfers. In Pennsylvania the state taxes family income at a proportional rate. I assume any marginal increase in this tax will have no significant effect on work effort and thus before-tax income (I). However, the tax does reduce after-tax income which in turn can affect housing decisions, school spending, and the relative attractiveness of private schools. These feedback effects of financing are explicitly incorporated into the analysis.

Each of the above subsectors of the metropolitan economy has been parameterized for the Philadelphia regional school economy, and the results below are based upon simulations with our model for this economy.[21]

4. An agenda for reform

The setting of a preferred agenda requires two crucial pieces of information: a specification of all possible alternative group choice functions, $U(x, \alpha)$, and a description of the group choice process adequate to assign a prior probability distribution for the emergence of any particular specification of $U(x, \alpha)$.

4.1 *The politics of fiscal reform in Pennsylvania*

Pennsylvania budgetary politics is currently undergoing a significant transition. Old-style bossism is on the way out (helped by the recent criminal convictions of the old-style bosses) and new-style coalition politics is on its way in.[22] No longer does a single leadership dictate the budget and all tax and school finance reforms. In the emerging new order, four major competing groups have surfaced as the significant voting blocs on all matters of finance: a bloc of moderate-conservative Republicans from the Philadelphia suburban counties, a bloc of pro-city Democrats from Philadelphia and (sometimes) Pittsburgh, a bloc of pro-western Pennsylvania Democrats from Pittsburgh and its surrounding counties, and a large, very conservative bloc of rural Republicans from the central and northern portions of the state.[23] Finally, there is a small group of rural Democrats and Democrats from the middle-sized cities in the state (Erie, Allentown, Scranton, e.g.) who can generally be brought within a Democratic coalition as needed.

In a series of interviews with knowledgeable legislative staff, staff within the Governor's office, and the two major lobbyists within the state, a composite picture of likely winning coalitions on the issue of metropolitian school finance reform was developed. It was agreed among all those interviewed that none of the four voting blocs described above could generate enough votes within its own bloc to pass a piece of legislation counter to the interests of the other blocs. Some coalition among the four groups is therefore necessary for reform. Three potentially winning coalitions were uniformily identified.[24] The first, and generally agreed to be the most likely winning coalition, involved the Philadelphia suburban Republicans and their Republican and Democratic suburban counterparts from the western counties in the Pittsburgh area (hereafter denoted as the SW coalition). The second, and next most likely, winning coalition involves Philadelphia suburban Republicans teaming with rural Republicans (denoted hereafter as the SR coalition). Finally, center city Democrats in Pittsburgh and Philadelphia can join forces with upstate Democrats to form a third coalition (the CD coalition) capable of passing finance reform legislation. While numerous alternative groupings of the four voting blocs are possible (6 pairs, 4 triples, and unanimity) only these three groups were judged to be both politically feasible and sufficient to insure passage of an agreed upon policy.

Having established the set of possible winning coalitions, it was necessary to then determine the likelihood for each coalition that it would form and agree on policy. By definition each coalition is a winning coalition, so once we establish the probability that the coalition will form we have also established the probability that the coalition will win. Again interviews with legislative and administration staff and the major lobbyists were conducted. Each was asked to assess the likelihood that the three coalitions – SW, SR, and CD – would form and agree on a policy for school fiscal reform in the metropolitan Philadelphia region. The procedure used to extract the individual assessors probabilities of coalition formation is described in Winkler (1967).[25] The requirement that at least one winning coalition form on this issue imposed the constraint that the coalition probabilities sum to 1 across SW, SR, and CD for each respondent. The results proved surprisingly robust across the three

Table 1. Estimated probability of winning coalition formation

Coalition	Probability of coalition formation		
	SW	SR	CD
Respondent 1	.60	.35	.05
Respondent 2	.50	.35	.15
Respondent 3	.60	.30	.10

respondents (see Table 1). The center city coalition was judged least likely; the suburban-rural coalition more likely; the straight suburban (Philadelphia suburbs plus western Pa. suburbs) coalition most likely. To see if a consensus might be reached on the differences in the probabilities, a brief final interview was conducted with each respondent explaining the results in Table 1. Respondents 1 and 3 generally deferred to the judgement of respondent 2, the respondent with the longest experience in Harrisburg. Respondent 2 was reluctant to alter his estimates and was pleased to hear of the support of the others. In the work which follows, the results in Table 1 for respondent 2 are taken as the likelihood that each of the three coalitions will form and win on a metropolitan school finance reform issue.[26]

4.2 *Assessing coalition preferences*

Having specified all possible winning coalitions on any metropolitan school reform issue, the next task is to specify each coalition's preferences for the outcomes of such reforms. The relevant outcomes are assumed to be the level of instructional services per child (E, measured in dollars) and the after-tax, after-education income in each family (y, measured in dollars). For this analysis, y is measured as before reform income (I) *minus* local school taxes *minus* state school and reform taxes *minus* any private school tuition paid *plus* the annual value of capitalized changes in the value of a family's residential plot. We adopt as our normalization for each coalition's preferences the following, reasonably general specification for $U(x, \alpha)$:

$$U(x, \alpha) = \{\sum u(E(x), y(x))^\gamma\}^{1/\gamma}, \qquad \gamma \leq 1, \tag{1}$$

where,

$$u(E(x), y(x)) = (\beta y(x)^{-\mu} + (1 - \beta)E(x)^{-\mu})^{-1/\mu}, \tag{2}$$

where the behavioral relationships $E = E(x)$ and $y = y(x)$ which connect policies to outcomes have been outlined briefly in Section 3.[27] The preference parameters γ, β, and μ now constitute the preference vector α. Through γ, equation (1) allows for varying degrees of aversion to inequality in the distribution of preceived family welfares, as measured by the household utility function in (2). When $\gamma = 1$, all families are weighted equally and the coalition's $U(\cdot)$ reduces to the familiar Benthamite evaluation rule. As γ falls in value and become negative $U(\cdot)$ weights more highly those families with low values of $u(E, y)$. As $\gamma \to -\infty$, $U(\cdot)$ approaches a Rawlsian maximin criterion. The preference parameters β and μ define a CES family utility function for constituents represented by the coalition. The value $\varepsilon = 1/(1 + \mu)$ measures the elasticity of substitution between education and private income, while the parameters β and μ jointly determine the share of each good, E and y, in before-tax income (I).

To obtain estimates of the preference parameters β, μ, and γ – and thus $U(\cdot)$ – for the three potential winning coalitions, current and past legislative staff for the leaders of each coalition were interviewed. One staff person each was interviewed for the CD and SR coalitions while a joint interview with a staff person for the Pittsburgh suburban group and a staff person for the Philadelphia suburban group was used to assess preferences for the SW coalition. As the reform policies to be considered here are designed to impact only within the Philadelphia metropolitan area (with possible extension to the Pittsburgh region in time), the preferences of the SR coalition were assumed to be those of the Philadelphia suburban representatives only.[28] The interviews employed the indifference curve mapping procedures of MacCrimmon and Toda (1969) to obtain estimates of β and μ while a procedure outlined in Inman and Wolf (1976) was used to obtain our estimate of γ.

The MacCrimmon-Toda indifference map procedure extracts from each respondent for each coalition a series of better-than, worse-than, or as-good-as comparisons over the space of alternative outcomes in E and y for 'typical' constituent families. Two separate indifference curves were developed, one for a low to moderate income constituent family and one for a moderate to high income constituent family. The respondents first defined a starting bundle of E and y for the low-moderate income constituent and then were asked to compare that bundle, as the constituent might, to a successive series of alternative bundles until five points of indifference had been established. Linear approximations between the five points were used to approximate the indifference curve. The procedure was then repeated for a moderate-high income constituent to obtain a second indifference curve. Under the null hypothesis that constituent preferences can be defined by (2), the five points of indifference on each indifference curve are sufficient to estimate the parameters β and μ. For the CES utility function:[29]

$$\ln\left(y/E\right) = \left(\frac{1}{1+\mu}\right)\ln\left(\frac{\beta}{1-\beta}\right) + \left(\frac{1}{1+\mu}\right)\ln\left\{(dy/dE)_{\bar{u}}\right\},$$

or (3)

$$= \theta + \varepsilon\ln\left\{(dy/dE)_{\bar{u}}\right\},$$

where $(dy/dE)_{\bar{u}}$ is the marginal rate of substitution between y and E evaluated at a given (y, E) point. Assuming an additive error term, (3) can be estimated from our approximation to each indifference curve obtained via the MacCrimmon-Toda procedure. The regression results are reported in Table 2; they are the summary results based on 8 observations – 8 (y/E) points and the corresponding estimate of $(dy/dE)_{\bar{u}}$ at each point – obtained by 'pooling'

Table 2. Coalition preferences for education and income

Coalition	Preference parameters					
	θ	ε	$\bar{R}^2$	μ[b]	β[c]	γ
SW	2.34	.24	.76	3.098	.9999	1.0 ($ 600)[d]
	(.07)[a]	(.03)				
SR	2.31	.29	.83	2.460	.999	1.0 ($ 700)
	(.08)	(.04)				
CD	2.31	.29	.98	2.460	.999	−.33 ($ 1200)
	(.03)	(.02)				

[a] Standard errors in parentheses.
[b] The parameter μ is estimated from the estimated ε as $\mu = (1 - \varepsilon)/\varepsilon$.
[c] The parameter β is estimated as $q/(1 + q)$, where $q = e^{\theta/\varepsilon}$.
[d] The maximal contribution from a 'typical' rich family within the coalition to support a transfer of $ 250/family to a 'typical' poor family within the coalition.

the observations from the low-moderate and moderate-high income indifference curves.

The results in Table 2 suggest that we have obtained reasonably precise estimates of the CES parameters, and overall the $\bar{R}^2$ values for each regression imply that the CES specification is adequate for the underlying indifference curves. Further, the behavioral implications of the parameters are consistent with the general pattern of school spending. The implied elasticities of substitution (ε) between income and education are within the .25 to .30 range, not very far from the elasticity of .4 obtained by Lovell (1978) in his cross-section study of Connecticut school spending. The implied preferred shares of after-federal, before-local tax income to be allocated to education for a two-child family are .11 for constituents in the SW coalition and .20 for constituents in the SR and CD coalitions, both reasonable values for U.S. families. Not surprisingly, the least precise estimates are those obtained for the SW coalition. For the SW coalition joint interviews were conducted in which representatives of the Philadelphia and Pittsburgh suburban groups were asked to compromise group preferences and agree on points of indifference for the coalition using the MacCrimmon-Toda procedure. In most instances the two representatives 'split the difference' between their individual responses leading to a coalition indifference curve which lay between the two group indifference curves. The Pittsburgh group (not reported in Table 2) had the lowest estimated elasticity of substitution between E and y ($\varepsilon = .17$) and was willing to allocate the smallest share of income to education ($\simeq .06$). The final result for SW ($\varepsilon = .24$ and a share to education of .11) reflects this compromise of the high education interests in the Philadelphia suburbs with the low education interests in the Pittsbugh suburbs. Yet apparently this is a compromise which the Philadelphia suburban representatives are willing to make to insure that their preferences for redistribution (measured by γ) will control policy.

Those redistributive preferences were measured through a series of questions designed to extract the coalition's maximal willingness to redistribute income from moderate-high income families within the coalition to low income families. The maximal redistribution was measured as the dollar amount a rich family within the coalition would contribute to insure a $\$250$/family transfer to a low income family.[30] Given this maximal transfer and the initial income and education levels of the rich and poor families (as defined by the respondent) it is possible to solve for an implied γ using (1) and (2), where the household utility function (2) is that estimated for the coalition. The maximal contribution (within parentheses) and the estimated values of γ appear in Table 2. For the SW and SR coalitions γ is estimated as slightly greater than one; for these coalitions γ equal to 1.0 will be used. The center city coalition is clearly more tolerant of redistribution; the implied γ value is $-.33$. The city coalition is more decidedly pro-poor.

4.3 Setting the agenda

Table 3 summarizes the search for an optimal agenda for a proportional property tax credit financed through a proportional tax on wages. The response of the metropolitan school economy to a positive tax credit from a status quo position of no credit $(\lambda = 0)$ is first simulated to predict new educational spending levels (E) and after-local tax, after-private schools income levels (y) for each family in the region.[31] The new vectors of E and y are then evaluated according to each coalition's evaluation rule given by (1) and

Table 3. Optimal tax credit agendas

Objective	Preferred policy	Mean spending	Coef. of variance	City spending	Suburb. spending	Tax rate	% Exit
Status quo	$\lambda = 0$	$\$805$	.133	$\$724$	$\$869$	.000	21%
SW	$\lambda = .20$	825	.111	786	872	.011	16
SR	$\lambda = .40$	876	.113	847	927	.026	10
CD	$\lambda = .40$	876	.113	847	927	.026	10
max $EU(x, \alpha)$	$\lambda = .25$	840	.109	801	885	.015	14
max $U(x, E\alpha)$	$\lambda = .025$	811	.131	731	873	.001	20
max $Eu(x_i, \lambda = 0)$	$\lambda = 0$	805	.133	724	869	.000	21
	$\lambda = .25$	840	.109	801	885	.015	14
max $Eu(<x>^2, \lambda = 0)$	$\lambda = 0$	805	.133	724	869	.000	21
	$\lambda = .2$	825	.111	786	872	.011	16
	$\lambda = .4$	876	.113	847	927	.026	10

(2) and the parameter values in Table 2. Optimal policies and optimal agendas can now be specified.

The status quo point is selected as the no-aid position to reflect the search for an entirely new means of financing local education. Without any state assistance the mean level of instructional spending per child in the region is $ 805/child with the center city child receiving $ 724 and the average suburban child receiving $ 869. These averages include expenditures on private education for the 21% of the children who exit to private schools. The coefficient of variation in school spending as a description of the system's equity performance is .133. The needed wage tax rate is of course zero when $\lambda = 0$.

Table 3 next lists the preferred proportional rate credits for property taxation for each of the three coalitions, SW, SR, and CD. (The search for optimal credits proceeded in increments of .025 from 0 to 1.) For each coalition a unique optimal value of was found. For the low-education coalition, SW, the optimal credit is $\lambda = .2$. The mean education level increases only slightly from $ 805 to $ 825 reflecting the relatively low price sensitivity of school spending to tax credits in this sample. Most of the increase is observed for children within the center city. The suburban residents use the resulting property tax relief from the credit to increase y not E. As a positive credit does stimulate at least a small increase in E, public education becomes relatively more attractive to the demanders of quality private education and a few return to public schools; the exit percentage falls from 21% to 16%. The needed tax rate on wage income to finance $\lambda = .2$ is .011. As we move to the relatively pro-education objective functions of the SR and CD coalitions the optimal tax credit rises to $\lambda = .4$. Significant education increases are observed in both the city and the suburb and exit falls to 10% of the pre-reform enrollment. Because of the constitutional constraint in Pennsylvania that the credit be proportional, the stronger redistributive preferences of the CD coalition cannot be expressed in their preferred policy.

Of more direct interest to us here is the matter of agenda design for a legislature composed of CD, SW, and SR coalitions. It is clear that a single policy will not satisfy all the potential winners in the debate over preferred tax credits. What recommendations might we then make to this diverse group to assist their search for a good policy? Any move from $\lambda = 0$ to positive credits (except $\lambda \geq .80$ which are rejected by both SW and SR coalition in favor of the status quo), will be preferred by each coalition. If we are limited to a single recommendation without first knowing the winning coalition from legislative deliberations, then that one recommendation which maximizes $EU(x, \alpha)$ is to be preferred. In this instance that preferred singly recommendation is $\lambda = .25$. It is rightly seen as a compromise between the two preferred policies, $\lambda = .2$ and $\lambda = .4$, of the potential winning coalitions. A clearly less attractive recommendation for all three coalitions is that policy based on the maximization of $U(x, E\alpha)$, where the expected values of the elements of α are $E(\beta)$ = .9995, $E(\mu) = 2.78$, and $E(\gamma) = .90$.[32] The implied objective function is modestly redistributive beyond the Benthamite criterion and very slightly more pro-education than the preferences of the SW coalition. The resulting optimal policy of $\lambda = .025$ is quite instructive of the dangers of suggesting reforms to fit some perceived *average* welfare function. No one is well-served by this advice. Efforts to favor the lower income groups ($\gamma < 1$) do so by giving them just what they do not want (relatively speaking), private income. The low tax credit offers no stimulus to education spending but it does keep the regional wage tax low. Private income levels, perceived here as valued by the poor, are thereby protected. Thus the relative unimportance of education coupled with a modest redistributive criterion discourages an expansion of educational spending which all groups would prefer. For all groups involved, a single recommendation base on the criterion $EU(x, \alpha)$ is distinctly superior to the recommendation based upon the maximization of $U(x, E\alpha)$.

Better yet, however, is an agenda of options. Table 3 lists the optimal two-item and three-item agenda of proportional tax credits. The optimal four-item agenda is the status quo ($\lambda = 0$) plus the preferred policy for each of the three possible winning coalitions. In this instance, because the optimal policy for coalitions SR and CD happen to coincide, the preferred three- or four-item agendas are identical. The preferred two-item agenda consists of our best single recommendation, $\lambda = .25$, plus the status quo. This will occur whenever the status quo policy is uniformily unattractive relative to all alternative policies for each coalition. This is almost the case here; only those policies where $\lambda \geq .55$ are ever dominated by the status quo. Finally, when we compare the expected welfare values across alternative recommendation strategies we find the anticipated ordering of strategies results – that is,

$$EV(\alpha) = E\upsilon(\langle x \rangle^3, \alpha; \hat{\lambda} = 0) = E\upsilon(\langle \lambda \rangle^2, \alpha; \hat{\lambda} = 0)$$
$$= 7390.2 > E\upsilon(\langle \lambda \rangle^1, \alpha; \hat{\lambda} = 0) = 7389.0 > EU(\lambda, \alpha) = 7388.\text{[33]}$$

Of interest, too, are the results themselves. The preferred proportional tax credits range from .2 to .4 and reflect the advantages of subsidizing local school spending in a political economy which underprovides public education for a significant portion of the population, at least relative to constituent preferences as perceived by their legislative representatives. Why the local political process might be less than fully responsive to these preferences – even in the suburb – is a matter we cannot pursue here, but Barlow (1970), and Sheshinski (1977) have offered potential explanations for such a 'political market' failure. It is also interesting to note that the optimal tax credits proposed here for the Philadelphia metropolitan region are significantly more liberal than any property tax credit plans or so called circuit-breakers now in place in other states (see Advisory Commission on Intergovernmental Relations, 1977). Why? It is tempting to argue that other reforms were simply based on bad advice using $U(x, E\alpha)$, but the real explanation lies in the fact that the reforms proposed here are for a metropolitan region only and exclude any impact on taxes of school spending in rural regions. Within Pennsylvania at least, and likely within other states as well, the rural bloc is extremely conservative on state-financed educational subsidies and they like the property tax! Farm and large land interests (lumbering, mining) receive favorable property tax treatment through special use classifications which would be lost if we shifted towards wage-tax financing of education. By limiting our reform package to metropolitan-wide taxation for metropolitan-only property tax relief we have isolated the potentially significant opposition of the rural bloc to meaningful reform. That alone has been an important lesson learned.

5. Summary and extensions

The matter of reforming the fiscal structures of metropolitan school economies is a pressing yet extremely complex policy issue now confronting most state legislatures in the United States. New, often radically different strategies for the funding of local schools are being sought. Good economic policy advice is at a premium. This paper has sought to outline a methodology for providing that advice which is sensitive to both the complexities of the policy problem and to the needs of busy decision-makers who must make a choice. An agenda-setting strategy which balances the gains from flexibility against the costs of policy deliberation has been proposed and then applied to the task of recommending a property-tax credit (λ) for local school finance. The best single recommendation ($\lambda = .25$) and the best agenda ($\lambda = .2, \lambda = .4$, plus the status quo) were calculated for the Philadelphia metropolitan school economy.

Numerous qualifications and extensions suggest themselves. First, our alternative objective functions consider only private income and education. Yet one of the central issues in reform of local finance is the potential efficiency losses associated with the effects of local property taxation on housing consumption. To confront this matter, housing services must be introduced explicitly into the household utility function. But if a wage tax is to be used to finance the reform, then, to avoid the trivial result of fully substituting an efficient for an inefficient tax, the allocative consequences of wage taxation must be made endogenous as well. A four-commodity household utility function over housing, leisure, education, and other goods would therefore be an important extension of this work. The parameterization of such a four-commodity utility function through our MacCrimmon-Toda indifference curve procedure is feasible but probably suspect. This fact suggests a second extension. While we have relied upon interviews to provide the relevant data to estimate constituent preferences, a more attractive option would be to estimate such functions econometrically from revealed household behavior for each constituent group. While such estimates will no doubt be statistically less precise than those presented in Table 2, they are likely to be a truer approximation of actual constituent preferences. Further, the uncertainty of such statistical estimates can be included in our analysis, as can the uncertainty attached to our behavioral models' predictions for the effects of policies on the valued outcomes of income, education, housing, and leisure. This work would constitute a useful third extension.

There remains an important final question, however, which has been purposefully pushed into the background. It's answer is fundamental to all the results developed here. *What is the correct agenda-setting criterion?* We have assumed for this analysis that the correct criterion is to maximize the expected value of agendas over alternative (winning) coalition preferences. That criterion has some appeal. From behind a veil of ignorance, a 'universal legislator' not knowing what coalitions he or she might fall within on any issue – yet wanting to insure that if they are a member of the winning coalition, there is an agenda which offers an attractive range of choices – might well choose our criterion of maximizing expected welfare across coalition preferences as the preferred agenda-setting rule. Yet this criterion is not the only candidate. The universal legislator might wish to design agendas which provide equal protection to all possible winning coalitions in which case our criterion becomes maximize the simple sum, rather than the probability weighted sum, of coalition preferences. From this extension it is easy to see the next step, the step which places the problem of finding a criterion for optimal agenda-setting within the larger context of designing an attractive social choice process. That is the arena in which we must look for an answer to our fundamental question of what is an optimal agenda-setting rule.[34] Hopefully the analysis here will convince others of the importance of such a search.

NOTES

1. *Serrano v. Priest* (Serrano II), 18 Cal. 3d 728, 557 P. 2d 929, 135 Cal. Rptr. 345 (1976) and *Robinson v. Cahill* 62 N.J. 473, 303 A. 2d 273, *cert. denied*, 414 U.S. 976 (1973). *Horton v. Meskill* (172 Conn. 615, 376 A. 2d (1977) reached a similar conclusion regarding the unconstitutionality of the Connecticut system of school finance. For a thorough review of these cases see Inman and Rubinfeld (1979).
2. For a useful overview of recent state reform efforts, see Education Commission of the States, *School Finance Reform in the States: 1978.*
3. This is not the place to review this literature, but the recent work of Black, Lewis and Link (1979), Feldstein (1975), Inman (1978a), Ladd (1975) and Friedman and Wiseman (1978) are all worth a look.
4. Geoffrion et al. (1972) has developed a computer interactive methodology which operationalizes Marglin's insights.

92

5. Or we can model explicitly the group choice decision process as a noncooperative policy game using known individual preferences and a well-specified solution concept such as a Nash equilibrium (see, for example, Kydland, 1976). This strategy to our problem presumes too much.

6. As Burmeister et al. (1977) point out, the criterion can be axiomatized following Harsanyi (1955).

7. The specification of $U(\cdot)$ above is based on the more natural specification $\tilde{U}(y, \alpha)$, where y are policy outcomes (e.g., education and income). However, the outcome variables are directly dependent on the choice of policy variables, $x - y = \varphi(x)$. Thus upon substitution, $U(x, \alpha) = \tilde{U}(\varphi(x), \alpha)$.

8. The economist's knowledge of the consequences of policy define the relationship between valued outcomes, y, and the policy variables, $x - y = \varphi(x)$. This information is crucial to defining $U(x, \alpha)$; see note 7 above.

9. The maximization of $U(x, \bar{\alpha})$ to find a single best policy using the most likely value of $\alpha (= \bar{\alpha})$ is probably a fair characterization of what economists now do when forced to give single recommendation advice. More often than not we simply use our own best guess for α. Sometimes we actually try to estimate $\bar{\alpha}$ using information on the distribution of preference parameters; see, for example, Eckstein and Krutilla's (1958) strategy for defining the social rate of discount for cost-benefit analysis.

10. The approach to agenda-setting adopted here is perhaps best seen as an exercise in constitutional design rather than an exercise in policy manipulation as in Plott and Levine (1978). For a possible motivation for the approach here, see Section 5 above.

11. It is important to note that the significant computor costs are likely to be incurred in calculating $U(x, \alpha)$ for each policy and not in finding the best agenda per se. Evaluating $U(x, \alpha)$ will require us to simulate the impacts of policies x on valued outcomes (see note 7 above). Once $U(x, \alpha)$ has been calculated for each x and each α value, however, this data simply becomes reuseable input in the search for optimal agendas.

12. The reader is referred to Inman (1980) for details.

13. When the group preference function is additive separable across policies – e.g. $U = u_1(x, \alpha) + u_2(z, \alpha)$ – where x and z are separate policies, then the value of agendas for deciding x and the value of agendas for deciding z will be independent of policies not within x and z's Pareto sets. We can then compare agenda values for the two policies and allocate the exogenous number of agenda items across the x and z policy areas until the marginal values of increasing the agenda in each area are equal. If separability does not obtain so that $U = U(x, z; \alpha)$, then agendas chosen for x will influence the value of the agenda for z, and conversely. The agenda problem then becomes part of the joint policy problem of choosing the best mix of x and z reforms, where each (x, z) package can now be called a new policy q with group preferences defined as $U(q, \alpha)$. A new, and considerably more complicated, agenda problem can now be defined using $U(q, \alpha)$ as the relevant group preference function.

14. See Inman and Rubinfeld (1979) for a survey of the evidence and arguments why such a pattern is likely to emerge.

15. The analysis developed here neglects an outcome variable of potential importance to any property tax reform proposal, housing investment. While the model itself predicts changes in housing consumption it is not evaluated separately from private income in our normative analysis.

16. For a more detailed and technical presentation of the following model see Inman (1977, 1978a).

17. See the report of Roger Schmenner (1978).

18. See the studies by R. Hall and D. Jorgenson (1967) and M. E. King (1974).

19. Romer and Rosenthal (1979) provide a useful review of the empirical literature on attempts to identify the political-structural determinants of local budgetary choice, and rightly conclude

that doing so from cross-section data is an extremely difficult task. This difficulty does not preclude the use of cross-section estimates of budgetary choice behavior as predictive models, however, anymore than our failure to identify the underlying structure of any process prevents the use of reduced form equations as predictors.

20. The term $\pi r(db/dE)$ is omitted here and is the cause of the approximation. In the simulation it is included and has only a trivial impact on τ.

21. The key behavioral relationships needed for these simulations are a demand for local education equation and a land value or capitalization equation. The specifications used for these two equations are described in Inman (1977). When estimated for the Philadelphia metropolitan school economy, the demand for education equation implied an income elasticity of demand equal to 1.47, a tax price elasticity of demand equal to $-.09$, and an exogenous lump-sum and elasticity of .12. Each elasticity is statistically significant. The land value or capitalization equation performed almost identically to that in Oates' (1969) original equation for New Jersey and to that in my replication (1977) for Long Island. Nearly full capitalization of tax rate variations – holding service levels constant – is observed in the Philadelphia school economy.

22. The transition has not been easy, however. Indeed passage of the first state budget following the conviction of the major leader in the General Assambly required the ex-leader to return to Harrisburg to fashion a last-minute, late-night compromise among the competing groups. For a fascinating description of the old-style, see Peirce (1972: Ch. 4).

23. The 'new order' described here applies only to the House of Representatives. The Pennsylvania Senate, as best as we could determine, remains largely under the control of two or three key Senate leaders, to the extent it can be controlled at all. The House is the central body for initiating finance reform and we have therefore concentrated our efforts on this body of the legislature.

24. The procedure for identifying possible winning coalitions on metropolitan school reform can be briefly summarized. In an initial series of interviews the four major coalitions were identified. They included the Philadelphia suburban Republicans (denoted S), the center city Democratic coalition (C), the pro-western Pennsylvania coalition (W), and the upstate rural Republican coalition (R). No coalition by itself had enough votes to prove decisive on their own in finance reform. Therefore all possible *winning* coalitions must involve varying combinations of members of these four groups. In a second interview all possible two and three group coalitions were discussed. Initially, two group coalitions were considered and those coalitions which were viewed as impossible on school reform issues – (C, R), (C, S), (W, R) – were dropped from subsequent consideration. Of the three which remained – (S, R), (C, W), (S, W) – we next determined whether the coalition had sufficient votes to insure a victory for its favored policy or whether additional coalition members (a three-group coalition) would be needed. The coalition (S, R) was felt to be sufficient and it becomes a potentially winning coalition, denoted as SR. The coalition (C, W) was viewed not as likely as the coalition of C plus a few rural Democrats plus the middle-sized cite Democrats. This coalition is a possible winning coalition and denoted as CD. Finally, the coalition (S, W) was seen as the major new coalition in the state, losing perhaps some Pittsburgh votes in any strict anti-city legislation. Even with this loss, however, this SW coalition was seen as sufficient to pass legislation.

25. The procedure used in Winkler's (1967) CDF-Fractile procedure. Respondents were first asked their best guess of the probability (p) that a given winning coalition would form. This value of p was called their 'most likely value' of p. It was then explained that they might not be absolutely certain of this probability and that most likely they have in mind a range of possible values for p. To assess this distribution, each respondent was asked for an assessment such that it is equally likely that p is greater than or less than the assessed value. This point describes the median of the respondent's estimates for p. Quartiles and the extreme tails (1/100

chance p is less than this value, and 99/100 chance p is less than this value) were also assessed. Separate assessments of the likelihood of each coalition were conducted, subject to the constraint that the most likely values across each coalition sum to 1. In all cases the distributions were symmetric; the most likely values of p equaled the median values. Further the distributions were reasonably tight about the most likely values. All agenda-setting results which follow are based on the most likely values of p.

26. For procedures when consensus is less easily achieved see Winkler (1968).

27. The welfare function specification in (1) has been used widely in the recent public finance literature on optimal fiscal policy as well as being recommended in the management science literature as a useful specification for problems involving group compromise (see Freimer and Yu, 1976). The household utility function specification is the simplest form which allows us to specify a variable elasticity of substitution between private goods and education (see Sato, 1972).

28. It was the feeling of all staff interviewed that the needed rural Republican votes to form SR would come along (for small favors at other times) if their suburban Republican counterparts liked the proposal.

29. Equation (3) follows from the first-order conditions for maximization of (2) subject to the constraint $I = y + \tau E$, where τ is the tax price per unit of education. Noting that the ratio of prices equals the marginal rate of substitution, $(dy/dE)_u$, (3) follows.

30. The questions designed to extract redistributive preferences first asked whether the coalition should respect the wishes of the recipient group as to how that group wished to receive a fixed sum transfer. All respondents answered yes, and this was taken as an indication that the coalition's revealed household utility function should be the basis for redistribution. Second, each respondent was asked what would be the maximal tax rate which the coalition might impose upon its typical moderate-to-high income family to fund a \$250/family transfer to a typical poor family. Finally each respondent was asked to give the after-tax income and education levels received by the typical moderate-to-high income family and the typical low income family in the coalition. This information is sufficient to specify γ.

31. The simulation is outlined in Inman and Wolf (1976).

32. Calculated from the coalition parameter values in Table 2 and the coalition probabilities in Table 1.

33. A word of caution is in order. The numerical values given here for the various expected utility specifications have meaning only as a means of ordering alternative agenda strategies. No inference as to the utility difference between strategies being 'large' or 'small' – and therefore worth ignoring – is possible from these numbers.

34. See for example the recent work of McKelvey (1976) and Plott and Levine (1978).

REFERENCES

Advisory Commission for Intergovernmental Relations. (1977). *Significant features of fiscal federalism, 1976-77*, Vol. 2 (m-110). Washington, D.C.

Barlow, R. (1970). Efficiency aspects of local school finance. *Journal of Political Economy* 78: 1028-1040.

Black, D. E., Lewis, K. A., and Link, C. R. (1979). Wealth neutrality and the demand for education. *National Tax Journal* 32: 157-164.

Burmeister, E., Jackson, J., and Ross, S. (1977). The evaluation of simple and optimal decision rules with misspecified welfare functions. In J. D. Pitchford and S. J. Turnovsky (Eds.), *Applications of control theory to economic analysis*. New York: North-Holland.

Eckstein, O. (1961). A survey of the theory of public expenditure criteria. In *Public finances: Needs, sources, and utilization*. Princeton, N.J.: Princeton University Press.

Eckstein, O., and Kruttila, J. (1958). *Multiple purpose river development.* Baltimore: Johns Hopkins Press.

Education Commission of the States. (1978). *School finance in the States.* Denver.

Feldstein, M. (1975). Wealth neutrality and local choice in public education. *American Economic Review* 65: 75-89.

Freimer, M., and Yu, P. L. (1976). Some new results on compromise solutions for group decisions problems. *Management Science* 22: 688-693.

Friedlander, A. (1973). Macro policy goals and revealed preference. *Quarterly Journal of Economics* 87: 25-43.

Friedman, L. S., and Wiseman, M. (1978). Understanding the equity consequences of school finance reform. *Harvard Educational Review* 48: 193-226.

Geoffrion, A. M., Dyer, J. S., and Feinberg, A. (1972). An interactive approach to multi-criterion optimization, with an application to the operation of an academic department. *Management Science* 19: 357-368.

Hall, R., and Jorgenson, D. (1967). Tax policy and investment behavior. *American Economic Review* 57: 391-414.

Harsanyi, J. C. (1955). Cardinal welfare, individualistic ethics, and interpersonal comparisons of utility. *Journal of Political Economy* 58: 309-321.

Inman, R. P. (1977). Micro-fiscal planning in a regional economy: A general equilibrium approach. *Journal of Public Economics* 7: 237-260.

Inman, R. P. (1978a). Optimal fiscal reform of metropolitan schools: Some simulation results. *American Economic Review* 68: 107-122.

Inman, R. P. (1978b). Testing political economy's 'as if' proposition: Is the median income voter really decisive? *Public Choice* 33: 45-65.

Inman, R. P. (1980). Giving advice to busy politicans: A decision-analytic approach. University of Pennsylvania. Mimeo.

Inman, R. P., and Rubinfeld, D. (1979). The judicial pursuit of local fiscal equity. *Harvard Law Review* 92: 1662-1750.

Inman, R. P., and Wolf, D. (1976). SOFA: A simulation program for predicting and evaluating the policy effects of grants-in-aid. *Socio-Economic Planning Sciences* 10: 77-88.

Johanson, L. (1974). Establishing preference functions for macroeconomic decision models. *European Economic Review* 5: 41-66.

King, M. (1974). Taxation and the cost of capital. *Review of Economic Studies* 41: 27-37.

Kydland, F. (1976). Decentralized stabilization policies: Optimization and the assignment problem. *Annals of Economic and Social Measurements* 5: 249-261.

Ladd, H. (1975). Local education expenditures, fiscal capacity, and composition of property tax base. *National Tax Journal* 28: 145-158.

Lovell, M. (1978). Spending for education: The exercise of public choice. *The Review of Economics and Statistics* 60: 487-495.

MacCrimmon, K. R., and Toda, M. (1969). The experimental determination of indifference curves. *Review of Economic Studies* 36: 433-451.

Mangasarian, O. L. (1964). Nonlinear programming problems with stochastic objective functions. *Management Science* 10: 353-359.

Marglin, S. (1967). *Public investment criteria.* Cambridge, Mass.: M.I.T. Press.

McKelvey, R. (1976). Intransitivities in multidimensional voting models and some implications for agenda control. *Journal of Economic Theory* 12: 472-482.

Mera, K. (1969). Experimental determination of relative marginal utilities. *Quarterly Journal of Economics* 83: 464-477.

Oates, W. (1969). The effects of property taxes and local public spending on property values. *Journal of Political Economy* 77: 957-972.

Peirce, N. (1972). *The megastates of America.* New York: Norton.

Plott, C., and Levine, M. (1978). A model of agenda influence on committee decisions. *American Economic Review* 68: 146-160.

Romer, T., and Rosenthal, H. (1979). The elusive median voter. *Journal of Public Economics* 12: 143-170.

Sato, L. (1972). Additive utility function with double-lag consumer demand functions. *Journal of Political Economy* 80: 102-124.

Schmenner, R. (1978). The manufacturing location decision: Evidence from Cincinnati and New England. *Harvard Business School Report*, March: 1-312.

Sheshinski, E. (1977). The supply of communal goods and revenue sharing. In M. S. Feldstein and R. P. Inman (Eds.), *The Economic of public services*. London: Macmillan. 253-273.

Wales, T. (1973). The effect of school and district size on education costs in British Columbia. *International Economic Review* 14: 710-720.

Weisbrod, B. (1968). Income redistribution effects and benefit-cost analysis. In S. Chase (Ed.), *Problems in public expenditure analysis*. Washington, D.C.: The Brookings Institution. 177-222.

Winkler, R. (1967). The assessment of prior distributions in Bayesian analysis. *Journal of the American Statistical Association* 62: 776-800.

Winkler, R. (1968). The consensus for subjective probability distributions. *Management Science* 13: 61-75.

Zellner, A. (1974). The quality of quantitative economic policy-making when targets and costs of change are mis-specified. In Willy Sellekaerts (Ed.), *Econometrics and economic theory: Essays in honour of Jan Tinbergen*. White Plains, N.Y.: IASP, Inc. 75-93.

Comments on R. P. Inman

J. A. MIRRLEES

Nuffield College, Oxford

Robert Inman presents a most interesting model of alternative educational policies, and has made believable estimates of the preferences of some groups who might in fact have to take these policy decisions. He goes on to select a list of policy alternatives to be presented to policy-makers, his selection criterion being expected utility, i.e. utility averaged over the population of possible governments. I do not believe that this procedure makes sense. My remarks will be devoted to explaining why.

By means of interviews, Inman has estimated – let us, for the sake of argument, concede that he has determined – the preference orderings of different groups, labelled α, among alternative outcomes, labelled x. He represents the preference orderings by utility functions of outcomes $U(\cdot, \alpha)$: outcome x has utility $U(x, \alpha)$. Inman happens to have specified a particular utility function for each α. But as far as his evidence or knowledge goes, he could just as well have used alternative utility functions $V(\cdot, \alpha)$ given by

$$V(x, \alpha) = W(U(x, \alpha), \alpha)$$

where W is an increasing function of its first argument. If it is claimed that expected utility is to be maximized, is it EU or EV that is to be maximized? These criteria would in general give different answers. It makes no sense therefore to talk about expected utility when there is no basis for selecting a particular function U representing preferences, a function comparable across groups.

Objections like this one have been used in social choice theory for decades. In particular, the attempt by Vickrey and Harsanyi to base utilitarianism on the expected utility of a randomly chosen member of the population has been attacked by Pattanaik and Sen on similar grounds. There is an account of all this in Sen's book, *Collective Choice and Social Welfare*, Chapter 9, Section 3. I happen to think that utilitarianism can be based on arguments similar to those of Vickrey and Harsanyi, and defended against the objections of Pattanaik and Sen. That defence must be based on showing how interpersonal comparisons of utility can be made. It cannot be used to rescue Inman's procedure, because he is deliberately and explicitly considering the economic advisor's role in a situation where there is no common standard by which the utility levels of alternative possible governments can be compared.

It is clear, in the first place, that the preferences over alternative distributive and educational policies are not statements of individual consumer preferences, but of political orderings, or what might even be called opinions as to what is right. A particular form for the function U is given in Inman's equation (1), but we are not told why that particular form was chosen – why, for example, the sum of individual utilities is raised to the power $1/\gamma$ rather than being multiplied by that number; or why it is not multiplied by β. Since the functions simply describe the groups' political orderings, Inman has no need to tell us why he happened to use that particular form. As soon as he uses expected utility, however, he is making his accidental choice of function determine his answers. Therefore the answers are meaningless.

Does this imply that the question, what advice to give when it is not yet known which preference ordering will rule, is meaningless? Not exactly. What it means is that an attempt to answer the question without deciding what is the relevant absolute standard is doomed to failure. One could adopt a narrowly prudential standard, and ask what advice will maximize the probability that the advisor will be kept in employment by the government when it sees the consequence of his advice. I am not prepared to spend time considering what the answers to that question would be. An alternative is to enquire what advice, whether in the form of a single option or a small set of alternatives, will do most good in the end. That explicitly requires a standard of value, as well as analysis of the choices that will actually be made under the various possible governments. Most economists, like other people, are frightened of the moral responsibility that implies, or perhaps suffer from the confused belief that discussing what is right implies a claim to be especially virtuous oneself. The alternatives, as far as I can see, are to be like the Vicar of Bray, or to determine policies by mathematical inadvertence, as in Inman's paper.

It is interesting to note that the particular form of U chosen by Inman has the property that utility is linearly homogeneous in education and in income: doubling both doubles utility, so that there is no diminishing marginal utility. The centre-city coalition might be much more aggrieved by inegalitarian policies than the other groups would be delighted by them. But the implied criterion takes no account of that. One could try to think about the issues I have raised along these lines, but I do not think it would get anywhere in the end. It might be more interesting to see whether one could find a utility function that all groups could be persuaded to accept, by way of compromise, for the determination of long-term policies. Certainly there are many fascinating questions, like this one, that are raised by the sort of study that Inman has attempted.

Comments on R. P. Inman

DANIEL McFADDEN

Massachusetts Institute of Technology

Consider the legislative process leading to school finance reform. Various coalitions of legislators have the potential to pass reform measures on which their members agree. The outcomes achievable by a coalition are constrained by the technology of school operation and by social and legal constraints on redistribution between coalition members. Subject to these constraints, the members of a potential coalition will bargain over the terms of reform. A coalition will fail if its members are unable to come to an agreement, or some members abandon the coalition to join a second which offers preferred outcomes.

The preceding discussion views the legislative process as a cooperative game without side payments. From this perspective, there are three possible roles for the economic analyst in the legislative process. First, the analyst may advise a potential coalition such as a political party on the technical feasibility of reform proposals, or may prepare reform measures taking into account the preferences and bargaining strengths of coalition members. This role emphasizes the mediation aspects of defining the bargaining set and achieving agreement on a position satisfactory to coalition members. This might be termed 'advising a potentially winning coalition in search of an acceptable proposal.'

Second, the analyst may advise a special interest group such as a teacher's union. In this case, the interest group has well-defined preferences. The analyst's task is to maximize these preferences subject to the compromises necessary to assemble a winning coalition. Term this 'advising a proposal in search of a winning coalition.'

Third, the analyst may advise an agency outside the legislature, such as a state department of finance, on the feasibility and social desirability of alternative reform measures. The objectives and problems of the analyst will depend on the relation of the agency to the legislative process. One possibility is that the agency determines a proposal which maximizes social preferences, and then searches for the least socially undesirable compromise which can achieve a winning coalition. Thus, the agency behaves like a special interest group where the interest is defined to be a particular measure of social preference. A second possibility is that the agency centralizes the 'advising of coalitions in search of acceptable proposals.' This role will differ from decentrallized advice on proposals only if the agency attempts to interject its own (or social) preferences into the judgement on what advice to give to which coalitions. When the agency is an active and interested participant in the process of formulating proposals, the rules governing its relationship to the legislature must be clarified. Control of the resources required to formulate and document proposals may give an agency considerable influence in structuring the measures considered by the legislature and the ease with which alternative coalitions might form. However, potential coalitions ordinarily have some power to reformulate proposals or utilize the resources of special interest groups if they are dissatisfied with agency recommendations. Then the agency must consider the strategic consequences of its positions, taking into account the ability of coalitions to turn elsewhere for the advice required to formulate a winning proposal.

These comments suggest that the task and objectives of the economic analyst will vary depending on which principal he represents in the school finance reform confrontation. Since most principals will be active participants in the cooperative game to determine the reform, the task of the analyst will almost always be defined in terms of the strategic consequences of his proposals. Starting from this framework, it should be possible to describe each analyst's job and determine the protocol he should follow in advising his principal.

Robert Inman considers the problem of a planner who, in my terminology, advises coalitions in search of acceptable proposals. Inman pictures a process in which this planner has centralized control over the agenda of reform alternatives to be considered, and faces a fixed list of potentially decisive coalitions. The cost of formulating alternatives is assumed to be sufficiently large so that a relevant question for the planner is how many alternatives to offer; this cost is presumably also the root of the planner's monopoly power over the agenda. Inman assumes that the goal of the planner is to maximize the preferences of the winning coalition. He is assumed to know the preferences of each coalition, and to have subjective probabilities for winners. The objective function is then taken to be the probability-weighted sum of the coalition utility functions.

There are two aspects of Inman's formulation which in my judgement could be improved. First, while Inman views the planner as being a very active player in the decision process, controlling via the agenda the alternatives each coalition can consider, he excludes some of the strategic options and considerations one would expect such a player to have: (1) The probability that a coalition can win is presumably influenced by the attractiveness to its members of the alternatives it might back. Thus, by setting an agenda in which a specified coalition can always be blocked by a second, the agent should be able to exclude some coalitions from contention. The subjective probabilities of success are then functions of the planner's strategy. (2) If the potential coalitions are active players, they may have the ability to force consideration of alternatives not on the planner's agenda, either by turning elsewhere for advice, or by forcing the planner to analyze added agenda items. The planner then no longer has a monopoly, and must consider the strategic consequences of his suggested agenda. I believe that a more realistic approach to modeling planner's actions is to make the gaming aspects of his role explicit. My introductory comments suggest one way in which the position of a planner in the decision process can be classified; a model should specify his position, the strategies he has available, and the strategies of other players. The nature of coalitions and rules for blocking should be specified – particularly with respect to the possibilities of forming joint coalitions, or of achieving coalition unanimity by excluding splinter members.

The second area for potential improvement in the Inman model is in the specification of planner's preferences. Plausible cases are when the planner is an agent for a specific coalition with well-defined group preferences and seeks to maximize these preferences, or when the planner is an agent for society and seeks to maximize a social welfare function. Either of these alternatives could be broadened to admit a classical theory of agency, with incomplete information on principal's preferences and possible incompatabilities between principal and agent preferences. Less plausible is Inman's assumption that the planner seeks to maximize the expected utility of the winning coalition. First, in a game theoretic view, the probability that a coalition will win depends on the planner's strategy. Then Inman's objective function is not a well-defined primitive of the model. Second, even if one can justify the assumption necessary for the comparability of utilities across individuals or coalitions so that it is meaningful to form a weighted sum, it is unclear why this sum should represent planner's preferences. It is a poor candidate for a social welfare measure, since one would expect the latter to weigh the outcomes to losers as well as winners and to be determined by ethical principles more fundamental than the structure of feasible coalitions or probability of winning. Alternatively, if one starts from the proposition that the planner's objective function is a result of self-interest in achieving compatability with the eventual winner, then one should make explicit the incentives generating this self-interest (competitive pressure from other planners, payment schedule contingent on performance). The tastes of the planner should be a primitive in this formulation.

The problem that Robert Inman poses of determining appropriate behavior rules for economic advisors to a legislative process is a fascinating one. Several aspects of Inman's approach, including the role of legislative coalitions in the decision process and the agency relationship between legislators and the economic analyst, seem sensible and plausible. In my judgement, it would be more fruitful in future research on this topic to develop more explicitly the objectives of the planner, and to consider fully the strategic aspects of planner's acts in a game theoretic setting.

Imperfect capital markets and the public provision of education

P. G. HARE   and   D. T. ULPH*

University of Stirling   *University College, London*

Summary

An intergenerational model of wealth distribution is the basis for an analysis of educational policy: specifically grants, loans and subsidies. Parents endow their children with education and/or cash bequest; the child's earned income and the cash bequest may be taxed. For given tax schedules and a given distribution of abilities in the population, the distribution of wealth eventually approaches an equilibrium. Initially we characterise the optimal tax schedules, using a welfare function based on the long run equilibrium wealth distribution. We then enquire whether grants, loans or subsidies would form part of an optimal distributional policy. It turns out that educational grants are desirable if they are the only additional instrument available, but loans appear to be superior, although the model needs further development to analyse them fully: the model is formulated for subsidies, but not solved in this paper.

1. Introduction

One of the grounds frequently advanced for some form of public intervention in the education market is the imperfection of the markets for loans to finance private provision. There has been a great deal of discussion of the precise nature and extent of these imperfections and of the welfare effects of various types of government intervention.[1] A lot of this latter discussion is conducted in terms of the standard considerations of 'equity vs. efficiency'. Illuminating though such discussion is, it has two drawbacks.

First, it is not clear how far some of the objectives, in particular the equity objective, could be better met by alternative instruments (e.g., income taxation). What one really wants to examine is the strength of the argument for

* We are grateful to J. Mirrlees and C. Pissarides, as well as other participants at the U.K./U.S. Conference on Collective Choice in Education held in Boston in December 1979, for valuable comments on the previous version of this paper. As usual, we accept responsibility for remaining errors and omissions.

public intervention against a background in which other possible instruments have been pursued to their limits (i.e., set at their optimal levels).

Secondly, the introduction of such alternative instruments inevitably takes the discussion into the realm of second-best analysis. This means that we cannot always appeal to first-best conditions as a guide to whether or not efficiency is being achieved. It also carries the implication that there may not be the tradeoff between efficiency and equity that is sometimes referred to. For example moves to reduce the inequity in the distribution of earning ability, which may in themselves involve some inefficiency, may reduce the need to rely on progressive taxation as the principal instrument of redistribution and may result in an overall improvement in efficiency.[2]

In some earlier work[3] we have attempted to provide an explicit second-best analysis of some issues in the economics of education. In that work we ignored the problem of capital market imperfections and concentrated instead on the optimal design of policies to offset the inequality arising from unequal dispersion of abilities. It is the purpose of this paper to introduce capital market imperfections into our earlier models and undertake some second-best analysis of various policies to offset both imperfect capital markets and the unequal distribution of abilities.

We had hoped to analyse a model in which the reasons for the imperfection of the capital market were embodied within the structure of the model, but unfortunately have only been able to make much progress so far with a model in which imperfect capital markets are imposed as an exogenous constraint. Indeed, we begin by making the extreme assumption that it is impossible for people to borrow to finance their education. In this case, in the absence of government intervention, the only way people could finance private education is from parental income. This leads us to formulate an intergenerational model very similar to one recently analysed by Loury (1979), with the major difference that we allow for the possibility of financial bequests.

The reason for allowing financial bequests is that we can then assess the merits of educational policy as an instrument for altering the transmission of wealth in the context of a model in which there is an alternative policy available.

In the next section of the paper we outline the basic model and establish the existence and uniqueness of a stable distribution of wealth. In Section 3 we introduce taxation and characterise the optimal tax scheme for the resulting model. Some important properties of the optimal tax schedules are derived. These are used in the subsequent section to analyse the case for educational policies involving loans, grants or tuition subsidies. In the final section we discuss a number of directions in which it would be useful to develop the analysis further.

2. Intergenerational transfers: Simplified version of the Loury model

In this section we introduce an intergenerational model based on Loury (1979), but somewhat simplified. Initially, the model contains no form of income or bequest taxation, but that complication, and its implications, are examined fully in section three, below. Strictly speaking, since each generation only receives income in a single period, we should always refer to lifetime income, or wealth, but for convenience in what follows we use the terms income or wealth interchangeably.

Parents in each generation use their wealth, w, to pay for the education of their offspring, to provide a financial bequest for their offspring and to finance their own consumption. To facilitate the analysis, we follow Loury in our neglect of the biological 'facts of life'. We thus assume that each parent has one child, whose income depends on its education, its basic ability and the cash bequest already mentioned. Parents have a utility function, $u(c_1, c_2)$, a function of their own consumption, c_1, and their offspring's income, c_2. Subsequently, we shall interpret c_2 as net income, but since there is no income taxation in this introductory version of the model, the distinction between net and gross income (or wealth) is unimportant.

Let us suppose that parents know the ability, α, of their offspring, and that α is distributed in the population according to the probability density function $\varphi(\alpha)$ defined on $[0, 1]$. For any particular individual, ability is assumed to be independent of parental characteristics. Given parental decisions concerning educational provision e, and bequests b, the individual's income,

$$y = h(\alpha, e) + b \tag{1}$$

where $h(\alpha, e)$ is an earnings function expressing market earnings in terms of α and e. The form of the function $h(\cdot)$ is also known to parents. It is helpful to introduce the following three assumptions concerning the functions $\varphi(\cdot)$, $h(\cdot)$ and $u(\cdot)$.

A. Ability α is distributed on the unit interval $[0, 1]$ with probability density function $\varphi(\alpha)$ satisfying the condition that $\varphi(\alpha) > 0$ for all $\alpha \in [0, 1]$. φ is continuously differentiable.
B. (1) $h(\alpha, e)$ is twice continuously differentiable for all $\alpha \in [0, 1]$, $e \geq 0$.
   (2) h is *strictly* increasing and *strictly* concave in e for all $e \geq 0$, $\alpha \in [0, 1]$ ($h_e > 0$, $h_{ee} < 0$).
   (3) h is strictly increasing in $\alpha(h_\alpha > 0)$, and increasing α raises the marginal product of education, i.e., $h_{\alpha e} > 0$.
   (4) $h(\alpha, 0) = 0$, for all $\alpha \in [0, 1]$; as $e \to 0$, $h_e(\alpha, e) \to +\infty$. Further
   $$-\frac{eh_{ee}}{h_e} \to \beta(\alpha), \ 0 < \beta(\alpha) < 1, \text{ as } e \to 0.$$

(5) h is bounded. Hence there exists $k > 0$ with the property that $h(\alpha, e) \leq k$ for all $\alpha \in [0, 1]$, $e \geq 0$.

C. (1) $u(c_1, c_2) = \upsilon(c_1) + \delta\upsilon(c_2)$.

(2) $\delta \leq 1$.

(3) $\upsilon(\cdot)$ is strictly increasing, strictly concave.

(4) $\sigma(x) \equiv -\dfrac{x\upsilon''(x)}{\upsilon'(x)}$ is non-decreasing in x, with $\sigma(x) \to k_0 > 0$ as $x \to 0$.

Assumption A is made in order to reduce the number of cases requiring separate examination later on. In particular the insistence on positive weight in the tails of the distribution ensures that, when we incorporate taxation into the model, standard results on tax rates at the upper and lower ends of the ability distribution go through.

Assumptions B(2) and B(4) say that education is necessary to get any earned income, and that it is productive, indeed highly productive initially. Moreover, diminishing returns set in immediately, and B(5) implies that their effect is sufficiently severe that there is an ultimate upper limit to earned income (k). These assumptions exclude the possibility that some people may be ineducable: this does not mean that such people do not exist, but simply that they can be identified and treated separately through an appropriate system of lump sum transfers. The overall bound on education possibilities (B(5)) is probably not unreasonable, and it serves to place a bound on the wealth distributions we shall be dealing with below. Also, B(4) rules out a case which might arise if $h_e(\alpha, 0) < \infty$: in that case, some people might decide not to buy any education at all.

Assumption C is clearly restrictive and is certainly much stronger than we need. Unfortunately we have found it difficult to obtain a simpler set of conditions that will enable us to prove all the results we need. For example, we need to rule out a utility function such as the C.E.S. function which gives equal weight to parent and child, but has a zero elasticity of substitution. For then $c_1 = c_2$ is the optimal solution; but since c_2 is the gross income of the child while c_1 is the gross consumption of the parent, then, the child's wealth is always less than the parent's and no equilibrium distribution exists. On the other hand, one doesn't want the parent to care too much for the child since, if the education system is fairly productive, the child may always end up with more wealth than the parent, and again no equilibrium distribution would exist.

Finally, we remark on the informational assumptions regarding α and $h(\cdot)$. Now it seems not too unreasonable to suppose that parents can estimate the ability of their offspring fairly well, as we assumed above. It is rather less reasonable, however, to suppose that this ability should be independent of parental wealth, but we have not been able to develop the analysis with a weaker assumption here. Similarly, it is probably very difficult for parents to estimate the education production function, $h(\cdot)$ and it would be desirable to explore the implications of imperfect information about this function. That issue is not pursued any further in the present paper.

Define the function

$$J(\alpha, x) = \underset{e, b \geq 0}{\text{Max}} \{h(\alpha, e) + b\} \text{ such that } e + b \leq x \tag{2}$$

Thus if x represents the amount of resources which a parent makes available either for the education of, or for a financial bequest to his offspring, the function $J(\cdot)$ tells us the maximum income the offspring can have if x is allocated optimally. The parent's optimisation problem therefore assumes the simple form:

$$\left.\begin{array}{l} \underset{x \geq 0}{\text{Max}}\, u(c_1, c_2), \text{ where } c_1 = w - x, \\ \qquad\qquad\qquad\quad \text{and } c_2 = J(\alpha, x) \\ \\ \text{i.e., } \underset{x \geq 0}{\text{Max}}\, u(w - x, J(\alpha, x)) \end{array}\right\} \tag{3}$$

Solving (3) gives the optimal level of x as a function of w and α, while solving (2) for that level of x gives the optimal values for e and b. The overall solution to (2) and (3) may be expressed in the form: $c_1(w, \alpha)$, $c_2(w, \alpha)$, $b(w, \alpha)$. Moreover, it is easy to check that $c_2(\cdot)$ is increasing in α. (See Appendix, Lemma 1.)

Given solutions of the above form for all parents, we can examine how the distribution of wealth changes between generations. Suppose that we set out from some initial wealth distribution, with probability density function $f^0(w)$, and that after i generations, the corresponding probability density function is $f^i(w)$. The solutions to (2) and (3), with our assumption that ability, α is a random variable independent of parental wealth, w, allow us to calculate the conditional probability, $L(z, w)$; this is the probability that offspring of a parent with wealth w will have less than or equal to z.

Clearly,

$$L(z, w) = \begin{cases} 0 & \text{if } c_2(w, 0) \geq z \\ 1 & \text{if } c_2(w, 1) \leq z \\ \Phi(\alpha) & \text{if } c_2(w, \alpha) = z \text{ for } \alpha \in (0, 1) \end{cases} \tag{4}$$

The conditions in (4) are easy to understand. $c_2(w, 0) \geq z$ implies that for any $\alpha \in [0, 1]$, $c_2(w, \alpha) \geq z$ so that wealth of the offspring must exceed z; hence $L(z, w) = 0$. A similar argument holds for the second condition. In the third condition, $\Phi(\cdot)$ is the distribution function corresponding to $\varphi(\cdot)$; i.e.,

$$\Phi(\alpha) = \int_0^\alpha \varphi(\alpha)d\alpha,$$

represents the probability that offspring ability is less than or equal to the specified α, where $c_2(w, \alpha) = z$.

The wealth distribution in the next generation thus has a density function which satisfies the conditions:

$$\int_0^z f^{i+1}(w)dw = \int_0^\infty L(z, w)f^i(w)dw, \text{ for all } z. \tag{5}$$

Equation (5) generates a sequence of wealth distributions in successive generations, which prompts us to ask two important questions.

(a) Does the sequence of distributions generated by (5) approach some limiting distribution, $f(w)$, independently of the starting point, $f^0(w)$?
(b) Does there exist a stationary distribution corresponding to (5)? If there is such a distribution, we call it an equilibrium distribution.

Of course, (a) implies (b), since if there is a limiting distribution for (5), then it must satisfy the condition:

$$\int_0^z f(w)dw = \int_0^\infty L(a, w)f(w)dw \text{ for all } z, \tag{6}$$

which is precisely the condition for stationarity, (b). On the other hand, however, (b) does not necessarily imply (a), since a stationary distribution may not be unique, and even if it is, it may not be approached from all initial distributions. But the assumptions made above allow us to state the following result:

Theorem 1: Assumptions A, B(1)-(5) and C(1)-(3) imply that there is a unique equilibrium distribution, $f(w)$. This distribution is the limiting distribution for any initial distribution of wealth, $f^0(w)$.

Proof: see Appendix.

This is the basic result which we shall be employing in models with taxation in the next section. But before moving on to that, it seems useful to comment briefly on the relation between our model and that of Loury (1979). There are some relatively minor technical differences between the two models, notably in the treatment of the utility function. A more important difference, however, is that our model allows financial bequests while Loury's does not. In both models, because there are no capital markets operating, the marginal return to education is different for different individuals even at the long run equilibrium position. Hence the allocation of resources to education is likely to be inefficient. On the other hand, the possibility of financial bequests in our model means that the dispersion of returns to education must be less than that which arises in Loury's model: in particular, the marginal return to education (h_e) never falls below unity in our model. The effect of this is that equilibrium solutions examined in this paper are likely to be closer to an efficient allocation of education than those considered by Loury, but somewhat less satisfactory in equity terms than his. For our narrower dispersion of returns to education is associated with cash bequests which make people better off than the corresponding amount of education could have done. These remarks should obviously be treated with some caution, since, although the apparent tradeoff between equity and efficiency is clear for any given generation, it is much less clear that the tradeoff applies to the long run equilibrium positions. Suitable combinations of policies may make it possible to improve equity and efficiency simultaneously, in the long run.

3. The introduction of taxes

We now assume the government can tax both an individual's earned income and the bequests he receives. We allow these to be taxed independently so that we have both an income tax and an inheritance tax. Given the structure of our model this includes the possibility that the government may wish to base an individual's tax solely on the sum of his inheritance and earned income, that is to have a wealth tax. We shall see that the government will not in fact wish to do this.

In the next section of the paper we introduce the possibility of educational grants that are related to parental net wealth. Clearly if this is the only instrument that can be related to parental wealth we would bias the argument in favour of such grants by making them more discriminating than the other tools available to the government. Accordingly in this section of the paper we also allow that the tax authorities know parental net wealth and can base an individual's tax payments on it.

We assume that individuals care about their own consumption and the *net* income of their offspring, so the tax system affects an individual's decision in two ways. Given his gross income and his bequests (predetermined by his parent) the tax system affects the amount that he has available to spend on his own consumption and on provision for his offspring. It also affects the private return to any expenditure the individual makes on his child. It then follows that in analysing an individual's decisions, we can again characterise him in terms of the two variables w and α, provided that w is now interpreted as parental *net* wealth rather than gross wealth.

If we let $z^1(w, y)$, $z^2(w, b)$ be the schedules which determine the net earned income and net bequests of an individual whose parent's net wealth was w, then a (w, α) parent (i.e., a parent with net wealth w and offspring of ability α) seeks to:

$$\underset{e \geq 0, b \geq 0, c_2 \geq 0}{\text{Max}} \quad u(w - e - b, c_2) \qquad \text{s.t.} \qquad \begin{cases} c_2 \leq z^1(w, y) + z^2(w, b) \\ y \leq h(\alpha, e) \end{cases} \tag{7}$$

As before, c_2 is the net income (wealth) of the offspring, given the tax regime represented by the first constraint of (7).

This is not the most convenient form in which to handle the individual's optimisation decision. From a mathematical point of view it turns out to be better to work in terms of utility and the variables which are being directly influenced by the tax schedule – offspring's consumption, gross wealth and gross bequests. It is also convenient to use utility as a control variable, and to express offspring's income in terms of utility and the other variables. Accordingly, let

$$\xi(\eta, y, w, \alpha) \equiv \underset{c \geq 0, e \geq 0}{\text{Min}} \quad c \qquad \text{s.t.} \qquad \begin{cases} u(w - e, c) \geq \eta \\ h(\alpha, e) \geq y \end{cases} \tag{8}$$

Here, because we have now suppressed the variable c_1, representing consumption of the parent, we drop the subscript on the offspring's income and simply denote it by c.

For future purposes it is important to note the following properties of the function, $\xi(\cdot)$, readily verified from (8):

$$\left. \begin{array}{l} \xi_\eta = 1/u_2 > 0, \\ \xi_y = u_1/(u_2 h_e) \quad \text{(if } y > 0, \xi_y > 0; \text{ if } y = 0, \xi_y = 0) \\ \xi_w = -u_1/u_2 < 0 \\ \xi_\alpha = -(u_1 h_\alpha)/(u_2 h_e) < 0. \end{array} \right\} \tag{8'}$$

We can now re-write the individual's problem as follows:

$$\underset{\eta, y \geq 0, b \geq 0}{\text{Max}} \quad \eta \qquad \text{s.t.} \quad \xi(\eta, y, w - b, \alpha) \leq z^1(w, y) + z^2(w, b) \tag{9}$$

If we let $\eta(w, \alpha)$, $y(w, \alpha)$, $b(w, \alpha)$ and $c(w, \alpha)$ be the solutions to this problem then we can characterise the constraint that these arise from individual optimisation through the equations

$$\eta_\alpha = -\xi_\alpha/\xi_\eta = u_1 h_\alpha/h_e \tag{10}$$
$$c(w, \alpha) = \xi(\eta(w, \alpha), y(w, \alpha), w - b(w, \alpha), \alpha) \tag{11}$$

(10) has a simple interpretation. If parents choose optimally, then parents with children of higher ability gain from the higher earnings of their children (earnings are h_α higher). This means they can hold their child's total income constant by reducing education by (h_α/h_e) which means they have this amount more to spend on their own consumption. This increases utility by an amount $u_1 h_\alpha/h_e$.

We can once again work out the probability that an individual with net wealth w has an offspring with net wealth less than or equal to z as the functional:

$$L(z, w, c) \equiv \begin{cases} 0 \text{ if } \underset{\alpha \in [0, 1]}{\text{Min}} \ c(w, \alpha) \geqq z \\[2ex] 1 \text{ if } \underset{\alpha \in [0, 1]}{\text{Max}} \ c(w, \alpha) \geqq z \\[2ex] \displaystyle\int_{A(w, z)} \varphi(\alpha)d\alpha, \text{ where } A(w, z) = \{\alpha \in [0, 1] | c(w, \alpha) \leqq z\} \end{cases} \tag{12}$$

Notice that because we no longer have any guarantee that $c(\cdot)$ is monotonic in its arguments, $L(\cdot)$ is defined in a slightly different way from the previous definition, given in Section 2. Moreover it is now no longer possible to guarantee that a stable net wealth distribution exists, nor that it would be unique even if such a distribution existed.

We therefore proceed as follows. We impose on our choice of admissible tax functions the constraint that they should be such as to guarantee the existence of a unique and stable distribution of net wealth. That is we constrain the function, $c(\cdot)$, to be monotonic increasing in both its arguments, and we also require that there be a level of wealth, $\hat{w}$, such that

$$c(w, \alpha) < w, \ \forall \alpha \in [0, 1], \ \forall w \geq \hat{w}. \tag{13}$$

In addition, we shall assume that at the optimum, these constraints are not binding, and consequently can be ignored. We have no justification for this assumption, and hope to be able to undertake a more careful examination of this step in our argument in later work.

With this caveat in mind, we can formulate the optimal tax problem[4] as that of choosing functions $\eta(w, \alpha)$, $y(w, \alpha)$, $b(w, \alpha)$, $c(w, \alpha)$, $f(w)$ and points $\underline{w}$, $\bar{w}$ so as to solve the following constrained optimisation problem:

$$\text{Max} \int_{\underline{w}}^{\bar{w}} \int_0^1 \eta\varphi(\alpha)f(w)d\alpha dw \ \text{(Social welfare function; utilitarian)},$$

subject to:

$$\int_{\underline{w}}^{\overline{w}} \int_0^1 [c - y - b] \, \varphi(\alpha)f(w)d\alpha dw \leqq 0 \tag{14}$$

$$\eta_\alpha = -\xi_\alpha/\xi_\eta, \; \forall \alpha \in [0, 1] \\ w \in [\underline{w}, \overline{w}] \tag{15}$$

$$c = \xi(\eta, y, w - b, \alpha), \;\; \alpha \in [0, 1] \\ w \in [\underline{w}, \overline{w}] \tag{16}$$

$$\int_{\underline{w}}^z f(w)dw = \int_{\underline{w}}^{\overline{w}} L(z, w, c)f(w)dw, \; \forall z \in [\underline{w}, \overline{w}] \tag{17}$$

The first constraint requires the tax scheme to be purely redistributive within each period, so that the gross wealth available for redistribution (the $(y + b)$ term) equals the total net wealth after redistribution (the c's). One might think that we should also impose the condition that gross wealth available for spending one period should equal the net wealth that was available in the previous period. But one can check from the definition of $L(\cdot)$ that, by making suitable substitutions in (17) and integrating over all values of z, the constraint

$$\int_{\underline{w}}^{\overline{w}} \int_0^1 c\varphi f d\alpha dw = \int_{\underline{w}}^{\overline{w}} wf(w)dw$$

is implied by (14): consequently an additional constraint is not needed.

Constraints (15) and (16) simply repeat (10) and (11) and are the conditions to be satisfied if each individual is maximising his own utility, given the prevailing tax schedules. Lastly, constraint (17) represents the requirement that the wealth distribution, $f(w)$ should be an equilibrium distribution. In other words, we are concerned with the welfare effects of alternative tax schedules (and later, alternative educational policies) on long run equilibrium allocations.

If we introduce Lagrange multipliers λ, $v(w, \alpha)$, $\mu(w, \alpha)$, $\pi(z)$ on constraints (14), (15), (16) and (17) respectively, then we have the following Lagrangean:

$$L \equiv \int_{\underline{w}}^{\overline{w}} \int_0^1 \eta f\varphi d\alpha dw + \lambda \int_{\underline{w}}^{\overline{w}} \int_0^1 [y + b - c]\varphi f d\alpha dw +$$

$$+ \int_{\underline{w}}^{\overline{w}} \int_0^1 \mu[c - \xi(\eta, y, w - b, \alpha)]d\alpha dw + \int_{\underline{w}}^{\overline{w}} \int_0^1 v\left(\frac{\xi_\alpha}{\xi_\eta} + \eta_\alpha\right)d\alpha dw +$$

$$+ \int_{\underline{w}}^{\overline{w}} \pi(z)\left\{\int_{\underline{w}}^z f(w)dw - \int_{\underline{w}}^{\overline{w}} L(z, w, c)f(w)dw\right\}dz$$

After integrating the term involving η_α by parts, and reversing the order of integration in the integral $\int_{\underline{w}}^{\overline{w}} \pi(z) \int_{\underline{w}}^{z} f(w) dw dz$ we obtain the following first-order conditions, by differentiating the Lagrangean with respect to η, y, b, c and f.

$$(\eta) \qquad \varphi f - \mu \xi_\eta + v \frac{\partial}{\partial \eta} [\xi_\alpha / \xi_\eta] - v_\alpha = 0 \tag{18}$$

$$(y) \qquad \lambda \varphi f - \mu \xi_y + v \frac{\partial}{\partial y} [\xi_\alpha / \xi_\eta] = 0 \tag{19}$$

$$(b) \qquad \lambda \varphi f + \mu \xi_w - v \frac{\partial}{\partial w} [\xi_\alpha / \xi_\eta] \leqq 0, \ b \geqq 0 \tag{20}$$

where these inequalities hold with complementary slackness.

$$(c) \qquad -\lambda \varphi f + \mu - \int_{\underline{w}}^{\overline{w}} \int_{\underline{w}}^{\overline{w}} \pi(z) \frac{\partial L(z, x, c)}{\partial c(w, \alpha)} dz dx = 0 \tag{21}$$

$$(f) \qquad \int_0^1 [\eta + \lambda(y + b - c)] \varphi(\alpha) d\alpha + \int_{\underline{w}}^{\overline{w}} \pi(z) dz - \int_{\underline{w}}^{w} \pi(z) L(z, w, c) dz = 0 \tag{22}$$

$$v(w, 0) = v(w, 1) = 0 \qquad w \in [\underline{w}, \overline{w}] \tag{23}$$

Equations (23) are standard boundary conditions for the problem. Now since L is a functional, changing a single value of c should not influence its value, hence (21) reduces to the simpler form:

$$\mu = \lambda \varphi f$$

Substituting this into (18), (19) and (20) we obtain

$$(1 - \lambda \xi_\eta) \varphi f + v \frac{\partial}{\partial \eta} [\xi_\alpha / \xi_\eta] - v_\alpha = 0 \tag{24}$$

$$\lambda(1 - \xi_y) \varphi f + v \frac{\partial}{\partial y} [\xi_\alpha / \xi_\eta] = 0 \tag{25}$$

$$\lambda(1 + \xi_w) \varphi f - v \frac{\partial}{\partial w} [\xi_\alpha / \xi_\eta] \leqq 0, \qquad b \geqq 0 \tag{26}$$

Now $(1 - \xi_y)$ is just the marginal tax rate on earned income and $(1 + \xi_w)$ is the marginal tax rate on inherited income. Hence (24), (25) and (26) tell us that, for $w \in (\underline{w}, \overline{w})$, the marginal tax rate on earned income is zero at the top and bottom ends of the income distribution for people whose parent had net wealth w. This is because the boundary conditions, (23) imply that v is zero at these points. For people with positive bequests, the same conditions also imply that the marginal tax rate on inherited income should be zero. These are standard results in optimal tax theory (Seade, 1977).

To learn more about the nature of the solutions it is helpful to express all the terms involving ξ in terms of the underlying utility and production functions. After some manipulation, making use of the conditions (8′), it can be shown that the three equations (24), (25), (26) above become

$$(1 - \lambda/u_2)\varphi f - \frac{vh_\alpha}{h_e u_2} \cdot u_{12} - v_\alpha = 0 \tag{27}$$

$$\lambda\left(1 - \frac{u_1}{u_2} \cdot \frac{1}{h_e}\right)\varphi f + \frac{vh_\alpha u_2}{h_e^2}\left\{\frac{\partial}{\partial c_1}(u_1/u_2) - (u_1/u_2)\left(\frac{h_{\alpha e}}{h_\alpha} - \frac{h_{ee}}{h_e}\right)\right\} = 0 \tag{28}$$

$$\lambda(1 - u_1/u_2)\varphi f + \frac{vh_\alpha u_2}{h_e} \cdot \frac{\partial}{\partial c_1}(u_1/u_2) \leqq 0, \qquad b \geqq 0 \tag{29}$$

(28) can be rewritten

$$\lambda\left(1 - \frac{u_1}{u_2}\frac{1}{h_e}\right)\varphi f = -\frac{vh_\alpha u_2}{h_e^2}\left\{\frac{\partial}{\partial c_1}(u_1/u_2) - (u_1/u_2)\left(\frac{h_{\alpha e}}{h_\alpha} - \frac{h_{ee}}{h_e}\right)\right\} \tag{30}$$

Both the terms in the curly brackets on the right-hand side of (30) are negative. Moreover, it is a condition of the optimisation that $v \geqq 0$. So (30) tells us that the marginal tax rate on earned income $[1 - u_1/(u_2 h_e)]$ can never be negative, and will be positive if and only if v is positive.

Re-writing (29) in a similar way we see that

$$\lambda(1 - u_1/u_2)\varphi f \leqq -\frac{vh_\alpha u_2}{h_e}\left[\frac{\partial}{\partial c_1}(u_1/u_2)\right], \qquad b \geqq 0. \tag{31}$$

So if the marginal tax rate on income is positive (i.e. $v > 0$), and if the individual is making positive bequests ($b > 0$), then the marginal tax rate on bequests $(1 - u_1/u_2)$ must be strictly smaller than the marginal tax rate on earned income; this follows from a comparison of (30) and (31).

If we multiply both sides of (30) by h_e and subtract from (31) we obtain

$$\lambda(1 - h_e)\varphi f \leqq -\frac{vh_\alpha u_1}{h_e}\left(\frac{h_{\alpha e}}{h_\alpha} - \frac{h_{ee}}{h_e}\right), \qquad b \geqq 0 \tag{32}$$

Since the right-hand side of the inequality in (32) is strictly negative whenever v is strictly positive we see that $h_e \geq 1$ and this inequality is strict whenever $v > 0$. Thus the marginal return to education (h_e) is not reduced to unity in the presence of income and bequest taxation, even when $b > 0$, in contrast to the model without taxation discussed in the previous section.

Since our results on tax rates depend on whether v is positive or zero, we need to know more about the behaviour of v.

Lemma: If $v(w, \tilde{\alpha}) = 0$ for some $\tilde{\alpha} \in [0, 1]$, $w \in (w, \bar{w})$, then there cannot be an interval around $\tilde{\alpha}$ on which $v(w, \alpha) = 0$.

Proof: Suppose the Lemma is false; then there are two cases to consider.

(i) $b(w, \tilde{\alpha}) > 0$. Then on an interval around $\tilde{\alpha}$ we have $b > 0$, $v = 0$. We then have $v_\alpha = 0$ on this interval, and so, from (27), $u_2 = \lambda$ on this interval. But then from C(1), c is constant on this interval.

But from (31) $u_1 = u_2$ on this interval, and so the parent's consumption is also constant. So utility must also be constant, which contradicts $\eta_\alpha > 0$.

(ii) $u_1/u_2 > 1$ at $\tilde{\alpha}$ implies that $b(w, \tilde{\alpha}) = 0$ and also $b(w, \alpha) = 0$ on an interval around $\tilde{\alpha}$. Hence on an interval around $\tilde{\alpha}$ we have $b = 0$, $v = 0$.

Once again c is constant on this interval. But then, with zero marginal tax rate on earned income, y must be constant on this interval, i.e.

$$h_\alpha + h_e \cdot e_\alpha = 0$$

or $\quad e_\alpha = -\dfrac{h_\alpha}{h_e} < 0$ \hfill (33)

Now from (30)

$$u_1(w - e, c) = u_2(c) h_e(\alpha, e) = \lambda h_e(\alpha, e)$$

Then

$$-u_{11} e_\alpha = \lambda(h_{e\alpha} + h_{ee} e_\alpha)$$ \hfill (34)

But from (33) the right-hand side of (34) is positive while (with $u_{11} < 0$) the left-hand side is negative – a contradiction.

Thus $v > 0$ almost everywhere, and consequently the marginal rate of income tax is positive almost everywhere.

This completes the results on the optimal tax structure that we need for our analysis of education policy in the next section, and to this we now turn.

4. Education policy

The question we want to consider is the following. If the government has all the tax powers we were attributing to it in the previous section, is there any role for educational policy as an additional instrument of redistribution?

There are a number of policies one could consider – tuition subsidies, grants, loans – either singly or in combination. In this section, we begin by considering the case for a scheme of educational grants which are related to (net) parental wealth; later on, we examine loans and tuition subsidies.

4.1 *Grants*

Since the government can channel income to people through the tax system, an educational grant has to be characterised as more than just an income handout to low income parents. We have to capture the requirement that it must be spent on education. We can do this by introducing lower bounds on the amount of education a parent can choose to buy for his children. That is, in asking whether a policy of educational grants is desirable, we can simply ignore the income transfer aspect of such a policy (since that is being handled through the tax system) and ask if it is desirable for the government to impose constraints on how people choose to spend their income.[5] In a first-best world such constraints are, of course, undesirable. But they turn out to be desirable in a second-best world, as we now show.

Consider the optimal educational choices, $\hat{e}(w, \alpha)$ of all individuals under the optimal income tax scheme discussed in the previous section. Suppose that for some $w \in (w, \bar{w})$ the minimum value of educational expenditure occurs at $\tilde{\alpha}(w)$. That is $\hat{e}(w, \tilde{\alpha}(w)) < \hat{e}(w, \alpha)$, $\alpha \in [0, 1]$. Suppose now the government requires individuals with net wealth, w, to purchase a minimum amount of education equal to $\hat{e}(w, \tilde{\alpha}(w)) + \Delta(w)$, where $\Delta(w)$ is some small positive number. Clearly, people who were previously purchasing this amount will be unaffected by this constraint. Those who will be affected have abilities defined by the condition:

$$A(w, \Delta(w)) = \{\alpha \in [0, 1] \mid \hat{e}(w, \alpha) < \hat{e}(w, \tilde{\alpha}(w)) + \Delta(w)\} \tag{35}$$

Any individual $\alpha \in A(w, \Delta(w))$ will now have to purchase an additional amount of education

$$e(\alpha) = \hat{e}(w, \tilde{\alpha}(w)) + \Delta(w) - \hat{e}(w, \alpha) > 0$$

We want to know how this will affect his utility and the total amount of tax he pays.

There are two cases to consider:

(i) $b(w, \alpha) = 0$.

Then

$$\Delta\eta(\alpha) = -u_1 \cdot \Delta e(\alpha) + u_2 \cdot \Delta c(\alpha)$$

where

$$\Delta c(\alpha) = z_y \cdot h_e \cdot \Delta e(\alpha)$$

is the increase in the net income of the son as a result of this change.

But given the conditions for utility maximisation, $u_1 = u_2 z_y h_e$ and so to first order, $\Delta\eta(\alpha) = 0$.

The change in tax revenue brought about by this constraint is

$$\Delta T(\alpha) = h_e \cdot \Delta e(\alpha) \cdot (1 - z_y)$$

This is positive if the marginal tax rate is positive. We do not know it is positive for any given α, but we do know that points where it is not positive are isolated. So for almost every value of α for which $b(w, \alpha) = 0$ there must be a positive increase in tax revenue.

(ii) $b(w, \alpha) > 0$.
Here we have to consider the possibility that the individual can offset the effects of the constraint by reducing his financial bequests.

We have

$$\Delta\eta(\alpha) = -u_1[\Delta e(\alpha) + \Delta b(\alpha)] + u_2 \cdot \Delta c(\alpha)$$

where

$$\Delta c(\alpha) = z_y h_e \cdot \Delta e(\alpha) + z_b \Delta b(\alpha) \tag{36}$$

Again we find from first-order conditions that whatever (small) adjustment the individual makes to his bequests the effects on his utility are, to first order, zero.

The effects on tax revenue are

$$\begin{aligned} \Delta T(c) &= h_e \Delta e(\alpha)(1 - z_y) + \Delta b(\alpha)(1 - z_b) \\ &= h_e \Delta e(\alpha) + \Delta b(\alpha) - \Delta c(\alpha) \end{aligned}$$

We see that there is a degree of freedom in this change depending on how we choose $\Delta b(\alpha)$, and consequently (from (36)) $\Delta c(\alpha)$. Since the individual is indifferent to how $\Delta b(\alpha)$ is chosen let us choose it so that $\Delta c(\alpha) = 0$.

Then

$$\Delta b(\alpha) = - \frac{z_y h_e \Delta e}{z_b}$$

and consequently

$$\Delta T(\alpha) = h_e \Delta e(\alpha) \left[1 - \frac{z_y}{z_b} \right]$$

Now as long as the marginal tax rate on income is positive, the marginal tax rate on bequests is positive, but smaller. That is $z_b > z_y$. Since, almost everywhere the marginal tax rate is positive, we see that once again $\Delta T(\alpha)$ is almost everywhere positive.

If we integrate over all $\alpha \in A[w, \Delta(w)]$ then we will achieve a gain in tax revenue which is positive to first-order.

Since this tax revenue can be redistributed to make people better off, we can achieve an overall welfare gain by bringing in this binding constraint.

This argument shows that, even in a model in which one source of inequality arises from the unequal dispersion of abilities, there is still a case for giving educational grants on the basis of parental wealth. This contradicts the assertion by Johnson (1972: 288-299) that it was wrong to concede an argument for such grants.

Of course we have not, as yet, fully investigated how these grants should vary with parental wealth. This is essentially the question raised originally by Arrow (1971) on the optimal distribution of public expenditure, but now set in a framework in which there are alternative procedures for redistributing income.[6] We comment on the formulation of this question in our model later in this section, when comparing loans and grants.

Notice that the above argument for grants rests crucially on the condition that $h_e > 1$ almost everywhere. If there were a perfect loan market, then in the absence of taxation, people would borrow up to the point where $h_e = 1$. And so at the margin, there would be no difference between bequests and education. When there is a tax system, whether or not people will choose to borrow up to the point where $h_e = 1$ will depend on the tax treatment of loans. If they can be fully offset against earned income for tax purposes then this argument will hold, and our argument in favour of grants will fail. To see whether or not it is desirable to offset loans fully against income for tax purposes, let us now turn to a model of optimal taxation in which there are educational loans.

4.2 *Loans*

Unfortunately, the analysis of loans within this model quickly runs into difficulties.

To see this, let us give an alternative, though equivalent, definition of the function $\xi(\cdot)$ to that given in (8).

Thus let

$$\xi(\eta, y, \omega, \alpha) \equiv \underset{c \geq 0}{\text{Min } c} \qquad \text{s.t. } u(\omega - H(\alpha, y), c) \geq \eta$$

Here $H(\alpha, y)$ is the inverse function to $h(\alpha, e)$ and measures the amount of education an individual with ability α needs to achieve income level y.

Then if we let E denote the amount of money the parent borrows to finance his child's education then his problem is to choose y, E, b so as to

$$\text{Max } \eta \qquad \text{s.t. } \xi(\eta, y, w + E - b, \alpha) \leq z(w, y, b, E) \tag{37}$$

$$H(\alpha, y) \geq E \tag{38}$$

To allow the tax treatment of the educational loans to be chosen rather than imposed on the model, we have written the tax function in (37) in a completely general form. Given this, the existence of loans is equivalent to an increase in the wealth of the parent combined with the requirement that the parent spend the loan on education, which is why the second constraint has to be introduced. To see how the difficulties arise, let us consider the first-order condition for an individual optimum at which $y > 0$, $E > 0$ and, for convenience, $b = 0$. These are

$$1 - \lambda \xi_\eta = 0 \tag{39}$$

$$\lambda(z_y - \xi_y) + \mu H_y = 0 \tag{40}$$

$$\lambda(z_E - \xi_w) - \mu = 0 \tag{41}$$

$$\mu(H - E) = 0 \tag{42}$$

where λ and μ are the Lagrange multipliers on (37) and (38) respectively.

If we differentiate (37) totally with respect to α we then get

$$\xi_\eta \eta_\alpha + \xi_y y_\alpha + \xi_w E_\alpha + \xi_\alpha = z_y y_\alpha + z_E E_\alpha \tag{43}$$

Now differentiate (42) totally w.r.t. α to obtain

$$\mu[H_\alpha + H_y y_\alpha - E_\alpha] = 0 \tag{44}$$

120

Combining (43) and (44) we obtain

$$\eta_\alpha = -\xi_\alpha/\xi_\eta + \mu H_\alpha \tag{45}$$

If $H > E$ $\mu = 0$ and (45) is just as before. But if the government can induce people to use only loan finance to finance education (so that (38) becomes an equality), then, through (40) and (41) by suitably choosing its marginal tax rates (and hence η), the government can treat η_α as a choice variable. This suggests that it could choose controls, in the form of an appropriate tax schedule $z(\cdot)$, so as to eliminate the dependence of η on α altogether, i.e., choose its tax schedule so as to make η_α zero. It is easily checked by substituting μ $= \dfrac{\xi_\alpha}{\xi_\eta H_\alpha}$ into (40) and (41) that the condition for η_α to be zero is that $z_y = z_E$ $= 0$. That is that there be a 100% marginal tax rate on earned income and a 100% marginal subsidy rate on loan debts.

In the model analysed in the previous section this could not have been optimal. For since education had a direct opportunity cost in terms of the foregone consumption of the parent, if there were 100% marginal tax rates on all income, parents would never buy any education, and in steady state there would be no wealth.

When all educational expenditure is loan financed, then even though buying more education through loans has no effect on the child's net income when $z_y = 0$, on the other hand, if $z_E = 0$, it does not reduce net income either. Since it is loan financed, additional expenditure has no effect on parental consumption so while the parent has no particular incentive to choose a positive level of educational expenditure, he has no incentive not to.

It therefore follows that the first-best optimum allocation of resources could be supported by a loan market with 100% marginal tax rates (subsidies) on income (loans).[7]

This is very different from saying that the first-best could actually be achieved through a loans market, since once the optimal tax scheme that would support the optimum with loans was introduced there would be no particular incentive to choose the optimum.

Previously, we showed that some grants would be desirable, but we did not examine the conditions which the optimal grants should satisfy. Because of this, it might be suspected that they too might lead to the same difficulties that we have just observed for loans, namely collapse to the first-best solution. To show that this is not the case, it is sufficient to compare the household problems corresponding to the two policies. For *loans*, we simply repeat (37) and replace (38) with the corresponding equality to ensure that all education is loan financed. Thus:

$$\text{Max}\,\eta \quad \text{s.t.} \quad \xi(\eta, y, w + E - b, \alpha) \le Z^1(w, y, b, E) \tag{46}$$

and

$$H(\alpha, y) = E \tag{47}$$

For grants, using equivalent notation, the household model takes the form:

$$\text{Max } \eta \quad \text{s.t.} \quad \xi(\eta, y, w - b, \alpha) \le Z^g(w, y, b) \tag{48}$$

and

$$H(\alpha, y) \ge g(w) \tag{49}$$

$g(w)$ is the lower bound on education (which we argued earlier to be the appropriate formulation for grants, since their financial aspects can be captured in the tax schedules); $Z^1(\cdot)$ and $Z^g(\cdot)$ are the tax schedules for the two cases.

Since the tax authorities observe E and y (which are both household choice variables) in the model with loans, they can deduce α; hence the optimal tax schedule is able to reproduce the first-best allocation. But in the grants model, $g(w)$ is merely a floor, and knowledge of this and y does not allow the value of α to be estimated. Consequently, the grants model cannot replicate the first-best solution and grants are not equivalent to loans. Indeed within the severe limits of the present model, loans appear to be superior.

Let us turn finally then to the use of educational subsidies.

4.3 Tuition subsidies

So far we have assumed that parents pay the full cost of providing education and public subsidy of education takes the form of income transfers. It is interesting to ask whether this is optimal and whether the government should not additionally or indeed solely provide educational assistance in the form of subsidised tuition fees. Such a mixed system of grants and subsidies operates in both the U.K. and the U.S., though in another paper presented at this conference Nelson and Breneman question the use of this mixed system for community colleges in the U.S. They argue that on equity and efficiency grounds it would be better to have smaller tuition subsidies and larger grants. Unfortunately, their efficiency argument seems to be a first-best argument, so, while our model does not capture all the considerations they raise in their paper, it seems worth while to use it to test out their argument in a second-best framework.

Accordingly, let us now assume that parents with net wealth, w, can purchase education at a price $q(w)$. Again, we allow q to depend on w simply so that we can consider the argument for or against subsidies independently of administrative considerations.

Our previous model then has to be modified in two ways. Firstly, q has to enter the $\xi(\cdot)$ function as follows

$$\xi(\eta, y, \omega, \alpha, q) \equiv \underset{c \geqq 0}{\text{Min}}\, c \qquad \text{s.t.} \quad U[\omega - qH(\alpha, y), c] \geqq \eta \tag{50}$$

Secondly, the constraint that the government raise no net revenue (equation (14)), now becomes

$$\int_{\underline{w}}^{\bar{w}} \int_0^1 \{c - y - b + (1 - q(w))\, H(\alpha, y)\}\, \varphi(\alpha) f(w) d\alpha dw \leqq 0 \tag{51}$$

The effect of these changes is twofold. Equation (25) now becomes

$$\lambda[(1 - \xi_y) + (q(w) - 1)H_y]\varphi f + v\frac{\partial}{\partial y}[\xi\alpha/\xi\eta] = 0 \tag{52}$$

The term $(1 - \xi_y) + (q(w) - 1)H_y$ is what we may call the 'full' marginal tax rate on earned income. For when a father decides to increase his son's earned income then the tax revenue is increased at a rate equal to the marginal rate of direct taxation on that income plus (minus) the additional tax (subsidy) on the additional education required to increase income. It is easy to show that all our previous results about the marginal direct income tax rate now go through for this full marginal tax rate. In particular, if the tuition costs of some wealth group are subsidised, the marginal rates of direct income taxation on the income of their sons should be *positive* at both ends of the ability distribution. It is also easy to show that our proof of the general desirability of grants still goes through in the presence of tuition subsidies.

It only remains to see whether the subsidies are desirable.

Unfortunately given the complexity of the model we have not as yet been able to say anything useful about this in general, and we suspect that this problem may also collapse to the trivial first-best solution. However, we would hope to reach more interesting conclusions in a model where this feature was precluded by, for example, introducing labour supply considerations to prevent the marginal tax rate going to 100%.

5. Directions of development

In earlier sections of this paper we have been exploring some issues in the financing of higher education, in a model containing general income and bequest taxation. While in the absence of loans, it turns out to be optimal to provide some educational grants related to parental wealth, the analysis is much less clear when loans are present. In particular, the last section suggested that 100% marginal income tax rates might be optimal, in association with a 100% marginal subsidy on educational loans. However, it is clearly certain unsatisfactory features of our model which give rise to this implausible conclusion. In order to provide a more adequate analysis of the problem under consideration, it seems necessary to extend the model in several ways. This section concentrates attention on two possible extensions:

(a) the introduction of variable labour supply (work/leisure choice);
(b) incorporating some uncertainty about the returns to education.

Variable labour supply means that the tax system not only influences educational decisions, but also affects the earnings which result from a given amount of education: the wage rate may be determined by ability and educational provision, but the time worked remains variable. This consideration alone is sufficient to eliminate 100% marginal tax rates from the list of candidates for an optimal solution. Also, in terms of its economic rationale, variable labour supply is a much better feature to build into the model than a rather *ad hoc* constraint on the admissible tax rates.

The model developed in this paper has assumed the returns to education to be known with certainty, making it hard to understand some of the features of capital markets which are frequently observed and regarded as imperfections.

Much of economic theory regards a perfect capital market as one in which individuals would be able to obtain loans of any size at the prevailing rate of interest. But even when loans are sought for the acquisition of fixed capital or real estate, capital markets rarely function in this simple manner. Instead, collateral would be required for any loan, and the size of loan obtainable, as well as the interest charges and timing of repayments would depend on personal characteristics of the would-be borrower. It is easy to see why this situation should obtain, though rather less straightforward to incorporate its full implications into economic theory. If, for example, individuals could obtain loans of any amount, they would have an obvious incentive to take very large loans, and finance repayments by taking out additional loans, with no intention of fully paying back the loans during their lifetime. The requirement to provide collateral is a simple device to inhibit this kind of behaviour and, given the lack of information possessed by financial institutions about their customers' motivations and intentions, it may be the least costly means of imposing the required budget constraints. Moreover, in the case of loans to purchase fixed capital or real estate, the collateral can be whatever is bought with the loan, and is usually readily marketable in the event of default. Consequently, financial institutions incur relatively little risk in granting loans on such terms.

The case of educational loans is a little more complex, however, and involves greater risks for all parties, as well as the possibility of high returns.

The fundamental problem is that individuals seeking educational loans are not normally in a position to offer collateral to lending institutions (Atkinson, 1973). The reason for this is that the human capital which the loan helps to create cannot be repossessed by the lender in case of default. Moreover, the risk of default may well be rather high, as compared to loans for the purchase of physical capital, for two principal reasons. Thus individuals may not be able to repay a loan if they turn out to have *lower ability* than they expected at the time of taking out the loan, or if, even though they have high ability, they *choose a low income* (but perhaps very pleasant) job.[8]

From a theoretical point of view, the lower ability case is really a problem of *insurance:* if individuals could take out insurance policies against the risk of turning out to have relatively low ability (and the resulting low income), then there would be no need for defaults on educational loans. As we know, however, insurance markets do not offer the required kinds of policy, and it is not hard to see why this is the case. For on the one hand, if policies required a payment from an insurance company in the event that an individual turned out to have ability below some specified level, there seems to be no information available to the company which it could use to identify the occurrence of such events. Income itself is an unsatisfactory indicator, for reasons discussed below, while standard measures of ability (e.g. I.Q. tests) are well known to be both imperfect and unreliable: it is precisely their unreliability which might call for the development of the kind of insurance market being examined here. On the other hand, even if there are ways of identifying the events requiring payment (i.e. low ability) a market in ability-related risks is likely to suffer from severe *adverse selection* problems. This is because people who are fairly sure that they have high ability would be unlikely to purchase insurance; but their absence from the market raises the risks associated with all the other policies and hence increases the price insurance companies must charge in order to cover their costs. This increase may well lead to more people withdrawing from the market, and so on. Consequently, an insurance market of the required sort may well not be viable.

Let us now turn to the low income case, the possibility that people may be unable to repay an educational loan because they choose to take a low-paying (but pleasant) job, even when they have high ability. There are some difficulties in explaining exactly why or how such a situation could arise. It is not clear, for example, whether the issue arises because certain people make a deliberate decision not to repay a loan at the time when they are seeking it: this decision not, of course, being communicated to the loan granting authority. Or it may be that people seek a loan in the expectation of repaying it, but that government policy operating through some form of social security system prevents consumption from falling below some minimum level: individuals at or near to this level could not be expected to repay an educational loan. Finally, some people may embark on an educational programme in the expectation of enhancing their earnings capacity, but also as a means of discovering more about their work/career preferences: if they finally opt for a low-paying job, then again, repayment of a loan might be difficult or impossible. And agencies providing loans have no means of identifying any of these situations in which repayment could be hard to enforce, for the standard reason that they normally have no powers to require people to take high-paying jobs. From the point of view of the loan agencies, this problem is really a form of *moral hazard*.

In developing the model introduced in this paper, therefore, we should seek to introduce some of the issues discussed in this section. Almost certainly, the resulting models will be a little more complex than the analysis above, but they should allow us to analyse a wider range of important policy issues more fully than we have been able to do here.

Appendix

We require to prove the theorem stated in Section 2, which we restate here for convenience.

Theorem 1: Assumptions A, B(1)-(5) and C(1)-(4) imply that there is a unique equilibrium distribution $f(w)$ satisfying the conditions:

$$\int_0^z f(w)dw = \int_0^\infty L(z, w)f(w)dw, \text{ for all } z \tag{A.1}$$

Proof: The proof involves a number of preliminary results which then allow us to appeal to general theorems from the theory of integral equations and Markov chains.

Lemma 1: Given the problem described in equations (2) and (3), the solution, $Z = c_2(w, \alpha)$ is strictly increasing in w and α. Moreover, at any point $\hat{w}$ such that $\hat{w} = c_2(\hat{w}, \alpha)$, $Z_w < 1$.

Proof: It is easily shown that the function $J(\alpha, x)$ defined by (2) is concave in x, and satisfies $J_x \geq 1$. Moreover it is strictly concave as long as $J_x > 1$. Consequently, invert J to get

$$x = R(\alpha, z) \tag{A.2}$$

Then $1 \geq R_z \geq 0$ for all $Z \geq 0$, and $R_z > 0$ when $Z > 0$. R is convex in Z and strictly convex whenever $R_Z < 1$. Moreover, from assumption (B.3) it follows that $R_\alpha < 0$, $R_{\alpha z} \leq 0$.

The problem in (3) can now be re-written

$$\underset{z \geq 0}{\text{Max}} \, U(w - R(\alpha, Z), Z) \tag{A.3}$$

It is easily shown that this always has an interior solution characterised by

$$-u_1 R_Z + U_2 = 0 \tag{A.4}$$

Differentiate totally w.r.t. α to obtain

$$(u_{11}R_z^2 + u_{22} - u_1 R_{zz})Z_\alpha = -u_{11}R_\alpha R_z + u_1 R_{\alpha z}$$

Given all our assumptions, this guarantees $Z_\alpha > 0$.

Differentiate (A.4) totally w.r.t. Z to obtain

$$(u_{11}R_Z^2 + u_{22} - u_1 R_{ZZ})Z_w = u_{11}R_Z \qquad (A.5)$$

(A.5) guarantees $Z_w > 0$, and also $R_Z Z_w < 1$.

Unfortunately, from (A.4) it follows that for any point $\hat{w}$ such that $Z = \hat{w}$

$$R_Z = \frac{u_2}{u_1} = \frac{\delta v'(\hat{w})}{v'(\hat{w} - R)} < 1,$$

so this last finding does not immediately enable us to deduce $Z_w < 1$.

However, notice that after some re-arranging, we can write (A.5) in the form

$$\left[\left(\frac{ZR_z}{R}\right)\frac{R}{w} + (1 - R/w)\left(\frac{\sigma(Z)}{\sigma(w - R)} + \frac{ZR_{zz}/R_z}{\sigma(w - R)}\right)\right]\frac{wZ_w}{Z} = 1 \qquad (A.6)$$

Now the term in square brackets is just a weighted sum of the two terms. The first (ZR_z/R) is strictly greater than 1 when R is strictly convex – which we know it is at $\hat{w}$ since $R_z < 1$ there. Again, given the strict convexity which prevails at $\hat{w}$, the second term is greater than $\dfrac{\sigma(\hat{w})}{\sigma(\hat{w} - R)}$, which, given assumption C(4) is greater than or equal to 1. Hence the term in square brackets is strictly greater than 1 and the Lemma is proved.

Lemma 2: For all $\alpha \in [0, 1]$ there exists a unique $\hat{w}(\alpha) > 0$ such that

(i) $c_2(w, \alpha) > w$ $0 < w < \hat{w}(\alpha)$
(ii) $c_2(\hat{w}(\alpha), \alpha) = \hat{w}(\alpha)$
(iii) $c_2(w, \alpha) < w$ $w > \hat{w}(\alpha)$

Proof: From B(5) and C(1)-C(3), it follows that for all $\alpha \in [0, 1]$ there exists $\tilde{w}(\alpha)$ such that for all $w \geqq w(\alpha)$, $R_Z = 1$ whenever $Z \geqq w - R(\alpha, Z)$. Hence in equilibrium $c_2(w, \alpha) \leq c_1(w, \alpha) < w$. Given that $c_2(\cdot)$ is monotonic increasing in w (Lemma 1), it maps $[0, \tilde{w}(\alpha)]$ into itself. If we can show $c_2(w, \alpha) > w$ for all w in a neighbourhood of 0, then, for all small enough ε we can map $[\varepsilon, \tilde{w}(\alpha)]$ into itself. This will have a fixed point which will be unique given the last part of Lemma 1, and our proof will be complete.

Clearly as $w \to 0$, $c_2(w, \alpha) \to 0$. Now, let us assume that $\lim_{w \to 0} Z_w < \infty$. If follows that $\lim_{w \to 0} R/w$
$= \lim_{w \to 0} R_z Z_w = 0$. Hence, since $\lim_{z \to 0} \dfrac{zR_{zz}}{R_z} = \dfrac{1 - \beta(\alpha)}{\beta(\alpha)}$, while $\lim_{z \to 0} \dfrac{zR_z}{R} = 1 + \dfrac{(1 - \beta(\alpha))}{\beta(\alpha)}$, it follows from (A.6) that $\lim_{w \to 0} \dfrac{wZ_w}{Z} = 1 + \dfrac{1}{\dfrac{(1 - \beta(\alpha))}{\beta(\alpha)k_0}} < 1$. Hence Z is locally concave around 0, and

so $Z_w \to k_0 > 0$ as $w \to 0$. But it then follows from l'Hôpital's rule that $\lim_{w \to 0} \dfrac{Z}{W} = Z_w$ so $\lim_{w \to 0} \dfrac{wZ_w}{Z}$
$= 1$ – a contradiction. Hence as $w \to 0$, $Z_w \to +\infty$ and this guarantees our lemma.

Thus $c_2(w, \alpha)$ looks as follows (see Figure 1):

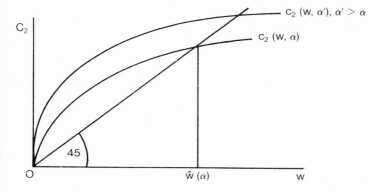

Figure 1. $c_2(w, \alpha)$

Lemma 3: There exists $\underline{w}, \bar{w}, 0 < \underline{w} < \bar{w}$ such that for all $\alpha \in [0, 1]$, $w \in [\underline{w}, \bar{w}]$, $\underline{w} < c_2(w, \alpha) < \bar{w}$.

Proof: Let $\underline{w} = \hat{w}(0)$, $\bar{w} = \hat{w}(1)$. These clearly satisfy the conditions of the lemma, and indeed are the only values of $\underline{w}, \bar{w}$ with this property.

Let $G(z, w) = \dfrac{\partial L}{\partial z}(z, w)$; then differentiating (A.1) and using Lemma 2, the condition for an equilibrium distribution may be expressed as follows:

$$f(z) = \int_{\underline{w}}^{\bar{w}} G(z, w)f(w)dw, \qquad z \in [\underline{w}, \bar{w}] \tag{A.7}$$

It also follows that:

$$G(z, w) = \begin{cases} \varphi(\alpha) & \text{if } z(w, \alpha) = z \text{ for some } \alpha \in [0, 1] \\ 0 & \text{otherwise} \end{cases} \tag{A.8}$$

By construction, $G(z, w) > 0$ when $z = w$, and is continuous except at points of the form $(z(w, 0), w)$, or $(z(w, 1), w)$, which are of measure zero overall.

The function $G(z, w) + \delta$, which we write as $K_\delta(z, w)$ is positive throughout its domain of definition. Hence we may employ a standard result in the theory of integral equations to assert that the homogeneous equation with kernel K_δ possesses a unique solution, $f_\delta(w)$, with corresponding characteristic value λ_δ (Cochran, 1972: Theorem 17.5-3). Without loss of generality, we can adopt the normalisation appropriate to probability distributions, namely

$$\int_{\underline{w}}^{\bar{w}} f_\delta(w)dw = 1$$

It follows immediately that

$$\lambda_\delta = \frac{1}{1 + \delta(\bar{w} - \underline{w})}$$

Letting $\delta \to 0$, $\lambda_\delta \to 1$ and the functions $f_\delta(w)$ approach a unique limit, $f(w)$. It is straightforward to verify that the limiting function, $f(w)$ has the following properties

- (i) $f(w)$ satisfies (A.7)
- (ii) $f(w) > 0$ for $w \in [\underline{w}, \bar{w}]$
- (iii) $f(w)$ is continuous.

Given these properties, it follows from the theory of Markov chains that for any initial wealth distribution $f^0(w)$ defined on $[w, \bar{w}]$, the sequence of distributions generated by the equation

$$f^{i+1}(a) = \int_{\underline{w}}^{\bar{w}} G(z, w)f^i(w)dw \tag{A.9}$$

tends to the unique limiting distribution $f(w)$.

This completes the proof of Theorem 1.

NOTES

1. See, for example, the special issue of *Journal of Political Economy* in 1972 (80(3): Part 2) and in particular the stimulating paper by Nerlove (1972).
2. This is a point we stressed in our earlier work (Hare and Ulph, 1978 and 1979).
3. See Hare and Ulph (1979).
4. To verify that the problem can be written in this way, one has to check that a number of conditions are satisfied – see Mirrlees (1971). It is straightforward to check that his conditions (C1), (C2), (C3) and (B) (CON) – require that the function

$$\sigma(\eta, y, b, w, \alpha) \equiv \frac{\xi_a(\eta, y, w - b, \alpha)}{\xi_\eta(\eta, y, w - b, \alpha)}$$

be *convex* in the variables η, y, b. We simply assume that the underlying utility and production function are such that this is so.
5. This way of looking at the educational problem was discussed in our earlier paper. Work has been done on the general form of this problem by Kevin Roberts (1978) and also by Guesnerie.
6. Other models in which the Arrow question is posed with explicit alternative redistributional tools are these of Bruno (1976), Ulph (1977), Hare and Ulph (1979).
7. Of course one could impose *ad hoc* constraints such as upper bounds on the marginal tax rates which would prevent the first best from being attainable, but that will not produce any interesting conclusions, since the desirability of the loans outcome as against the grants allocation will depend entirely on how the bounds on the tax rate are set.
8. Another important source of uncertainty about the returns to education arises in individual choices about the number of hours to work. Thus a model with variable labour supply actually covers both of the extensions referred to at the start of this section.

REFERENCES

Arrow, K. J. (1971). The utilitarian approach to the concept of equality in public expenditure. *Quarterly Journal of Economics* 85: 409-415.
Atkinson, A. B. (1973). *The economics of inequality*. Oxford: Oxford University Press.

Bruno, M. (1976). Equality, complementarity and the incidence of public expenditures. *Journal of Public Economics* 6: 395-407.

Cochran, J. A. (1972). *The analysis of linear integral equations.* New York: McGraw-Hill.

Hare, P. G., and Ulph, D. T. (1978). On the optimal distribution of public and private education: Models with taxation. *Stirling University Discussion Paper*, No. 55, March.

Hare, P. G., and Ulph, D. T. (1979). On education and distribution. *Journal of Political Economy* 87: S193-S212.

Johnson, H. G. (1972). The alternatives before us. *Journal of Political Economy* 80: S280-S289.

Loury, G. C. (1979). Intergenerational transfers and the distribution of earnings. *Northwestern University.* Mimeo.

Mirrlees, J. A. (1971). An exploration in the theory of optimum income taxation. *Review of Economic Studies* 38: 175-208.

Nelson, S. C., and Breneman, D. W. (1979). An equity perspective on community college finance. Mimeo. Also in *Public Choice* 36(3): 515-532.

Nerlove, M. (1972). On tuition and the costs of higher education: Prolegomenon to a conceptual framework. *Journal of Political Economy* 80: S178-S218.

Roberts, K. (1978). The treatment of the poor under tax/transfer schemes. Mimeo.

Seade, J. (1977). On the shape of optimal tax schedules. *Journal of Public Economics* 7: 203-225.

Ulph, D. T. (1977). On the optimal distribution of income and educational expenditure. *Journal of Public Economics* 8: 341-356.

Comments on P. G. Hare and D. T. Ulph

C. A. PISSARIDES

National Bureau of Economic Research, Cambridge, Mass.

In the model of this paper children cannot make their own education decisions, because they cannot borrow to finance their education. Parents, however, care about children's income, so, if the rate of return to education is higher than the rate of return to financial assets, parents will invest in their children's education rather than pass on financial wealth. Under the assumptions that there is a stationary distribution of abilities, and that each parent knows his child's ability, the authors are able to show that there is a stationary distribution of wealth. In equilibrium wealth inequality exists because more able children receive more education, and as a result accumulate more wealth.

It follows from this that if a government is interested in reducing inequality by taxing labour income and financial wealth differentially, it will have to tax labour income more heavily. Individuals will respond to the differential tax treatment by reducing investment in education, the source of the inequality, and so in the new (second best) equilibrium society will spend 'too little' on education. Thus, in the second-best equilibrium, if the government can induce low-income (and hence low-ability) individuals to spend a little more on education, it will be to society's advantage to do so; the small rise will be efficient and, because it will not be taking place everywhere, it may be chosen so as not to raise inequality.

Hare and Ulph call the ability to induce a small increase in the demand for education a 'grant'. They do not consider the financial aspects of the grant, because these are 'handled through the tax system'. A loan, on the other hand, is equivalent to a grant with a specific financial commitment; the full cost of the loan is repaid out of the returns to the education that it helped finance. If loans are allowed the model breaks down, because the outcome is a 'first best' where all education is loan-financed and the marginal tax rate is 100 per cent. The government 'produces' income optimally via education, and then redistributes it through the tax system equitably.

As far as public policy towards education is concerned the question of grants versus loans is probably the most interesting question raised in the paper. Essentially the difference between them is that a grant is treated as a gift by the recipient, even if he realizes the need for financing, in the sense that if he does not claim the grant he will not save any tax payments. Hence financing grants through general taxation biases the bequest decision in favour of education. In a perfect world, however, the government can eliminate this bias, if it wants, by taxing individual income to finance the grant according to the individual's use of the grant system. But if this is done then a grant is not different from a loan, since in the latter case the government is giving money to be spent on education and collecting it later from the individuals that made use of the system. Thus, if we allow taxation (as well as eligibility for grants) to depend on the individual's income, it is possible to structure grants as loans. The government will have an incentive to structure grants in this way, because, as the authors show, with loans the economy is able to reach a first-best.

The reason the authors do not reach this conclusion appears to be their failure to consider the full question of financing a non-trivial amount of grant. Under the heading of grants they consider only the question of whether it will be advantageous for some individuals to increase infinitesimally their education expenditure – not how much should be spent on education when this expenditure can be financed with discretionary taxation.

In practice, it is probably the case that if grants are financed through general taxation, individuals perceive them as a pure subsidy to higher education. As a result, when grants are introduced the numbers going into higher education increase, and this increase in numbers reduces relative earnings of qualified workers after a lag of three to four years. The increase in numbers will continue until a new equilibrium situation is reached, where the present value of earnings from education is higher, but not by the full amount of the grant.

Thus it seems that eventually students are made to pay for part of the grant through reduced earnings, except that there may be some cycles because of the lags involved in higher education. If grants are not offered to all individuals, but only to low-income groups, their introduction will raise the return to education for grant recipients, and reduce it for non-recipients. In this respect, the effect of grants is probably not different from that of progressive taxation; the latter also reduces the return to education for high-income groups relative to low-income groups. A loan is not likely to involve these distortions in the relative rate of return to education. It can be arranged in such a way that the full amount is deducted from the graduates' future pay along with other taxes, and the present value of the net returns from education need not change by its introduction.

Thus, in conclusion, there seem to be two problems here, which are best treated separately. First, capital market imperfections, for which the best policy is obviously the introduction of loans. Second, the optimal allocation of resources to education, given the efficiency and equity objectives. Once loans have taken care of imperfect capital markets, the second problem could be tackled by taxation under the assumption of a perfect capital market.

Comments on P. G. Hare and D. T. Ulph

J. A. MIRRLEES

Nuffield College, Oxford

Paul Hare and David Ulph have considerably advanced the theoretical analysis of educational policy. I do not claim, nor would they, that their model supersedes less precise arguments about education. It is still possible for informal discussions to keep in play more considerations than their mathematical model does. But the greater apparent realism of purely verbal discussions makes it impossible to derive clear and definite conclusions. Plainly the question how and to what extent education should be subsidised can be answered satisfactorily only in the context of an economic model where income taxation exists, and has a reason to exist. Such a model can be handled only by means of mathematics. Hare and Ulph show how this can be done. In my remarks, I shall concentrate on their model's limitations, which they have themselves emphasised, and speculate about the conclusions that would flow from a yet more realistic model.

The formal analysis of educational policy tends to generate the following unacceptable argument. Suppose educational expenditures can be observed by the government; and that the government wants decisions about these expenditures made by parents because, as Hare and Ulph assume, parents know their children best. Then almost the right decisions will be made if parents pay only one per cent of educational costs, and children receive a correspondingly small proportion of their earnings after tax. Thus the government can, if it wishes, almost equalize incomes; and yet educational choices are not distorted. The distributional consequences of providing incentives for the right human investments are made negligibly small by leaving tiny fractions of the costs and benefits in the hands of private individuals. This is a slight generalisation of the familiar argument that nearly complete taxation of profits is optimal.

The Hare-Ulph model leads to this conclusion. No-one thinks it is the right educational policy. How must the model be modified to meet the objections to that policy? One objection is that people do not make optimal economic decisions when both costs and benefits are very small. I am aure that is true, but it is not a consideration that our economic theories allow us to handle, and we have no empirical evidence as to its magnitude. If, on other grounds the ninety-nine per cent tax-subsidy method must be rejected, perhaps decision-cost considerations can be neglected.

The most important feature lacking in the Hare-Ulph model is unobservable behaviour – the educational effort of parents (and teachers), the learning effort of children, and the performance effort of adults. It is presumably desirable that the economy provide financial incentives for unobservable effort, for example through the income tax being less than one hundred per cent. As a consequence, there must also be a substantial private return to education. If nevertheless educational expenditures are fully subsidised, through free provision and grants, such rational parents as appear in the Hare-Ulph model will provide their children with too much education. An optimal policy would, most probably, subsidise educational expenditures, but not fully: government and parents are both shareholders in the child.

A model that added to the Hare-Ulph model unobservable labour-supply decisions would still have omitted matters of great moment. It is a well established fact that in many societies, most manual workers (for example) make negligible expenditures of money and effort for their children's education. We need a theory to explain that fact. It is not because their children have nothing to gain from such expenditures. A substantial proportion of innately able children are born to such parents. It is partly true that these parents do not know what expenditures would bring substantial returns, and that little is done to tell them. (Surely able children of low-income parents should get extra tuition, just as similar children of high-income parents get help from their parents.) It may also be true that low-income parents see little reason to invest in increasing the future incomes of children who can in any case expect higher incomes than their parents. At any rate, the capital market does not correct matters. Surely the bias towards over-expenditure on education, which one might correct through reducing educational subsidies, applies much more to high-income parents than to low-income parents.

Another feature of the Hare-Ulph model that one would like to see modified is the theory of private educational decisions. In the model, parents (or governments) decide. In the world, parents, schools and colleges, and children decide; and each category has different information, and different benefits to consider. For example, the scale of university admissions might be decided in the light of social benefits, admission decisions on the basis of information not used for tax-subsidy purposes; while the student determines his effort on the basis of private returns and his private knowledge of the pains and pleasures of study and its opportunity cost. A typical, and central question is whether admission should be selective; whether, that is, the private returns to education should induce an excess demand for, say, university places. I think that is a feature of the optimum system. The reasons have not yet crept into our models.

I might mention one peculiarity of the Hare-Ulph model, with utility a function of parental consumption (net of bequests) and child wealth (gross of bequests). If that were right, then everyone could be made better off by greater wealth combined with greater bequests (induced by subsidy, perhaps). It is hard to believe that is true. This feature of the model is not, I think, essential. Certainly it need not divert us from the real merit of Hare and Ulph's work, that it provides a framework for the central questions of educational policy, and techniques that can be used for yet more realistic models.

An equity perspective on community college finance

SUSAN C. NELSON and DAVID W. BRENEMAN*

Brookings Institution, Washington

More than any other institution in the United States, community colleges have been assigned the task of carrying out society's often-stated goal of equality of opportunity for postsecondary education. This spirit is evident in the educational policies of most two-year public colleges: in their 'open door' admissions, in their flexible scheduling of classes in the evening and on weekends and at locations that are convenient for the students, and in the practice of offering almost any educational experience that students feel they need. Community colleges have been more successful in attracting populations traditionally underrepresented in higher education. Compared to their four-year counterparts, community college students of 1976 were more likely to be black or hispanic (20 percent vs. 12 percent), to be attending part-time (43 percent vs. 15 percent), to be first-generation college-goers (59 percent vs. 48 percent), to have low family incomes (25 percent with less than $ 10,000 in family income vs. 16 percent), and to be older (more than 29 percent over 25 years old vs. 13 percent) (BC, 1978). On the financial side, the tradition of low tuition made possible by substantial public subsidies from state and/or local taxes was designed to bring a community college education within the reach of almost all families.

This evidence of a commitment to equality of educational opportunity does not, however, constitute proof that the goal has been realized. This paper examines the equity implications of the four main sources of community college revenues, with an eye to recommendations that could make the financing more equitable. In particular, what are the effects of tuition and student aid policies on access to a community college education (or to any higher education)? Is the intersectoral distribution of state subsidies for higher education inequitable to community college students relative to their counterparts at senior public institutions? Do federal student aid programs treat recipients (and potential recipients) at community colleges inequitably, compared to similar students at four-year colleges? And finally, in states where

* The authors are Research Associate and Senior Fellow, respectively, in the Economic Studies Program. The views expressed here are those of the authors and not necessarily those of the trustees, officers, or other staff members of the Brookings Institution.

local taxes provide support for community colleges, do variations in local wealth constitute a source of interdistrict inequity as court cases such as *Serrano v. Priest* have held they do at the level of elementary-secondary education?

Equity, of course, is not the sole concern of policy. In all matters of public finance, efficiency considerations play a crucial role in justifying any subsidies. Higher education has traditionally though not universally been viewed as producing substantial societal benefits that merit support from some level of government.[1] The goals of equity and efficiency often conflict, however, requiring that a balance be struck between the two. Arthur Okun (1975: 2) has called this choice '... our biggest tradeoff (which) plagues us in dozens of dimensions of social policy. We can't have our cake of market efficiency and share it equally.' While economists and policy makers have paid increasing attention to equity in recent years, the concept and its application to policy are often mishandled, with almost any difference in treatment being branded an inequity. We hope to contribute some clearer thinking on equity as it applies to community college finance.

1. A theoretical perspective on equity

Equity can be viewed (1) in terms of the effect of the subsidies on the lifetime distribution of income (Conlisk, 1977; Pechman, 1970; Hartman, 1972); (2) in terms of the net effect of the taxes and benefits of the relevant subsidies on the current distribution of income;[2] or (3) the equity implications of the costs and the benefits of a set of subsidies can be examined separately, with taxes being judged according to their progressivity and benefits according to their contribution to equalizing educational opportunity in society – the approach advocated by Pechman (1970). Of these three alternatives, the lifetime income approach is ultimately the most appealing basis for judging a service, like education, in which so many of the benefits come as future earnings. Unfortunately, this approach cannot provide any guidance for current policy because, as John Conlisk's elaborate theoretical model of the intergenerational transfer of income shows, presently available data and techniques are inadequate for determining the redistributional effects of higher education subsidies. While the second (net benefit) approach has been most widely used, it can be rejected for both theoretical and technical reasons. The third alternative, which judges the taxes separately from the benefits, emerges as the strongest. Before applying this approach to community college finance, we briefly summarize the reasoning that led to this choice.

Following the lead of many economists concerned with the effect of public policies on the distribution of income, the bulk of the literature on the equity of public subsidies for higher education has focused on the income distribution of net benefits (subsidies minus taxes paid). If net benefits were positive for low income classes and negative for the more affluent, the subsidies were pronounced equitable since they contributed to a more equal distribution of income in society; if the net benefits were the reverse, the subsidies were judged inequitable. Hansen and Weisbrod used a similar but slightly different approach: they compared the net benefits and the family income of the median student attending California's community colleges, state four-year colleges, and universities, plus the net benefits of the median family with no children in public higher education.

The conclusions reached by these studies were mixed. While Hansen and Weisbrod found a regressive distributional effect, matched by Windham (1970) and Zimmerman (1973), many studies including those by Pechman (1970), Machlis (1973), and Crean (1975) concluded just the opposite. The studies by Pechman and Machlis used Hansen and Weisbrod's data but looked at net benefits by income class rather than by the type of college attended (if any). This change in definition and methodology thus reversed the earlier conclusion. For his analysis of Florida, Windham compared the distribution of subsidies for 1967 with a distribution of tax burdens for 1960 and 1961 without adjusting for inflation or growth in real incomes. His finding of a regressive redistributional effect would also have been overturned if appropriate tax data were used, as Nelson (1980a) indicates. The results of net benefit studies are quite sensitive to the data employed. Since the main redistribution from higher education subsidies is a transfer from non-students to students, the lifecycle of earnings will also strongly influence the conclusions from net benefit studies as long as parents of college students tend to be near the peak of their age-earnings profiles.

A final problem inherent in the net benefit approach is that its conclusions can be misleading for public policy. It is possible that an apparently 'good' situation (in terms of net benefits) can emerge from a regressive tax system and an anti-poor distribution of educational benefits, while a 'bad' distribution of net benefits can arise even with progressive taxes and a benefit distribution that favors the poor. The first anomaly results from the fact that even with regressive taxes, higher income people still pay higher taxes. The second anomaly is due to the life-cycle of earnings: if students come from families whose incomes are higher simply because they are older, then the transfer from non-students to students could appear to redistribute income from poor to rich, even if the lowest income students receive the largest benefits. (Examples are given in Nelson, 1980a.)

Such problems with the net benefit approach point to the advisability of examining taxes separately from the benefit side of the subsidies. This method implicitly recognizes that society views one dollar paid in taxes as different from a dollar's worth of education received. It assigns the task of redistributing current income to the tax system and of equalizing educational opportunities to the benefit side. Most of the equity issues raised in relation to community college finance – including those examined in this paper – focus on the benefit side. Central to such an analysis is the concept of 'equality of educational opportunity'. 'Equitable opportunity' may be another way of stating this idea, perhaps more consistent with the general definition of horizontal and vertical equity as an equal treatment of equals and suitably unequal treatment of unequals, with distinctions based on 'relevant' characteristics such as income or educational background. 'Opportunity' implies that an element of volition is involved;[3] opportunities can be equal, or equitable, even if outcomes are not, which is consistent with Okun's description of equality of opportunity. 'Basically it is rooted in the notion of a fair race, where people are even at the starting line. . . . Presumably, it would be desirable to have fairer races' (Okun, 1975: 75 and 84). Unequal outcomes can suggest but do not prove inequity in opportunities.

Our analysis of community college finance proceeds in two stages. We begin by focusing on pricing policies as facilitating or impeding access to higher education. We then look at the subsidies from each level of government separately, examining their equity implications in the context of the other purposes they are designed to serve.[4]

2. Tuition and pricing policies

Community colleges in most states take pride in themselves for adding only minimal financial barriers onto the unavoidable costs of foregone earnings for any student who wants an education. This tradition survives in some states more than in others. Tuitions exceeding $ 700 in New York, Pennsylvania, and Ohio were well above the national average of $ 374 in 1979, and contrasted sharply with the negligible (or zero) tuitions in California and Hawaii. With rising costs and tightening state budgets, pricing policy remains a controversial subject in all states and poses what arguably is the most important equity issue in community college finance: What effect do financial barriers have on access of low income populations to a community college education? Translated into policy terms, this becomes a choice between the traditional strategy of low tuition/low aid or a higher tuition/higher aid approach (assuming the constraint of a fixed budget) as the better way to reduce the positive correlation between income and the probability of receiving higher education. Economists have frequently advocated the latter method on Pareto efficiency grounds. Assuming positive marginal externalities, en 'efficient' level of tuition presumably would still be less than full-cost tuition. If the higher tuition/higher aid strategy were also considered more equitable, one of the rare opportunities would exist to improve both equity and efficiency with the same policy change. This indeed seems to be the case.

From an equity perspective, the choice between the two pricing policies hinges on a comparison of the effectiveness of a dollar of tuition subsidy and a dollar of student aid in affecting the enrollment decisions of potential students at various income levels. While the demand for higher education in general has been examined in considerable detail, only a few studies on the tuition sensitivity of demands for higher education among various sub-populations are directly relevant to this policy question, and none focus separately on community colleges. Work by Bishop (1977) indicates that economically and educationally disadvantaged populations in general have larger price elasticities than their more advantaged counterparts. Adults too seem to be more price-sensitive, and presumably part-time students are as well (Bishop and Van Dyk, 1977). These findings strongly suggest that any increase in tuition – without an offsetting increase in student aid – would disproportionately affect those groups that community colleges were designed to attract into higher education.

Before rejecting the higher tuition strategy as an inequitable way to finance community colleges, the use of student aid to offset the higher tuitions for low income students needs to be explored, including the possibility that student aid could be more effective than low tuition in reducing barriers to access. Again, the existing literature does not provide much help. Not only have community colleges not been examined separately; most of the estimates are already obsolete since they are based on student behavior before the massive federal program of need-based student aid (the Basic Educational Opportunity Grant program – BEOG) was fully operational and came to be well-known (see Jackson, 1977, and Nolfi et al., 1978).

The day that students view net tuition – not posted tuition – as the relevant financial barrier to attending a community college will be the day that tuition below the level dictated by efficiency considerations can no longer be justified. The ideal world where only net tuition matters has not yet been reached. Substantial information barriers still remain. Many high school students and even more adults are not aware of federal and state aid programs, and few know, without applying, the amount of aid for which they qualify.[5] The application process itself poses a further hurdle for many students, particularly first-generation college-goers whose parents might be intimidated by the complicated forms, or those for whom English is a second language.

Even in the real world, a higher tuition/higher aid strategy might deal more successfully with financial and nonfinancial barriers than universal low tuition. Without increasing total subsidies, a movement toward a higher tuition/ higher aid strategy could focus more of the subsidies on low income students. It could relate the subsidies directly to need, without asking the others to pay more than the level of tuition dictated by efficiency considerations. Some high income students who put relatively little value on their education might withdraw, but if information was well diffused, there could be a net increase in the number of low income students enrolling. Outcomes would depend on the success of attempts to reduce the non-price barriers. But unquestionably there is some combination of higher tuition/higher student aid that would improve equity and reduce the differences in the college-going rates of various income groups.

3. State intersectoral subsidies

Community college leaders and other concerned observers often claim that community college students are treated unfairly – 'inequitably' – by the state because, even though they pay a lower price of attendance, they also receive lower subsidies and lower total expenditures for their education than do students who attend senior public institutions. The assumption is that this lower level of support provides community colleges students with inferior educational opportunities, which is particularly undesirable from an equity standpoint in view of community colleges' less affluent student bodies. This section examines the validity of this assertion of intersectoral inequity, first empirically, and then conceptually.

Three types of evidence are often cited in discussions of intersectoral equity. First, according to most sources of data, institutional spending per student is lower at community colleges than at public four year colleges or universities. This discrepancy holds true for the narrower category of 'educational and general' expenditures as well as for total spending, compared to either full-time equivalent (FTE) or to total enrollment, and reflects the patterns of state and local subsidies for public higher education as well. For instance, in 1977, educational and general expenditures per full-time equivalent student in the public sector averaged $5318 at universities, $3899 at other four-year colleges, and only $2085 at community colleges (see Brandt and Ni, 1979, and Pepin, 1978).

Looking beyond this simplistic intersectoral comparison, a second type of evidence of inequities comes from the rates at which states reimburse institutions for students ostensibly taking comparable courses (at least receiving the same credit toward a bachelor's degree). In states where the comparison can be drawn, community colleges receive a lower payment than do senior institutions. For some critics, these two types of evidence – lower spending per student and lower subsidies from the state, relative to what four year colleges and universities receive – provide sufficient proof of inequitable treatment, of a lesser concern for the education of the community college student, and of an implicit state intention that a community college should offer a less expensive education.

A third, more sophisticated type of evidence of intersectoral inequity compares the resources actually spent on a student's education at a community college with what he would receive at a senior public institution, recognizing that differences in the purposes of the institutions unavoidably contribute to some spending differentials. A number of researchers have attempted to isolate the resources devoted solely to the education of first- and second-year undergraduates at each type of institution, although the joint product nature of teaching and research at universities makes this a difficult, if not impossible, task. The two primary modifications to educational and general expenditures per FTE that are necessary are: (1) to exclude expenditures for research and public service, and (2) to derive an enrollment measure which reflects the fact that most institutions, public and private, devote more resources to upper level and graduate students than to freshmen and sophomores.[6]

Analyses that adopt this better specified approach generally contradict the simplistic comparisons and find no basis for asserting that fewer resources are systematically devoted to educating a community college student than to his counterpart at a senior public institution. Results from three studies in this category – by June O'Neill (1971), Estelle James (1978), and Howard Bowen (1979) – appear in rows 1 through 3 of Table 1. While O'Neill and Bowen do find community colleges with the lowest instructional costs, a differential of approximately 10 percent or less between the lowest and highest cost sectors

Table 1. Comparison of 'instructional costs' and 'subsidies' per 'standardized lower-division undergraduate' at public institutions

Author/data	Date of data	Community college	Other four year	University
A. *Instructional costs*				
1. O'Neill (per credit hour)	1966–67	$ 31.20	$ 32.20	$ 34.70
2. James	1966–67	874.00	857.00	583.00
3. Bowen (median)	1976–77	1959.00	2025.00	2020.00
Hansen and Weisbrod:				
4. Including capital costs	1964	721.00	1348.00	1464.00
5. Excluding capital costs	1964	441.00	578.00	709.00
B. *Subsidies – instructional costs – tuition*				
6. James	1966–67	764.00	558.00	284.00
Hansen and Weisbrod:				
7. Including capital costs	1964	721.00	1248.00	1214.00
8. Excluding capital costs	1964	441.00	478.00	459.00

Sources: See references in text.

does not seem large enough to warrant a verdict of intersectoral inequity, particularly since tuition differentials would more than offset these spending disparities. Indeed, when James focused on subsidies (i.e., instructional costs minus tuition) she found community colleges most favored (see Table 1, line 6).

Some detailed analyses, such as the Hansen and Weisbrod study of California, have concluded that intersectoral inequity is indeed a problem. Upon careful examination, however, their study, too, questions more than it supports this conclusion. The key is their estimate of capital costs, which account for two-thirds of the difference in instructional costs and nearly all of the difference in subsidies to students in community colleges, compared with those in four-year institutions (compare line 4 with line 5, and line 7 with line 8, Table 1). While capital costs and benefits should not be ignored, more importance should be attached to operating costs as better reflections of current rather than past policies. Furthermore, the accuracy of Hansen and Weisbrod's figures is questionable since they are grossly inconsistent with O'Neill's calculations, which were more carefully prepared and defined. If capital costs are omitted, the Hansen and Weisbrod claims of intersectoral inequity are substantially weakened in reference to expenditures and are virtually refuted in terms of subsidies for public higher education.[7]

The evidence from these four studies (and from our own simple adjustments to spending data, shown in Table 2) persuades us that, in general, community college students have approximately the same level of resources spent on them

Table 2. Instructional costs and subsidies per lower-division undergraduate in selected states, 1976-77: By type of public institution

	Instructional costs[a]			Subsidies[b]		
	Community colleges (1)	Other four year (2)	University (3)	Community colleges (4)	Other four year (5)	University (6)
Aggregare U.S.	$2036	$2148	$2234	$1682	$1495	$1360
California	1986	1977	3224	1937	1514	2694
New York	2832	2857	3404	1969	1823	2437
Illinois	1946	2415	2450	1534	1810	1732
Florida	2252	2029	2360	1720	1395	1625
Texas	1903	2220	1991	1591	1876	1534
All other states and territories	1962	1945	2160	1550	1274	1244

Sources: Norman J. Brandt and Anne Ni, *Financial Statistics of Institutions of Higher Education, Fiscal Year 1977* (Department of Health, Education, and Welfare, National Center for Education Statistics); Andrew J. Pepin, *Fall Enrollment in Higher Education 1976* (HEW, NCES, 1978).

[a] Instructional costs per lower-division undergraduate =

$$\frac{\text{Educational and General Expenditures} - (\text{Research} + \text{Public Service})}{\text{weighted FTE enrollment}}$$

[b] Subsidies = Columns 1-3 minus (tuition and fee revenues per unweighted FTE enrollment).

and receive about as much subsidy as their counterparts at senior public institutions. Does this then mean that a freshman at a community college faces the same educational opportunities as his counterpart who chose a senior institution? The answer to this question depends on the relationship between dollars and educational opportunities. While it is generally assumed that spending differentials reflect educational differentials, several arguments challenge this assumption.

First, there is the question of efficiency in the narrower sense of effective teaching (in contrast to societal optimizing in resource allocation). Lower spending per student could be viewed either as a sign of greater productivity or as evidence of inferior services. Lacking the pressures of the marketplace, public colleges and universities (and private ones too, for that matter) presumably seldom operate on their production possibility frontiers, making it far from certain that an increase in an institution's budget would translate fully into an increase in output. And what constitutes a higher level of output is itself subject to varying interpretations in a world where, as Howard Bowen phrased it (1979: 24), 'Revenue, rather than need, becomes the primary determinant of cost per student unit. There is no limit to the amount that can be spent in search of "quality" or "excellence".' One institution's higher quality could be another's waste and inefficiency.

Second, even apart from problems of efficiency and definitions of outputs, studies that have attempted in a variety of ways to examine the relationship between spending and educational results fail to produce convincing evidence that more spending leads to higher quality education.[8] In part this reflects a poor understanding of the relationship between real resources (such as class size) and educational outcomes. This finding also could be attributed to the variety of technologies with which undergraduate education can be produced: large or small classes, taught by a tenured faculty member, a junior professor, a part-time teacher, or a graduate student are obvious alternatives. While the costs of these options vary widely, 'educational value-added' may not follow suit.

Third, the fundamental differences between two- and four-year institutions further complicate the relationship between costs and educational opportunities. At universities, undergraduate education is jointly produced with research and graduate, making the cost of a unit of each dependent on the quantity of the other outputs. At community colleges, a different mix of services is produced with, for example, freshman English accompanying community- and work-place-oriented programs. Given an institution's mission, the technological choices it faces are constrained. Consequently, intersectoral comparisons of instructional costs, even if carefully calculated as in the studies discussed above, provide an even weaker indication of relative educational quality than would such comparisons within a given sector.

What, then, can be said about intersectoral equity in light of this analysis?

First, the strongest conclusion is that state funding patterns, in general, do not systematically favor lower-division students in senior public colleges and universities at the expense of their counterparts at community colleges. This finding does not mean, however, that freshmen and sophomores face comparable educational opportunities at two- and four-year institutions, the links between spending on educational inputs and outcomes remain unknown. Until researchers can describe that relation, the absence of serious expenditure differentials at least moves the burden of proof onto critics of the current funding patterns.

4. Federal student assistance

Several equity questions can be raised about federal programs of student aid: How effective are they in equalizing educational opportunities for low income populations? Do the neediest students receive the most benefit from these programs? While these and other similar questions are fundamental to any evaluation of the programs, it also seems appropriate to pose a corollary question from the perspective of community colleges: Do federal student aid programs enhance access and choice as much for low income students who happen to attend community colleges as for their counterparts who have chosen other types of institutions? In other words, do community colleges receive 'their fair share' of federal student aid funds? While this section cannot definitively answer this question, it does offer some tentative conclusions on underutilization.

Observers who believe that community colleges receive less than their fair share of aid often point to the fact that 22 percent of federal student aid funds goes to community colleges while they enroll 34 percent of all students and serve a less affluent clientele. This comparison oversimplifies the issue by ignoring the lower costs associated with community college attendance. To determine whether community colleges are receiving an appropriate share requires a notion of how aid should be distributed, and a comparison of the actual distribution of aid with that ideal standard.

The ideal distribution depends on a measure of 'need,' the difference between the cost to the student of his education and what he can contribute toward it. Since both components of need are subject to differing interpretations, no theoretical consensus exists on what community colleges' share should be. In particular, should costs of attendance include all necessary costs that a student incurs while enrolled, or only the additional (marginal) expenses of enrollment? This question is particularly relevant for students who attend community colleges right after high school graduation and still live at home, imposing almost no new financial burden on their parents besides tuition and books. If foregone earnings are included in costs as conceptually they should be, in place of living costs, does that increase or decrease the estimated need of community college students relative to others? On one hand, foregone earnings for community college students are probably lower since they tend to be less able than students attending senior institutions, although foregone earnings may constitute a larger fraction of total family income since community college students also tend to come from less affluent backgrounds. Elements in choice of an appropriate contribution are more numerous. How much should parents be expected to contribute from their resources? What if they do not meet that expectation? What circumstances end a parent's obligation to contribute? For the student, should there be an explicit self-help requirement, and if so, what form should it take? The official need analysis systems necessarily provide answers to these and other questions, but those answers and their legitimacy are increasingly being challenged by analysts and by parents pushing for middle income assistance. Without a consensus on these questions, no single standard can be identified against which the actual distribution of student aid funds can be compared.

The lack of data presents a further obstacle in a comparison between the ideal and actual distributions of aid. It is currently impossible to make any adequate approximations of student need at various types of institutions, primarily because of inadequate information on student incomes. Consequently, we must settle for indirect evidence.

The picture that does emerge from examining several pieces of information suggests that community college students are adequately represented in the important basic grant program,[9] but it shows that they are less apt to participate in the campus-based programs. These conclusions result from comparing student aid funds under each of the four main Department of Education programs (basic grants, and the campus-based programs of Supplementary Educational Opportunity Grants, College Work-Study, and National Direct Student Loans) for each type of institution and adjusting them separately for: (1) enrollment, (2) costs of attendance, and (3) family income plus tuition level (for further elaboration and evidence, see Nelson, 1980b). It can be shown that community colleges receive a share of basic grant funds that is slightly larger than their share of enrollment, while for each of the campus-based programs they receive much less than their share of enrollment. Secondly, when federal student aid is compared to tuition revenue plus an estimate of costs of attendance, basic grants cover a larger fraction of costs for community college students than for those at other types of institutions, while the campus-based programs offset a smaller fraction of costs for students at two-year public colleges. The third conclusion arises from examining data for first-time full-time freshmen at institutions in a given tuition range. Students at a given income level are about as likely to receive a basic grant award if they attend a community college as if they attend a four-year institution, but they are substantially less likely to receive aid under one of the campus-based programs. This says nothing about the size of the basic grants, however.

From an equity perspective, the finding that community college attendance reduces participation in the campus-based programs but not in BEOG (if generally true) can be interpreted in either of two ways. One view would hold that BEOGs and campus-based programs should be judged according to the same standard. In that case, the distribution of campus-based funds appears inequitable because the fact of community college attendance reduces the probability of receiving an award, while no such problem seems to exist for BEOGs. Alternatively, a different standard could be applied to campus-based programs. If 'access' is the purpose of basic grants, and 'choice' for low income students one of the goals of campus-based aid, under this interpretation campus-based funds improve educational opportunities by helping low income students afford the more expensive institutions, if they so desire. An equitable distribution of campus-based funds would then find them concentrated at more expensive institutions, as indeed they seem to be. From this perspective it is not surprising and is perhaps even desirable that community college students participate more in basic grants than in campus-based programs.

5. Local support: The Serrano case goes to college

In 1971, the California State Supreme Court ruled that the method of financing public education that prevailed in California was illegal because the quality of a student's education depended on the wealth of the district in which he lived. A fiscally neutral system of finance was to be placed in its stead. John Serrano, the plaintiff in that landmark case, was 11 years old and a student in Los Angeles at that time. His younger brother David graduated from high school last year and is currently attending a community college. Will the issue of interdistrict equity associated with the name of Serrano accompany David to college?

This question is relevant not only in California but in as many as 20 other states where community colleges, like the public schools, receive a significant portion of their support from the local property tax. In those states, does the variation among community college districts in taxable wealth lead to an inequitable distribution of educational opportunities? Leaving the legal answer to the lawyers,[10] we argue in this section that from a policy perspective interdistrict equity in community college finance does not warrant major concern, although it should be included among several goals of a state finance formula.

When we talk about interdistrict equity at the community college level, we have in mind a notion quite similar to that propounded by the school finance reform movement, where attention is focused on the relation between educational opportunities (measured by educational expenditures or revenues per student) and district affluence (measured by equalized assessments or personal income). Several characteristics of the mission and finance of community colleges dictate some modifications in the empirical approach, however.

(1) As was discussed in greater detail in Section 3 of this paper, financial statistics of community colleges are poor reflections of the real educational opportunities available. While this is a problem for quantifying inequities in public schools as well, it is more severe at the community college level, where the variance in program costs and mix of programs is much greater, and where the choice of educational technology is wider (part-time or full-time faculty, lecture or small classes, etc.).

(2) Student equity needs to be distinguished from taxpayer equity. While both were important to the success of the school finance reform movement, only the former is relevant to the analysis in Section 1 and the main concern of this paper, i.e., an equitable distribution of educational opportunities.

(3) The presence of tuition complicates any examination of interdistrict equity at the community college level. Not only might students in poor districts have an inferior educational opportunity available to them, they might be forced to pay more for it too. Hence the relationship among district affluence, tuition, and institutional spending (or income) merits examination.

(4) It is unclear whether actual students or all adult residents of the district are the appropriate base for interdistrict comparisons. Unlike elementary-secondary education, where potential students are clearly identifiable by age, community colleges view all residents within their 'service areas' as potential students, and administrative and educational policies can play an active role in determining total enrollment.

In spite of the furor of the school finance reform movement and the plethora of research studies that have accompanied it, the empirical evidence on interdistrict equity in community college finance is sketchy at best. Although one of the common types of finance formulas is called 'equalization funding' or 'minimum foundation funding,' we are aware of only two recent empirical analyses of interdistrict equity at the community college level. John Augenblick (1978) examined the relationship among property wealth, tax rates, personal income, tuition, and total revenues – mainly on a per student basis – for California, Illinois, Mississippi, and New Jersey in 1975. Among his more interesting findings are the following: (1) Property wealth and total revenues (per student) were positively related in all states, though the strength of the correlations varied substantially. The relationship between per capita wealth and revenues per student was much weaker and perhaps negative.[11] (2) Only in Mississippi did students in low wealth districts also appear to pay higher tuitions. (3) It does not seem to matter whether a measure of district wealth or personal income is examined – both variables were positively related to total revenues per student and to tuition.

Catherine P. Clark (1980) expanded on the analyses performed by

Augenblick for California. She found variations in spending and revenues per student to be persistent and substantial over the years 1975 to 1979, and like Augenblick she found a strong correlation between total resources and equalized assessed property values (both on a per student basis). Unlike Augenblick, however, Clark's analysis showed virtually no relation between a measure of personal income and institutional spending.

The sum of evidence from these two studies implies that interdistrict inequities do exist in the financing of community colleges in the states examined, in that low wealth districts also tend to have low revenues available (per student). Augenblick's work in states where tuition is charged shows that wealth and revenue inequalities are not generally compounded (or offset) by variations in tuition rates. Clark's finding of no relation between personal income and spending per student suggests that low income families may not systematically face more poorly financed community colleges in spite of the interdistrict inequities related to wealth.

Since public policy, to economists, is largely a balancing of equity and efficiency concerns, it is important to put these tentative findings in the perspective of other public services. While community colleges in a number of states (including California) originated in the public school system, and even though the education they provide is sometimes viewed as grades 13 and 14, there are several important differences between high schools and community colleges that make a simple extension of school finance reform to the colleges unwise. The most obvious and fundamental distinction is that community college attendance, or even any higher education, is not compulsory. This reflects a societal judgment that, unlike elementary and secondary schooling, postsecondary education is not essential for functioning or succeeding in life. This judgment reflects practice too, since postsecondary attendance is still far from universal. In 1977, 86 percent of the population aged 16-17 was enrolled in school below the college level (of whom approximately 8 percent attended private schools), while only 36 percent of those aged 18-19 were in college, and about 10 percent of that age group was attending public two-year institutions. These statistics highlight a further distinction between secondary and postsecondary education: in the former sector a student faces little choice among institutions, and is essentially constrained to his local public school, whereas substantial choice and mobility exist in higher education. Similarly, most community college courses are not tuition free (except in California), posing a financial barrier unknown to public elementary-secondary education and again indicating that they are deemed less essential. Finally, perhaps the greatest spatial inequity exists for residents outside any community college district or beyond commuting range.

Instead of viewing community colleges as an outgrowth of the public schools, they could also be seen in the context of other local services. The protection of life and property through fire, police, and medical services could certainly be considered as essential a right of citizenship as a basic education, yet no attention comparable yo that of the school finance reform movement has focused on making the financing of these services more equitable across districts. Since a community college education is clearly less of a fundamental right than life and property, we might expect public policy to attach a higher priority to fiscal neutrality for those basic services than for community colleges, but such seems not have been the case.

To suggest that interdistrict equity has only secondary importance in the financing of community colleges is not to deny it as a worthy goal of public policy. Garms (1977) included it as one among nine criteria for judging a finance system for community colleges. Interdistrict equity should not be a dominant goal, however, the pursuit of which leads to a total revision of financing patterns as it did in the elementary-secondary school systems of many states.

6. Toward more equitable financing of community colleges

The main conclusion from this analysis is an ironic one. The area of finance often considered the most important contribution of community colleges toward equity in higher education – low tuition – is actually the one most vulnerable on equity grounds. Informational and procedural barriers undoubtedly do deter some low income students from enrolling and should not be ignored if a higher tuition/higher aid strategy is adopted. The potential is so great, however, for using the revenues generated from higher tuitions to offset these non-financial barriers, to lower the net price for low income students, and to reduce or even eliminate the positive correlation between family income and the probability of attending college that we believe that equity should not be used to justify universal low tuition. Indeed, our analysis suggests that a higher tuition/higher aid strategy, the pricing policy traditionally supported by economists on efficiency grounds, also provides more equitable opportunities.

Comparisons between per student expenditures at public four-year and two-year colleges have frequently been thought to display inequities, but in our analysis the structure of subsidies receives better marks then does low tuition. Among students in public higher education, those attending community colleges do not seem to be placed at a disadvantage in terms of federal, state, or local subsidies. The evidence on expenditures in the two- and four-year sectors that community college spokesmen interpret as inequitable support for their students can in fact be explained by the different purposes of the institutions and by the common pattern, in both the public and private sectors, of institutions spending more for the instruction of upper level and graduate students than for lower division undergraduates. Community college students do not receive lower subsidies or expenditures than do their counterparts at public universities; all lower division undergraduates regardless of where they enroll tend to have less spent on their education than more advanced students.

While the information needed to reach a definite conclusion is not available, federal student aid programs do not seem to be biased against community college students. From an equity perspective, it is most important that this conclusion apply to the basic grant program, the federal government's main contribution to access for low income populations to higher education. That program has apparently done well in its coverage of low income students whatever the institutions they attend, but the half-cost provision constrains awards for low-income students attending the lowest priced colleges. It appears that the reauthorization of the federal Higher Education Act will take an important step in that direction by moving towards a 70 percent limit on grants as a fraction of costs. The campus-based programs are another story, but one that is consistent with one of their primary purposes of providing lower income students with some ability to choose more expensive institutions. While this leads to an appearance of community college students receiving less than their 'fair share,' the result seems to us to contribute to broader educational opportunities.

The significance of interdistrict equity is not nearly as great at the community college level as it is for elementary-secondary education, but the available evidence suggests that it may indeed be contributing to spending differentials among districts that work to the disadvantage of less affluent jurisdictions. Since state governments contribute a larger share of community colleges' support than do local districts, considerations of interdistrict equity have a place in (any) criteria determining how state subsidies should be distributed, but this is less important than other elements in a policy designed to ensure greater equity in the distribution of opportunities for all kinds of higher education.

NOTES

1. Some economists have argued that the marginal conditions required to justify below-cost tuition on efficiency grounds are not met, that the externalities associated with the additional enrollment are not worth the tuition subsidies (see, for instance, Schultz, 1972).
2. The study of Hansen and Weisbrod (1969) and many of the responses to that work fall in this category. For references see Nelson (1980a), which includes also a more detailed discussion of net benefit studies.
3. See the discussion of equal educational opportunity in Burbules and Sherman (1979).
4. There is, of course, a broader equity issue involving those who do not enroll for any post secondary education, and thus receive no subsidy at all. However, the financing policies discussed in this paper are intended to emove low income as a barrier to college attendance.
5. The college, not the federal government, selects recipients under the three campus-based

programs – Supplemental Educational Opportunity Grants (SEOG), College Work-Study (CWS), and National Direct Student Loans (NDSL).

6. This practice of spending more on higher level students could be, and indeed has been, challenged on equity grounds, but it is a separate issue of 'appropriately' unequal treatment of unequals.

7. According to O'Neill's careful estimates, capital costs amounted to about 18 percent of current instructional costs in both the public and private sectors of higher education. Hansen and Weisbrod, who neither define nor describe their measure of capital costs, show them as exceeding current educational expenditures for universities and the CSUC system and equalling about two-thirds of current operating expenses at the community colleges.

8. On this topic Bowen (1979) refers to Bowen and Douglas (1971), Astin (1968), and Jackman and Layard (1973).

9. This appears true in spite of a provision limiting awards to half the cost of attendance, a constraint that has the effect of reducing awards for only the lowest income students attending the lowest cost institutions (generally community colleges).

10. The lawyers from the original *Serrano* case at the Western Center for Law and Poverty are considering a legal challenge to California's system of financing community colleges. They interpreted the provisions in the state constitution instructing the state to provide a system of community colleges as requiring that the institutions be supported in a fiscally neutral way.

11. Augenblick suggests that the link between the per capita and per student analyses is the community college participation rate: enrollment as a fraction of the district population. Apparently participation rates are lower in more affluent districts, presumably because young people there are more likely to select a four-year college. This in turn implies that if the main concern in analyses of interdistrict equity is the student (as it is in this paper) rather than the taxpayer, comparisons of the financial resources of districts should be made on a per student basis because low wealth districts need higher per capita spending on community colleges than do more affluent districts.

REFERENCES

Astin, A. (1968). Undergraduate achievement and institutional excellence. *Science* 161: 661-668.

Augenblick, J. (1978). Issues in financing community colleges. Education Finance Center, Education Commission of the States, Report F-78-4. October.

Bishop, J. (1977). The effect of public policies on the demand for higher education. *Journal of Human Resources* 12: 285-307.

Bishop, J., and Van Dyk, J. (1977). Can adults be hooked on college? *Journal of Higher Education* 48: 39-62.

Bowen, H. R. (1979). Assessing the benefits and costs of higher education. Presentation delivered at symposium on Efficiency and Equity in Educational Finance, University of Illinois, Champaign-Urbana, May 3-5.

Bowen, H. R., and Douglas, G. K. (1971). *Efficiency in liberal education.* New York: McGraw-Hill.

Brandt, N. J., and Ni, A. (1979). *Financial statistics of institutions of higher education, fiscal year 1977.* Washington, D.C.: Department of Health, Education, and Welfare, National Center for Education Statistics.

Breneman, D. (1978). The outlook for student finance. *Change* 10: 48-49, 62.

Burbules, N. G., and Sherman, A. L. (1979). Equal educational opportunity: Ideal or ideology? Stanford University, Institute for Research on Educational Finance and Governance. May.

Bureau of the Census. (BC). (1978). School enrollment: Social and economic characteristics of students, October 1976. *Current Population Reports, Population Characteristics*, Series P-20, No. 319. Washington, D.C.: Government Printing Office. February.

154

Bureau of the Census. (BC). (1979). School enrollment: Social and economic characteristics of students, October 1977. *Current Population Reports, Population Characteristics*, Series P-20, No. 333. Washington, D.C.: Government Printing Office. February.

Clark, C. P. (1980). Two-year colleges and finance equity: The case of California. Los Angeles: Western Center for Law and Poverty. February. Draft.

Conlisk, J. (1977). A further look at the Hansen-Weisbrod-Pechman debate. *Journal of Human Resources* 12: 147-163.

Crean, J. F. (1975). The income redistributive effects of public spending on higher education. *Journal of Human Resources* 10: 116-121.

Garms, W. I. (1977). *Financing community colleges*. Teachers College Press, Columbia University.

Garms, W. I. (1980). On measuring the equity of community college finance. University of Rochester. February.

Hansen, W. L., and Weisbrod, B. A. (1969). *Benefits, costs and finance of public higher education*. Chicago: Markham Publishing.

Hartman, R. W. (1972). Equity implications of state tuition policy and student loans. *Journal of Political Economy*, Supplement, 80(3, pt. 2): S142-171.

Jackson, G. A. (1977). Financial aid to students and the demand for postsecondary education. Ph.D. dissertation, Harvard University.

Jackman, R., and Layard, P. R. G. (1973). University efficiency and university finance. In M. Paskin (ed.), *Essays in modern economics*. London: Longman.

James, E. (1978). Product mix and cost disaggregation: A reinterpretation of the economics of higher education. *Journal of Human Resources* 13: 157-186.

Machlis, P. D. (1973). The distributional effects of public higher education in New York City. *Public Finance Quarterly* 1: 35-57.

Marmaduke, A. S. (1978). Implementing the student financial aid partnership. Paper prepared for the Conference on Student Aid Policy of the Aspen Institute for Humanistic Studies, July.

Nelson, S. N. (1980a). Community colleges and their share of student financial assistance. Washington, D.C.: College Entrance Examination Board.

Nelson, S. N. (1980b). Equity and higher education finance: The case of community colleges. In Walter W. McMahon and Terry G. Geske (Eds.), *Efficiency and equity in educational finance*. Forthcoming.

Nolfi, G. J., et al. (1978). *Experiences of recent high school graduates: The transition to work of postsecondary education*. London: D. C. Heath and Co.

Okun, A. (1975). *Equality and efficiency: The big tradeoff*. Washington, D.C.: Brookings Institution.

O'Neill, J. (1971). *Resource use in higher education*. Berkeley, Calif.: Carnegie Commission on Higher Education.

Pechman, J. A. (1970). The distributional effects of public higher education in California. *Journal of Human Resources* 5: 361-370.

Pechman, Joseph A. (1971). The distribution of costs and benefits of public higher education: Further comments. *Journal of Human Resources* 6: 375-376.

Pepin, A. J. (1978). *Fall enrollment in higher education 1976*. Washington, D.C.: U.S. Department of Health, Education, and Welfare, National Center for Education Statistics.

Schultz, T. W. (1972). Optimal investment in college instruction: Equity and efficiency. *Journal of Political Economy*, Supplement, 80(3, pt. 2): 32-33.

Windham, D. M. (1970). *Education, equity and income redistribution*. London: D. C. Heath and Co.

Zimmerman, D. (1973). Expenditure-tax incidence studies, public higher education, and equity. *National Tax Journal* 25: 65-70.

Comments on S. C. Nelson and D. W. Breneman

SIV GUSTAFSSON

Arbetslivscentrum, Stockholm

In their study of community college finance Nelson and Breneman arrive at what they call an ironic conclusion. They conclude that contrary to the general notion a low tuition policy is vulnerable on equity grounds. They conclude that their analysis suggests that a higher tuition policy combined with higher aid is not only the pricing policy supported by most economists on efficiency grounds but is also the most equitable one.

The first step in analyzing which type of finance is the more equitable is to decide what is to be meant by equity. This step is achieved by reviewing the literature on the topic beginning with the Hansen and Weisbrod (1969) study of California higher education, which is quoted as a pathbreaking study. This study later resulted in the 'Hansen-Weisbrod-Pechman debate' on whether community colleges get a fair share of state and federal subsidies. I find the arguments of the authors convincing in their conclusion that community colleges do not get lower subsidies for the same level of education than do other state colleges and universities. The empirical evidence supports this conclusion.

For judging equity Nelson and Breneman suggest three alternative standards:

1. Net effect of subsidies on lifetime distribution of earnings.
2. Net effect of taxes and subsidies on the current distribution of income.
3. Consider the effects of taxes and subsidies separately, subsidies by their contribution to equalizing educational opportunity, and taxes by their progressivity.

The authors conclude that we must rule out the first standard because John Conlisk has shown that 'currently evailable data and techniques are inadequate for determining the redistributional effects of current subsidies.' However, they find the approach appealing. Since data can be collected and methodology can be improved, I do not think this is a reason for rejecting the lifetime standard. I would like to carry the life-cycle equity concept further, to focus on individuals without regard to family background.

The Swedish equity concept is in the process of changing from a re-distribution of incomes from rich families to poor families to a redistribution of incomes over the life-cycle of individuals. Students can by definition not sustain themselves because they cannot simultaneously do full-time work and full-time studies. Sweden has a policy of no tuition at all for any kind of schooling. Moreover, for financing costs of living of university students state-subsidized student loans with a grant part that is equal for everyone is offered. The educational subsidy does not depend on parents' income. The advantages of the system are that parents do not have to carry a heavy financial burden that is concentrated in a few years and individuals do not depend on their parents for receiving a higher education.

It is easily seen that this equity concept is based on the individual as opposed to the family. Student loans were being made dependent on spouse's income for a longer period than they were being made dependent on parents' income before this change. The effect had been discrimination against adult women who wanted to educate themselves after having raised a family. Incomes of their husbands were too high for them to get student finance, but they needed extra financing to make up for their work in the household, for which they must substitute goods or services bought on the market.

Nelson and Breneman conclude that a higher tuition policy is more efficient and also more equitable than a lower tuition policy. But why is the high tuition policy more efficient? A well-known finding of economic theory is that a free market leads to a Pareto-efficient solution. A policy of providing no tuition subsidy is a free market policy, and a higher tuition policy could come closer to this. But for this policy to be Perato-efficient it also requires that the capital market be completely free; that is, students should be able to take loans against the security of their future earnings. Since this is unlikely to be considered a good enough security by the bankers, government loans to students have been introduced in many countries (with or without outright subsidies or grants as well). Support of students eligible only on grounds of their family background requires much more bureaucracy for administration than does the Swedish system. Before we have analyzed the functioning of the capital market and differences in administrative costs we cannot draw valid conclusions about the efficiency of alternative systems.

Is it true that by limiting aid to poorer students in higher education the effects would be more equitable? As every economist knows, Pareto efficiency is no guarantee of equity; it is compatible with any income distribution. I am not prepared to draw conclusions about equity without more evidence about the lifecycle income distribution effects that would be implied by the policy changes advocated by Nelson and Breneman.

PART III

Perspectives on recurrent education

The finance of recurrent education: Some theoretical considerations*

MAURICE PESTON

Queen Mary College, London

In this short paper I wish to concentrate on two matters: (a) the analytical basis of government involvement with the financing of recurrent education, and (b) certain practical aspects of this involvement whatever its analytical foundation. In doing this, there are two background assumptions to be noted. Firstly, I shall discuss only the mixed economy as we know it, rather than an idealised system which may or may not be possible, but certainly does not actually exist. Secondly, I shall not go out of my way to distinguish 'education' from 'training', either in terms of content specifically of use to the individual or firm, institutional location, or method of instruction.[1] The first of these assumptions do not mean that I shall refrain from drawing our attention to policy changes of a fundamental kind, and the second does not cause me to ignore the usual questions of 'who benefits?' and 'who pays for?' recurrent (or any other kind of) education.

In addition, the chief assumptions that I shall make concerning the general economic environment are as follows:

(a) The economy will continue to be a mixed one with the public sector comprising some twenty to forty per cent of total economic activity. (As a first approximation I would measure the relative size of the public sector by the share of the labour force employed by it, i.e. in the case of the U.K., 25%-30%) (Peston, 1980).
(b) The economy will continue to contain a large trades union element.[2]
(c) The share of net output in manufacturing contributed by the 100 largest firms will remain at about its present size, i.e. about 40 per cent, or will increase (Prais, 1976).
(d) Economic growth will continue, encouraged by technological advance of a labour-saving nature but possibly constrained by continual energy shortage.
(e) Left to itself, the economic system will adjust to offset external shocks either of an expansionary or of a contractionary kind, but this process of

---

* This paper has benefitted significantly in several places from Mark Blaug's criticisms, although our views on this subject in general rarely coincide.

adjustment will be exceedingly slow. In particular, the economy left to itself will spend a disproportionate amount of time in under-employment conditions both because of its inability to offset contractionary shocks in the short term, and because its automatic offset to inflation will also be contractionary.[3]

(f) Wants as expressed by households will partly be a reflection of something correctly to be called underlying preferences, and partly the reflection of preferences created in society by a number of forces including the efforts of all kinds of private enterprise, but also public sector institutions.

(g) At the very least the decline in aggregate work input of the past one or two decades will continue. This decline for men comprises a reduction of length of working life, working year and working week, and, according to my calculations for the U.K., amounts to no less than and probably more than 10% of the work input over the past decade and a half or so. The position for women is confused by the growth of female labour force participation. This is surely correctly to be interpreted as the substitution of paid work in the office or factory for unpaid work in the home. Unfortunately, it is not possible, because of this complication, to estimate the change in total female work input, but it is hard to believe that this would be qualitatively different from the male.

If we consider the long run adjustment process in these conditions, we would expect it to have the following characteristics:

(i) A change in the level of real wages and their structure together with associated changes in employment. In particular, the demand for most labour, but especially the unskilled and semiskilled, will fall relative to the supply, but real wages may not adjust accordingly. Nonetheless, there will be pressures to expand labour-intensive activities.

(ii) A continued reduction in work input along all three of its dimensions, but here too the reduction will not be the same for all occupations and skill levels.

(iii) A continuation of, and probable increase in training specific to the firm in some sectors of the economy, specificity here being often connected with complementarity to the new technology.

(iv) A greater demand for general training, because of uncertainty concerning what specific skills will be demanded, and what the requirements of different parts of the new technology will be.

(v) An expansion in the demand for services complementary to leisure activities, of which education is the most relevant to the present discussion.

In connection with this kind of adjustment process, economists have tended to focus firstly on the benefits of education and training as they accrue to the individual. He will compare these with the costs he bears (both suitably discounted) and decide whether to use his leisure time, some of his working time, or even to give up work temporarily, to attend an educational institution. Alternatively, the relevant activity may take place within the firm, the costs being borne by the individual via the payment of lower wages. Secondly, economists have looked at the benefits received by the firm, i.e. whether they are specific to it even though they are embodied in the individual, so that it is willing to pay for and actively encourage education and training.

It should be recognised in many actual cases that education is a sort of payment in kind, deductible in cost by the firm but not taxable as a benefit to the individual. Thus, especially for employees with high marginal tax rates, notably management, educational opportunities may be offered in place of nominal salary increases.

Turning now to the supply side, economists have assumed that, as long as the demand for recurrent education exists, appropriate institutions will emerge in the private sector to meet it. Some have gone further and asserted that there will always be potential profit seekers in this area who will encourage an inchoate demand to emerge.

The result of this sort of approach has been to leave the economist floundering somewhat when it comes to government financing and provision. Sometimes he ducks out of the issue altogether by referring vaguely to political and sociological considerations. On other occasions he sees some justification of public financing of education in terms of so-called externalities. He also acknowledges that there may be an income distribution facet of the problem, arising from an inability to deal more generally with inequities as they arise in the economic system.

Concerning provision, the majority of economists in this field note the possibility of market failure, but tend not to be convinced by it. Instead, they assume that state schools and colleges of further and higher education exist for ideological reasons.[4]

If this view is accepted, certain consequences can immediately be deduced. The most obvious is that public financing of recurrent education must be directed at the external benefits it generates. Taking the simplest standpoint, and, therefore, ignoring all considerations of second best, if there are relevant externalities, it will be desirable for the state either to subsidise the individual who is considering extending his education after a shorter or longer period of work experience, or the institution that might provide that education. In addition, if, as is typical of this part of economics, full employment is taken for granted, the finance itself must be raised in ways that do not excessively distort overall allocations in the economy, or impede the very education that it is supposed to be fostering. What should be noted is that public financing does not imply that recurrent education should be provided without charge, only that it be subsidised.

The second consequence of the standard approach is that the government need have no plan for recurrent education, or set up institutions to provide it.[5] The most that may be required is encouragement, the spreading of information on the possibility of profit to be made here, and, perhaps, a further subsidy on infant industry lines. In other words, what must be done is to optimise the private sector response, not to replace it.

To summarise, it might be argued that there is no special problem of the finance of recurrent education at all. It is part of the general problem of education finance, involving a balance between user charges and taxation, and the usual principles of public finance must be applied to it. It may well be that, if nothing else changes, there will be increasing pressure on the public sector arising from growing demand for recurrent education with its associated externalities. There is also the decision at what level to raise this money, i.e. by central or local government. But these are all conventional issues, implying quantitative but not qualitative variations on existing themes.

Let me turn to some criticisms of this approach. The most obvious is that it is in danger of trivialising the subject. An example is the classification of 'equality of opportunity' or 'social cohesion' as non-economic considerations. This is not to say that they cannot be treated in that way, but to point out that since 'economic' is usually not defined in the first instance, they become so by decree, so to speak. Of course, if 'economic' is defined as 'appertaining to markets', it follows all too inevitably that phenomena which have not clearly and directly to do with markets must be excluded. But even here it can be argued that 'equality of opportunity' or 'social cohesion' may be demanded by individuals as members of groups (rather than isolated on desert islands), and that an unaided market system is unable to provide them. Then, paradoxically enough, the question of supply, to meet social demands, and the creation and responsiveness of appropriate institutions falls fairly and squarely within economics, and not on its periphery or even outside it altogether.

A similar comment may be made on externalities (Peston, 1972). No-one doubts that these may exist, and they can be identified in reality. But what is an externality is not entirely (or even at all) objective. It depends on individuals' perceptions and responses. These in turn may not be independent of government actions and political pronouncements. It follows once again that we are verging on the purely definitional – what the state concerns itself with must evince some externality or other, i.e. what is of public interest must be of public interest.

Thus, at the purely theoretical level, while rejecting neither of the concepts, 'market failure' and 'external benefits', I resist their too-easy application on the grounds that they tend to be ragbags and divert attention from serious issues. If they are to be of use, they must be formulated in empirically discernible and testable terms. It should be recognised that the state becomes involved in education and accepts a financial responsibility for a whole host of reasons. While we all have the technical skills to fit these into the standard categories of 'market failure', 'externalities', 'non-economic considerations', and 'ideology', little or no insight or practical understanding is gained from doing so.

Let me, therefore, go back to the beginning and consider the question of public sector involvement and financing without being totally committed to the usual preconceptions to be found within the textbooks of the economics of education. The easiest place to start is by considering demand. Instead of postulating that individual workers and firms have a well-defined set of preferences and demands for recurrent education, consider the alternative that most of them are rather vague about both what they want or might have. Typically, they would like more of what they are used to, and tend to be fearful of anything different. The worker is accustomed to an existence in which he works for a continuous period for most of his adult life, most weeks of the year, most days of the week, and most hours of the waking day. Anything other than brief interruptions to this work experience is abnormal, and to be rejected. Such interruptions are designated as unemployment and *ipso facto* are to be regarded as undesirable. They are especially undesirable if a severance of the link between the worker and the firm occurs; thus, going on a special course is made more acceptable if the connection with the firm is maintained.[6]

Related to these attitudes which are, of course, strongly socially determined, is the fact that the organisation of firms tends to be such that all workers have to be treated in much the same way. The individual worker who would wish to demand more education as an adult cannot easily organise his working life accordingly.[7] In addition, existing institutions within the labour market may inhibit his ability successfully to retrain. Even ignoring all the genuine externalities, a firm which wished to organise a programme of permanent education and training might find the costs too high simply because it would be unable to distinguish between different workers according to their needs and tastes.

Now, neither of these factors, the formation of preferences and the responsiveness of firms subject to existing institutional restraints, would necessarily be very important on their own. They become more significant when some further possibilities are taken into account. One is that the kind of technical change that is beginning to influence the advanced industrial world is of such magnitude as to have consequences of revolutionary character. There are two ways of looking at this. Firstly, attention may be paid to the potential that may be missed because of the way the economy adjusts at the margin. Secondly, at the other extreme, consideration may be given to the possible damage to society of very rapid but uncontrolled adjustment. We do not possess the ability to predict whether the danger is ultra conservatism concentrating on job preservation or ultra liberalism devoted to efficiency maximisation without any regard to job destruction. One group of experts utter warnings about the dire consequences of the micro-chip while paying too little attention to its potential for good. A second group emphasises the system's ability to cope without appreciating that its piecemeal accomodation to external shocks may not lead to an overall optimum.

A key role for government is not primarily to overcome this dilemma or to pronounce in other than the long term on the correctness of one view or the other. Rather it is to act as a continuous monitor moderating or encouraging change as the occasion demands. Given that, its role in demand enhancement becomes a central one. To use another technical term (albeit also one which is often used to trivialise a whole area of discourse), government has the task of creating merit wants.[8] Politicians aware of the technical feasibility of reducing total lifetime work input may decide to encourage this, and to persuade the electorate of the desirability of its consequences, social and individual. They may, in particular, note that workers' attitudes to change may be influenced by fear and excessive devotion to the status quo.

Given the present institutional structure of the mixed economy, and possibly given any feasible institutional structure, existing workers' organisations at all levels have considerable influence on the introduction of new techniques and methods of working. Of course, they are not all powerful, but there is no need to take such an extreme position to infer a serious role for government in assisting technical advance by moderating its impact on those workers who are likely to suffer from it.

Let us make the assumption that the new technology does enable the economy to return to past growth rates and to exceed them. Assume also that the technology is labour saving in the short and medium term. (There is no problem, if that is not the case. And it must be added that the evidence, albeit rather unsystematic and illustrative, is that in practice displacement of labour services tends to occur much less than is predicted or feared.)

The fact that new technology can lead to (or is predicted to lead to), redundancies and chronic unemployment is why some workers resist it, and also operate it much below its true potential. That it does have such potential means that those who gain from its introduction can compensate those who lose. Some may argue that this is neither necessary nor desirable, technical progress being one of those random shocks that people must accept, taking the rough with the smooth, so to speak. They would say that compensation tests do not apply in such a case. Counter-arguments depend on such value judgements as protecting the innocent bystander or giving first priority to the poor in any division of an increment in the national cake. More to the point, it must be accepted that, if those who lose from the change can prevent it or restrict it, they *have* to be compensated, whether or not on other grounds they deserve to be.

This is important for recurrent education in two ways. Firstly, workers may be willing to accept redundancy, and a shorter working lifetime in any or all of its various dimensions, if by recurrent education they are guided to make constructive use of their additional leisure, or by recurrent training they become more employable on average. Secondly, the increased productivity on which this whole argument is based means that the resources are there to support such a programme, the role of the government being to tax the nominally employed in order to support those in recurrent education.

Related to this would be a reinterpretation of the opportunity costs of recurrent education. If we consider why 'normal education' consists for the overwhelming majority of people of a continuous period of schooling followed by a continuous period of work followed by retirement, the justification must lie in maximising the period in which the investment pays off, and realising that the interruption of work for later education is extremely expensive in terms of production foregone. In the crudest terms, a year of schooling at age 18 can pay off over 45 years; foregoing that year and taking it at 28 can pay off over 35 years. Moreover, the value of output foregone at 18 is less than that foregone at 28.

There are two assumptions that our assessment of the economic future allows us to change which undermine this preconception. One is that the typical person will be fully employed over his working lifetime. A second is that investment in his education will pay off over his whole working lifetime. If, instead, we predict that he has a high probability of being unemployed as an adult, it may be cheaper to give him the opportunity for so-called optional education later rather than earlier. Moreover, if it is predicted that his earlier schooling becomes obsolete and needs refurbishment or even replacement, our estimate of its value relative to delayed schooling will be diminished.

All of these considerations together with the proposition that the economy left to itself cannot take full cognisance of them (and to the extent that it does, cannot act appropriately) add force to the central role of the government in planning the education system, and especially recurrent education in the foreseeable future. Curiously enough, it may well be that the government's role should be transitory until the economy can adjust fully to the changes required. Once wants have been established and both sides of industry see what needs to be done (and, especially, what new educational institutions are required to supply the appropriate services), the role of government may start to be diminished. Happily or unhappily, what is transitory has a tendency to become permanent in the public sector, partly for ideological reasons, and partly because of the costs of unsettling an institutional structure. In sum, the textbook view of the role of government in education may be theoretically correct in full equilibrium, but public policy is a series of temporary equilibria (which in education may, anyway, last a century or more) and may cause the government to stay in this field permanently.

Let me now turn to the existing institutional structure of education. Presumably, although an expanded programme of recurrent education may lead to the creation of new institutions, it will be based in its initial stages on existing schools and colleges.[9] Apart from that, its ramifications will affect them in a variety of ways. It is possible, for example, that there will be a decline in the scale or rate of growth of various forms of optional education for people in the age group 16-21 if it becomes possible (or they are encouraged) to defer some or all of this until later. There is the further possibility that even the last year of compulsory education could be abolished to be replaced by an equivalent period of compulsory education later in life. In either case there must be a reconsideration of the curriculum in those countries such as the U.K. where the dominant tendency is to view it as an integrated whole.

To be set against this potential decline will be an expansion of education for adults. Here too there is a major curriculum problem. It is one thing to talk about education for constructive leisure or retraining to improve employability. It is quite another to determine precisely what curriculum actually achieves those ends. There is also the organisation question of whether recurrent education can or ought to be altogether as rigidly controlled in its timetabling and teacher dominance as conventional education. If it is to be connected at all closely with unemployment, the relevant institutions must be able to respond to demand when and where it appears. A person unemployed in November will want help then, and will not take kindly to being told that he must wait until a new course starts at the beginning of the next academic session nearly a year later.

Obviously, the best way of looking at this is that recurrent education comprises a variety of services. Some of these are broadly the same as those currently being offered; others will need to be quite different. Some adults, therefore, will attend existing courses and be no different from other pupils and students. Others will require quite different treatment, located in new schools and colleges or in separate departments of existing ones. It may even be that the education service must reach out much more to the workplace, so that in broad terms workers on a particular course will continue to attend their accustomed place of work.

As far as the financing of institutions is concerned, the questions confronting the government are largely standard ones. These are as follows:

i. Should public finance of recurrent education be restricted to existing state schools and colleges or should it be extended to the private sector, the emergence of new institutions being encouraged there?

ii. Should public finance be available to subsidise firms who wish to reorganise their labour force and take on some of the burden of recurrent education themselves?

iii. Should a programme of recurrent education be regarded as essentially national in character involving central government financing, or should it be turned over to local government and be financed jointly by local and central taxation?

iv. Since many of the benefits of recurrent education are private in character, should the state meet the full cost or should user charges be levied on the individual or his employer?

v. Is it useful to distinguish the grant or maintenance side of expenditure from the capital and running costs of educational institutions?

I do not propose at this stage to attempt to answer these questions. It is highly likely that in the present stage of discussions of the subject they are unanswerable. Nonetheless, certain aspects of the eventual set of answers may be pointed to. Unfortunately, these seem to raise even more questions.

Let me, therefore, at the outset reiterate the proposition stated above, that there is no financial problem in the sense of the country being unable to afford the education. The whole subject arises because we can afford to use time and available productive capacity for this purpose, especially when the alternative is simply that they will be wasted. The issues are whether we should, how we set about doing it, how we determine the financial arrangements in detail, and how we manage the distribution of net benefits.

On the public-private division, obviously if one sector can provide the appropriate service and the other cannot, there is no problem. To state that the issue is ideological may mean no more than that the service is defined by its origin, and, for example, that private sector education is a different sort of thing from public, and not at all a substitute for it. While this view can be elaborated on and is almost certainly valid for compulsory schooling, it is difficult to see it as compelling for recurrent education. Thus, the issues can be seen as more practical ones of comparative costs, the need for inspection, proper accounting for the use of public money etc. In the United Kingdom it is also worth recognising that there may be excess capacity in the state education sector in the 1980s, and that at least for a while the least cost solution would be to make use of that capacity for recurrent education.[10]

On the question of subsidies, since governments already subsidise firms in a variety of different ways, ranging from capital investment allowances to industry training schemes, no new point of principle arises when it comes to their participation in a programme of recurrent education. While it will be true that the precise education and training offered will vary in nature depending on the relative mix of firm and college involvement, and this will affect the mode of financing, the decision itself will surely be taken on grounds much broader than that and will have little to do with public finance.

Similarly, although the economist can point to the advantages and disadvantages of either centralised or decentralised solutions to the control problem, only a detailed study in association with experts in government and education could hope to come up with a definitive answer. What must be noted, however, is that availability of sources of financing may themselves influence the decision arrived at. Thus, in the U.K., a failure to reform local taxation and to find new sources of funds for local educational authorities might cause a government to seek a centralised solution when on all other grounds a decentralised one would be right.[11] This consideration is not limited to the problem of recurrent education, but may be specially germane in that case.

Beyond that, a programme of recurrent education will introduce new factors into the labour market, and, if it happens on any kind of large scale, will disrupt all sorts of conventional procedures in collective bargaining, and in hiring and firing. This possibility will itself hold back new developments, especially if the costs of such innovations look very large compared with the benefits at the local level. It is likely, therefore, that any major step forward will require central government involvement, taking the lead in setting out principles of action and offering to meet the initial funding.

The allocation of costs and benefits depends partly on what is regarded as the starting point. Although it is not necessary that there should be a strong connection between recurrent education and decline in employment, we have argued that in practice there will be. Whether or not there will be an acceleration of developments in this field depends to some extent on forecasts of rising unemployment of a structural and chronic kind.[12] If, therefore, the state already accepts responsibility on behalf of its citizens to offset the personal costs of unemployment by social security payments, and to try and use various policy devices to reach full employment, nothing new emerges when it comes to discussing the same sorts of expenditure within the context of recurrent education. This is especially so if it is agreed, as we have suggested, that offering workers this option will change their attitudes towards the introduction of new methods of working and new technology. On grounds of efficiency, of equity (i.e. the displaced workers are in that condition as a result of external forces they cannot control) and of social stability (i.e. workers being reeducated and retrained are less likely to be disruptive and prone to anti-democratic influences), the benefits of recurrent education, while they accrue *ex definitione* to the individual, are sufficiently social in character to justify national financing.

This does not mean that user charges should be ruled out in their entirety but in the development stage of the next decade or so they are surely an irrelevance.

What of another kind of argument, that the workers we are talking about are merely taking up their delayed rights?[13] They could have stayed on at school and proceeded to college and university, but chose not to, because they could not afford it or because they were not ready psychologically. Can they legitimately consider that they are owed certain maintenance grants and some extra education? This subject of educational rights and educational endowment has been widely discussed in recent years. It is clearly political in nature, but does bring into focus the issue of what is a private benefit. Students gain from going to university, but if the state does not finance university education accordingly, why should it apply a different principle to recurrent education?

Apart from the quasi-philosophical point that the distinction between the 'private' and the 'social' is not as clear-cut as the proponents of welfare economics make out (i.e. if we are obliged to regard the 'social' as equivalent to what the state chooses to do, then it is not something which explains what the state does or justifies it), there are two other matters of interpretation of grants and recurrent education to be cleared up. They are concerned with the interpretation of what is meant by 'income' and 'employment'.

Now, many of us, influenced largely by Popper and being devotees of 'positive economics', have allowed ourselves to be persuaded that questions of meaning are extra-scientific, and words can be used within a science in any way we choose. All of this in turn is connected with claims about the value-free nature of economics. While this may be a valid position within the abstractions of philosophy and methodology, it is both incorrect and naive in the real world. Connotation has overwhelming social significance, and actions (including public policy) depend on the words used to describe them.

All this is a prelude to raising the question whether payments to adults undertaking recurrent education ought properly to be described as transfers (and designated either as social security or student maintenance grants) and whether the people themselves should be designated as unemployed. Since 'transfers' are regarded as inferior to 'incomes' and being unemployed is undesirable compared with being employed (no matter how much effort is put into studying and acquiring new skills), the whole of the recurrent education programme will be seen as something acceptable only *faute de mieux*, when the objective of policy is to establish it as something worthwhile in its own right. The use of one terminology rather than another, and the placing of certain activities in one category rather than another, may undermine policy or even prevent the best policy being adopted.[14] (If a programme of recurrent education is adopted, it is reasonable to infer that it will be financed in ways that encourage it to be successful. This means that those who go on such a programme should not lose out, or expect to lose out, in ordinary material terms compared with what otherwise might be the case. It is also suggested that they should suffer no loss of social status.)

It is certainly puzzling that a man attached to a firm is regarded as employed no matter how little work he does while someone else not so attached but studying hard is not employed. The former receives a payment called an income; the latter gets a grant or is on social security. Given the values built into our society, men will tend to prefer to fight for their jobs and their incomes, no matter how wasteful this is, to preserve what they regard as their independence and their dignity. Equally, policy makers may be loth to support a programme which actually enables the economy to work better simply because they are afraid of being soft.[15]

As economists we would define incomes as what is received for valuable economic activity. In a purely market economy we might then be tempted to define a valuable economic activity as whatever is traded across a market.

170

I myself have some doubts about that, but they are irrelevant in a mixed economy where there is no simple test of what is economically valuable other than what various decision makers accept as such. In the private sector this is what people do or would pay for, but in the public sector (which makes a whole variety of transfer payments), economic activity is simply what the government says it is. As far as the financing of recurrent education is concerned, the simple conclusion is that it may vary in difficulty partly in the way it is interpreted and justified. To dismiss such considerations as merely presentational would be a mistake which is not unusual, but is surprising in an economics profession which long ago accepted the subjective theory of value.

In concluding, I am aware that this essay has been much more an exercise in asking questions than answering them. Its main purpose has been to establish the seriousness of the role of public policy, and to argue that, although a financing problem exists, it raises few special problems for recurrent education. In particular, insofar as the subject becomes important because of technical advance and raising productivity, financing should not be thought to be unusually held back by resource constraints. Equally, if recurrent education is simply to be seen as the next stage of social policy (i.e. if nothing specially to do with new developments in the economy), its finance becomes merely a part of general public finance, of who is willing to pay for what.

NOTES

1. By recurrent education I mean education occurring during what is otherwise regarded as working life. I would not myself include work experience within normal schooling or even within higher education (e.g. as part of sandwich degrees or in vocational courses such as medicine and engineering). In addition, it is probably correct to exclude education occurring during working life but not at the expense of actual working; although this does leave the position of housewives somewhat blurred. For an excellent analysis of the economics of training see A. Ziderman (1978).
2. The unionised sector of the U.K. economy is currently equal to 51% of the labour force. It was equal to 42% a decade ago. It should also be recognised that unionisation of public sector employees is much more than that of private sector ones.
3. However else the experience of the 1970s is interpreted, it is difficult to interpret it as favouring the view that the economy has a tendency to move towards full employment, let alone an optimum, in any but the long run, if then.
4. 'Enough has now been said to suggest that one can make out a perfectly good case for State education based on the role of schools in providing a non-legal type of "social control". . . . As we have seen, there is, in fact, no convincing economic case for State ownership of the education industry' (Blaug, 1970: 119-120). '. . . There is no purely economic factor that would justify government operation of schools' (Cohn, 1979: 267).
   Both of these books appear to identify economics with neo-classical economics, and, therefore, to come to the trivial conclusion that anything else is non-economic. See also Ziderman (1978: Chs. 4 and 5). He notes that 'traditionally in Britain the methods of persuasion, dissemination of information and legislation in the realm of industrial training have been preferred to the more overt forms of intervention via direct state finance and

provision of training. However, in more recent years a greater reliance on the latter forms of intervention has been evident' (p. 38).

5. To revert to our earlier remark on definitions, it might be useful to distinguish between recurrent education', but in few if any countries is there yet a recurrent education system. circumstances, and recurrent education as a system and as a set of principles which are recognised explicitly as an integral part of the country's education as a whole. In other words, in almost all countries it is possible to point to something and say 'that is an example of recurrent education', but in few if any countries is there yet a recurrent education system.

6. This is not the place to deal with the question of the origin of preferences, but no discussion of the economics of education can ignore the matter entirely. Within the neo-classical frame-work and its associated welfare economics individual preferences are taken as given. Policies not sensitive to such preferences are defined as paternalist or even dictatorial. It is recognised even then that paradoxes can arise, and that these are exacerbated when preferences vary. But once preferences are dependent on past choices and are to some extent socially determined, their position at the foundation of welfare economics is imperilled. This is not to say that we should go to the other extreme and argue that preferences are irrelevant. It is simply to query whether preferences of the moment, so to speak, are all that are relevant.

7. While his pay may be regarded as a private good quality of working life is more akin to an indivisibility or public good.

8. A serious political question is whether a subject such as recurrent education gets on the agenda for debate, and what broader political issues (e.g. unemployment) it is connected to. Once on the agenda of politics the nature and extent of future development will be determined to some extent by a party-political process. Preferences and what people are willing to pay will be important here, but so will other factors of a less specifically economic nature. The most obvious of these are the need for politicians to be seen to be active, and to be offering solutions to present difficulties.

9. We have already pointed out the significance of producer power in the economy as a whole. Nowhere is it more important than in education where developments such as those discussed here will be welcomed by some teachers but will be regarded as a threat by others. In the U.K. it should be remembered that teachers in secondary schools, the demand for whose services may decline, are not all organised in the same trades unions as teachers in further and higher education.

10. This is partly due to the decline in size of various age groups, but also because expectations of the growth of the non-compulsory sector have been revised downwards.

11. At the present time the government cannot make up its mind whether it favours local autonomy or not. The local authorities have limited powers of revenue raising which central government politicians have been in favour of increasing, but only if they are not exercised, it seems.

12. At the time of writing (1980), forecasts of U.K. adult unemployment for 1981 centre about 2m., i.e. approximately 8.5% of the labour force. For the medium term beyond that there is no consensus, but the most optimistic prediction would be about 6% of the labour force, and many forecasters do not see any significant improvement at all. (It should be recalled that the U.K. method of estimation of unemployment gives a figure which is a whole percentage point less than would be arrived at by (say) the U.S. method.)

13. This is sometimes called 'second chance education', and is associated with paid educational leave. Mark Blaug has pointed out that these considerations have been accepted to some extent in Europe and hardly at all in the U.S.A. His explanation of the difference would depend on differences in the political circumstances of the two parts of the world, and is connected with other aspects of working class behaviour.

14. Presumably, this is why some people have found 'paid educational leave' such an attractive expression.

15. This is one very powerful reason why recurrent education has not advanced as rapidly in the past decade as its importance warranted. A second is the antipathy to public expenditure which has intensified in many countries in that period. This, of course, is paradoxical because over anything but the shortest period an increase in employability and a rise in productivity will make it easier to reduce a fiscal deficit.

REFERENCES

Blaug, M. (1970). *An introduction to the economics of education.* London: Allen Lane/The Penguin Press.

Cohn, E. (1979). *The economics of education.* Cambridge, Mass.: Ballinger.

Peston, M. H. (1972). Public Goods and the public sector. London: Macmillan.

Peston, M. H. (1980). The ratio of public to private expenditure and the relative price effect. *British Review of Economic Issues* 2: 46-51.

Prais, S. J. (1976). *The evolution of giant firms in Britain.* Cambridge: Cambridge University Press.

Ziderman, A. (1978). *Manpower training: Theory and policy.* London: Macmillan.

The role of the state in financing recurrent education: Lessons from European experience

HOWARD GLENNERSTER*

London School of Economics

Abstract

This paper first considers what recurrent education is and what economic case might be made out for the State finance of adult education. The traditional arguments on grounds of efficiency and equity are difficult to sustain but a case can be made out that the imperfections in the present State finance and provision of higher education in Britain discourages a free choice amongst individuals between work, education, leisure and retirement. The second part of the article reviews European development in the finance of recurrent education. The third section draws some policy conclusions for Britain and the United states.

The theme of this paper is that recurrent education will never become a practical proposition until the issue of its finance is more fully debated. Advocates normally take it for granted that the extension of education into adult life should be either provided or financed by the State. Neither on traditional efficiency nor on equity grounds is that proposition at all convincing. A case can be made out for some State involvement.

The major issues, it will be argued, cross the traditional boundaries between discussions of income maintenance and education. What is essentially at stake is the case for widening individuals' capacities to move their income streams through their own lifetimes whether by education or not. At the moment there are significant market imperfections both in the education and social security systems which limit or prejudice individuals' choices. The case for State finance of recurrent education will rest, therefore, not on an attempt to replace one institutional orthodoxy for another, but in devising institutional means for widening the amount of flexibility and control individuals have over their working lives in a profoundly changed labour market. Some European experience provides evidence that some institutional innovations are possible and practical, but individually they do not go far enough to achieve more than a limited set of objectives.

* I would like to express my appreciation for the research assistance provided by Lisa Lynch, a graduate student at the School, and to those who contributed to the discussion at the Boston conference and in later comments, in particular Mark Blaug, C. A. Anderson, David Metcalf and Donald Verry.

173

1. Recurrent education – definitions and rationale

Numerous and frequently vague definitions of recurrent education (RE) are to be found in a wide ranging literature. It and the similar concept of *education permanent* were expounded at international conferences in Europe from the late 1960s. As an OECD report put it in 1973: 'the essence of the recurrent education proposition ... is the distribution of education over the lifespan of the individual in a *recurring* way' (OECD/CERI, 1973).

Beyond that, agreement is limited (Stoikov, 1975; Blaug, 1977). Some advocate postponing higher education for young people, others have seen it merely as a second chance for those who missed out on the first occasion. Some see it as full time formal education, others as involving part time, block or sandwich courses, alternating work and education, others see education in the work place and in the home as natural developments aided by new technology. 'There is a striking lack of consistency in the use of the term over time and between different spokesmen, not only in terms of the indiscriminate use of the various concepts, "recurrent", "permanent", "lifelong", but also in the use of the same concept' (Kallen, 1979).

From an economic point of view, however, the goal is clear enough. It involves spreading educational investment over a lifetime rather than concentrating it, usually full time, in the early stages of life. It is usually taken to involve the granting of rights to educational leave of absence to some or all workers for specified periods and free or subsidised provision. Traditional economic justifications for such a change on grounds of efficiency are difficult to make. If post compulsory education is seen as an investment, the earlier it takes place the better. Stoikov (1975) has shown, on normal rate of return calculations, that the cost of postponing education rizes very sharply with time. Some degree of 'second chance' education could be justified on rate of return grounds. Ziderman (1969) produced evidence of a positive return on adult training in the U.K. The U.S. Post Office has undertaken a series of cost benefit studies on its educational leave programme which suggests a healthy rate of return measured in terms of these employees' higher earnings (OECD, 1978). Leaving aside whether such earnings measures tell us anything about the efficiency of a public monopoly, the existence of a potential rate of return on adult education tells us nothing about who should finance it. If the training is specific and the firm benefits, it should presumably finance it. Insofar as the benefits are general and can be captured by the individual, the first presumption is that he should finance it unless wider social benefits can be identified, and we are back with the normal argument about the finance of higher education.

Nor is the traditional equity case much better. Proponents of RE have argued that the recent expansion of publicly financed higher education has given benefits to the younger generation which the older generations have not

Table 1. Highest qualification gained by economically active population (in %)

Age	20-29	30-39	40-49	50-59	60-69
Men					
Higher education	18	19	13	11	7
Other qualification	48	39	34	28	28
No qualifications	34	42	53	62	65
				50-69	
Women					
Higher education	15	12	10	7	
Other qualifications	48	34	23	17	
No qualifications	37	54	67	76	

Source: OPCS (1979).

shared. This disparity should be evened out in pursuit of intergenerational equity. However, this ignores the question of equity between those who receive public support for higher education and the great majority who do not. The considerations of equity involved in increasing access for the 13 per cent of forty-year-old men who have received higher education up to the comparable figure for twenty-year-old men of 18 per cent are swamped by the equity considerations involved in placing the financial burden of such a move on the 30 per cent of the British population who received *no* State support beyond school and the 50 per cent who received little (see Table 1).

The other equity case often advanced is that greater provision of finance for adults would encourage more disadvantaged students to extend their education and thus help to redress the social class imbalance in entry to further education experienced in all industrialised countries for which we have data. Evidence from existing and varied forms of adult education does not lead us to suppose that such equalisation will occur. Indeed the reverse. Students taking Open University courses have been predominantly middle class, indeed a large proportion already have some higher qualification. In a survey of adult students, two sociologist colleagues at the LSE concluded that such students were from higher status groups and for one reason or another failed to get selected for further education at the first attempt. They were certainly not from deprived groups (Hopper and Osborn, 1975). The universities are, moreover, most concerned to attract students who already have some higher education to give them 'post experience courses'. Merely to extend finance to older students attending conventional forms of higher education is, in short, more likely to extend inequalities of access by social class than the reverse. Recent interest in adults exhibited by education Ministries and institutions of higher education is however entirely consistent with the Niskanen model of bureaucratic and professional self-interest explaining budget strategies (DES, 1978; Niskanen, 1971). Both demographic trends and application rates have

176

Table 2. Higher education in the United Kingdom (in thousands) 1976/77

A. All full time students in universities and on advanced courses in further education	Age of students: Full or part time status				
	18 and under	19-20	21-24	25 and over	Total
Men	32.4	108.0	111.6	58.6	310.6
Women	29.0	90.1	61.8	33.6	214.5
All	61.4	198.1	173.4	92.2	525.1

B. Part time students	Men	Women	Total
Universities	19.9	7.5	27.4
Open University	35.8	25.4	61.2
Further education: Colleges and Polys			
Day	82.6	17.8	100.4
Evening	33.9	6.2	40.1
Total	172.2	56.9	229.1

Source: *Social Trends 1979*.

declined through much of Europe, endangering the maintenance of existing levels of spending and staff employment. The search for an alternative market is entirely understandable, but the self-interest of the academic community is scarcely a good case in equity.

The less traditional case for recurrent education falls into two distinct parts. The first rests on predictions of high levels of unemployment resulting from rapid technical change. It sees education as both a means of retraining and as a way of making 'unemployment' more socially acceptable and boosting effective demand. It is essentially a macro argument and it is elaborated by Peston in the accompanying paper.

I wish to argue that a case can be made out for forms of finance which are more favourable to the recurrent model without recourse to speculation about the future pattern of the economy, though their force is increased if Peston's prognosis proves correct. It might be called the 'free choice case'. It rests on a critique of the 'market imperfections' brought about by the present system of publicly provided and financed systems of higher education and student support which favour the present 'front-loading' model, and limit individual freedom of choice and are inequitable for those who do not benefit at all from such State support. Four kinds of market imperfection can be identified:

1.1 imperfect or biased information available to the young school leaver;
1.2 institutional rigidities and perverse financial incentives that exist in pub-

licly financed educational institutions, combined with an imperfect capital market;

1.3 arbitrary administrative divisions between categories of income maintenance provided by the State which prevent individuals exercising a rational choice between work, education, retirement and leisure;

1.4 social conventions which dictate 'normal behaviour' including time taken off work.

1.1 *Imperfect information*

Children of sixteen have scant information on which to base decisions about further education. We know that the most important variable associated with the wide variations in staying on patterns in British schools is the length of educational experience of their parents (Higher Education, 1963). Teachers and the general ethos of the child's school also affect aspirations for further education. It is recognised in the literature of health economics that one of the distinguishing features of health care is that demand is to a significant extent determined by the suppliers – the professional in whom the diagnostic expertise resides (Alan Maynard, 1979). The General Practitioner is the gatekeeper to all other forms of medical care. A similar though less extreme case of this kind exists, I suggest, in the case of school children faced at the ages of 16 and 18 with major educational choices, largely dependent on the advice of their school teachers. The subjects chosen, the type of institution, the decision to stay on at all, are at that age not personal choices in the full sense. This view makes no *a priori* judgment about the nature of the 'welfare loss' – whether individuals on balance choose 'too much' further education, too little or the 'wrong' kind, it merely suggests that with wider experience and maturity the process would conform more closely to the pure economic model of free choice.

1.2 *Institutional rigidities*

The pattern of institutional finance in the United Kingdom favours the direct school – higher education link. The number of university places which governments have undertaken to finance through direct grants to the institutions reflects the number of qualified school leavers the government wishes to see gain places, and since approved fees have formed a small percentage of total income, the institutions have had no incentive to promote courses designed to meet the needs of mature students. Evening or part time courses are more costly in administrative terms and in inconvenience for teaching staff. With no financial incentives there was no reason in the past why institutions should have adapted to these students' different and more costly demands and they have not done so in the main. Finally, British universities and the polytechnics too are very rigid about the packages they offer. Taking part courses or credits on the U.S. pattern at different times and accumulating a total qualification is rarely possible.

1.3 *Barriers to redistributing income streams through time*

The State is involved in varied forms of income maintenance including that for educational purposes. Each has different eligibility conditions, levels of benefit, and in some cases compulsory contributions. All these systems are essentially ways in which individuals' and families' income streams are redistributed through time but they bear no relation to one another. Official thinking about the interactions between educational maintenance and social security is precluded by administrative boundaries and conventions while individuals' freedom to shift their own incomes through time is restricted. The confusions that arise can best be appreciated with a few examples. It is financially advantageous for a young person to leave school and draw supplementary benefit as an unemployed person rather than to stay and receive a much lower, if any, educational maintenance allowance (Maclure, 1979). Those on training courses for unemployed young people receive more support than those attending as part of their normal education. The State forces individuals to save for retirement either through the state retirement scheme or an equally generous private scheme. It makes no provision for staff saving for educational or other voluntary leave in mid-career. Many of those in semi- or unskilled jobs never enjoy the fruits of this compulsory saving – they die first.

On the other hand, everyone is forced to pay through general taxation for a relatively tiny proportion of the community to delay entering the labour force at the beginning of their careers – a process from which the beneficiaries subsequently benefit further. Discussions of the cost of grants to students – mature or otherwise – rarely include an assessment of the off-setting savings in unemployment benefit that may result. These are merely some of the illogicalities and imperfections of the public sector.

On the other hand, the private capital market provides almost no facilities for taking time off work for education, training or other purposes in the U.K. 'Having a secure job', i.e. salaried, 'with prospects' or some financial assets is usually a precondition for any kind of personal loan.

1.4 *Social and institutional conventions*

Economic theory has little or nothing to say about social conventions. Men and women are individual decision-takers maximising their own welfare. Yet to the sociologist man is a social animal, and organisations have accepted rules and practices that relate only partially to economic factors. In some occupations, leave of absence in mid-career is accepted – indeed favoured – but these are exceptions. In most, I would suggest, such an activity is likely to be treated as rather odd or questionable and given the traditional patterns of hiring and promotions, someone who takes time out in mid-career is likely to lose in career terms or not be hired again very easily.

Conversely individuals and labour unions in the United Kingdom, to a lesser extent in Europe, are extremely reluctant to accept changes in work patterns which involve moving into different *kinds* of job in different *locations* and in different *social* settings. These barriers seem much more important in the older and more closely knit communities of the United Kingdom which does not have the 'frontier traditions' of the U.S.A. Moreover, trade union organisation is stronger and more extensive and can make this resistance effective and hence hold back productivity growth. Education and training for mature students could have the effect of changing old attitudes by widening experience. (Rarely do our mature students wish to return to their old jobs.) Longer education is associated with greater career mobility (Goldthorpe et al., 1979). More education later in people's careers could extend that mobility and hence the flexibility of the labour market. But it is not in the interests of private employers to provide training for those who might leave. It is on grounds such as these that some countries have introduced national legislation giving rights to educational leave following the ILO Convention of 1974. Britain has not done so.

The following section of the paper reviews recent European developments which have been largely ignored in Britain to ascertain what they can tell us about the reasons for State involvement in extending educational experience into adult life.

2. European experience – a significant start or a 'pricked balloon'?

In an article a few years ago Blaug (1977) reviewed progress towards more recurrent forms of education in Europe and concluded there was really very little to be found. It was no more than a 'gigantic political balloon which collapses as soon as it is pricked'. Of course, the more you inflate the balloon the easier it is to deflate and to some extent Blaug does just that by suggesting there is a grandiose RE Master Plan. If the 'movement' is seen instead as a piecemeal process of removing the kind of market imperfections discussed earlier and of finding ways of widening individual choice, we would expect progress to be slow. Moreover, the period he was studying was very short. As he points out, the concept of recurrent education was only put on the map in political terms by the Swedish Education Commission Reports of 1969 and 1970. To expect major changes in six years on an international scale is asking a lot. Most educational reforms in Britain seem to take about 40 to 50 years. A more favourable set of accounts appears in the *1979 World Yearbook of Education* (Schuller and Megarry, 1979) but it is not primarily concerned with financial issues. Our contention is that the reason for the disappointing demand Blaug notes may lie in the imperfections we have noted rather than in an intrinsic lack of interest by adults.

The following survey covers ten European countries and focuses on two related aspects, the rights to educational leave that have been established and such financial arrangements as have been made to pay for leave and education. First, an overview of the main development (summarised in the Annex: Table A1).

Of the ten countries, five have national legislation which covers *both* rights to leave and some kind of finance for leave and training costs. Others have one but not the other, the United Kingdom has neither. In some countries, developments have been mainly through trade union agreements with firms on an industry-wide basis. The Netherlands is an example. Such agreements also supplement national legislation. In virtually every case where finance is made available it relates to courses of vocational training relevant to the particular occupation or industry, or it relates to re-training in cases of redundancy, but there are wider social purposes in some cases and that trend has increased.

Blaug suggests that a combination of rights to educational leave, entitlement to payment while on leave and free education would produce a vast explosion in educational costs which no government could contemplate. Yet as European experience shows governments, employers and trade unions have devised rules about entitlements, types of course and limits to expenditure that have kept costs within reasonable bounds. The U.K. has remained aloof from even these changes. In the U.K. it is rather *more* innovation that is needed at this point, rather than more scepticism.

Belgium

Under the Law of Credit Hours 1973, participants in vocational training have the right to be absent from work on full pay. The costs are borne by the State and the employer on a 50/50 basis, but the government imposes strict controls, first on the courses it designates for inclusion in the scheme. These must be recognised, created or supported by the Department of National Education. Second, there are personal conditions of eligibility – workers must be under 40 if courses are undertaken in the day, and evening and weekend courses had to have been successfully pursued for a year. There is a maximum and minimum number of hours that can be spent attending courses and, finally, there are limits to the monthly sums paid out per worker. In the early years these controls were all too successful and demand was disappointingly small. In the first year after the law was introduced only 0.4 per cent of the total work force participated, or 10 per cent of those eligible. It has subsequently been extended to cover agricultural workers, the self-employed, first year students and employees following courses for the improvement of specific skills. Numbers on the course have risen and the rules have been regularly amended by ministerial order. The last order dates from April 1979 (*Moniteur belge*, 20.9.79). It lays down fairly detailed guidance on the content of permitted courses in 'general' education.

Belgian experience does suggest a number of administrative lessons: (a) Rationing total demand by eligibility and course criteria is perfectly feasible. (b) The Social Security system can be used as a vehicle for the funding. Employers pay 2 per cent of their total salary bill to fund the scheme and this is collected by the Department of Social Security and put in a separate account to which the State also contributes.

Denmark

No general rights to work absence exist in Denmark but some interesting precedents do emerge from the scheme of vocational training. Those who do not possess a recognised skill or are semi-skilled and attend training centres as well as those who are up-dating or improving on a recognised trade qualification, are paid out of government funds at a rate equivalent to 125 per cent of unemployment benefit (OECD, 1976). This is in itself fairly generous (about £7000 per annum in 1979). Thus the level of 'education benefit' is roughly equivalent to the average wage. The majority of those who benefit from this system are the semi-skilled (public employees are in a separate more generous scheme). Thus the Danes have accepted the logic of integrating educational benefit levels with unemployment pay. Moreover, they believe generous unemployment benefit rates are likely to increase labour mobility and prevent social and family disruption (Discussion with Danish official).

France

France has gone further than other European countries in introducing a national scheme of 'continuous' vocational training which includes rights to leave and financial compensation. This befits the country which is most associated with the Faure Report (UNESCO, 1972). A major impetus seems to have been the 1968 crisis and the agreements made with the trade unions in May 1968. The discussions that were initiated then led to the Bipartite Agreements of 9th July 1970 to the Law of July 1971 and to important modifications to that Law in 1976 and 1978. These were built on legislation which had created a Fund for Vocational Training and Social Mobility in 1966 and the Law of 1968 which established the right of workers to take unpaid leave for up to a year. The combined effect of over ten years gradual development is now considerable, and illustrates the effect of 'organic growth', spiced with some traditional French militancy. The essence of these laws is that employed workers have rights to leave of absence from work for periods of up to one year or 1200 hours on a part time course. Longer courses for special categories of employees are possible. The 1978 legislation designated six kinds of activity to which these rights applied: these related to change of employment and retraining, preparation for work, promotion, refresher training, initial training of young people who have no job, and general training and education for citizenship. The last was an extension of previous practice. If the training is approved by the State or local employer – trade union committees – the employer pays the worker his previous wage and part can be recovered from the government. In other cases the benefit is equivalent to the National Guaranteed Income. There are limits to the number of people who can be absent from a firm – usually 2 per cent of the labour force. Before the new law, few workers entered courses on their own initiative as opposed to those organised by employers – only about 60,000 in 1976 of which about half received paid leave (Schuller and Megarry, 1979). Categories who have been given rights include particularly needy groups, for example: those wishing to change their jobs or who have been made redundant; young people receiving unemployment benefit; mothers, single or separated women who wish to return to work and those facing redundancy.

In 1978 contributions paid by employers amounted on average to 1.1 per cent of their wage bill. (0.7 per cent payroll tax for employers of 10-19 people, 2.5 per cent for firms of 2,000 plus.) This is the sum every firm (at least those with more than 10 employees) had to spend on continuous training. This obligation could be discharged in four ways: (i) by making a contribution to the State; (ii) by training their own workers; (iii) by contributing to a training insurance fund; (iv) or by contributing to training associations run by employers' organisations.

The French case shows that a national scheme of entitlements is feasible, though it can be extremely bureaucratic. Its rationale is primarily that of increasing labour mobility but it is directed at disadvantaged groups.

Federal Republic of Germany

The Federal Republic has been more innovative in removing the institutional barriers to mature entrants than in legislation about leave or finance (Blaug, 1977). Some of the German states (*Länder*) have promoted correspondence and television courses not unlike the British Open University. The *Volkshochschulen* are local adult education centres quite distinct from technical or professional training.

There are two interesting precedents worth noting in the *Labour Market Promotion Act 1969*. Eligibility for assistance depends on having a full contribution record in the unemployment insurance scheme, and the course must be 'relevant to labour market policy' as well as to the individual's aptitude. These are very rough criteria and the whole scheme is administered by an independent public corporation – the Federal Administration of Labour Agency. This agency is financed by equal contributions from employers and employees – 1 per cent earnings from each. In some cases assistance takes the form of loans.

Some individual *Länder* have gone further in granting rights to leave of absence more generally, though for fairly short periods, typically between 5 and 10 working days a year and only for young workers – under 25. What is interesting is that rights to leave are for political education as well as vocational and in some cases general education.

Italy

Like France the 'troubles' of 1968 and trade union pressure seem to have acted as a catalyst for study leave proposals. Despite the existence of a national law (No. 300, 1970) which gives a general right to 'worker-students' that allows them to follow their courses, the detailed entitlements have been negotiated on an industry by industry basis. Engineering has been the pace-setter and pattern for many that have followed. Each firm agrees to provide up to a certain total number of 'credit hours' which are calculated according to the number of people it employs. The maximum benefit is 150 hours over 3 years for any one person, and no more than 2 per cent of the work force can be away simultaneously. Courses are organised in the afternoons and evenings. In 1974 the average duration was 350-400 hours. Of this 150 hours were the responsibility of the employer and were paid at normal salary levels. The determination of the appropriateness of the courses lies with the unions and their guiding principle is that the courses must add to the workers' culture – to ensure basic educational standards had been reached by all workers, to increase workers' capacities to control the processes of production and a series of strongly political objectives.

In the early stages very few workers were involved, but the numbers began to increase in the mid 1970s. The number of workers on courses financed by the Ministry of Education rose from 14,000 to 77,000 between 1974 and 1976. The major restraint appears to be the availability of publicly provided courses (OECD, 1978).

The Netherlands

Collective agreements between employers and trade unions which cover larger enterprises are really the only form of regularised provision in the Netherlands. Moreover, these are very limited. They are primarily concerned with short courses for members of the new works councils preparing them for their roles as workers representatives. A very small pay roll levy is exacted (.014 per cent) added to by the central government who finance two thirds of the educational costs while employers pay for loss of income and travelling expenses (OECD, 1976). Some agreements also cover leave for professional examinations and occupational training. One of the striking features of the Dutch situation has been the wide variety of institutions providing vocational and general education, including correspondence and TV and radio. A report published in 1974 suggested a combined participation of 1.2 million adults. (Total adult population 10 million.)

In 1975 the P.E.N. Commission was given the task of recommending ways of coordinating these varied activities and as a result in 1976 local munici-palities were encouraged to review the needs for adult education in their areas compared with existing provisions and set out a plan for extended and coordinated provision which could form the basis of a bid for funds from the government – 90 per cent grant for teaching and 50 per cent of other costs.

The Open School Commission is experimenting with so-called 'multi-media' courses for under-privileged groups in Dutch society.

Norway

Original government initiatives in Norway date back to the mid-1960s, but the Adult Education Act of 1976 only became effective in August 1977. The Act is concerned with the finance of educational provision and not leave, but the range of courses subsidised or fully financed by government is interesting.

  i) 'Fundamental' or basic education up to secondary level provided for adults – a catching-up process designed to ensure a basic subsistence level of competence required for full citizenship.
 ii) Vocational training provided as part of general labour market policy.
iii) Vocational training given as part of a company's training programme, but involving more general training and external instruction.
 iv) Other education and short courses reflecting the individual's own needs. The costs of instruction and travel to be provided by the State at various administrative levels.

Rights to leave are left to negotiation between trade unions and employers, but the National Basic Agreement encourages such local agreements.

Sweden

Sweden has taken a lead in promoting recurrent education. It was a Swedish Commission which popularised the idea and it has pressed ahead in a cautious way with implementation. In his article Blaug (1977) argued that to give both rights to education leave and to finance it in an open ended way could 'guarantee a run-away inflation of education expenditure', and that was why Sweden had not done both. The Swedes have now managed to finance adult leave within careful limits without falling into the trap Blaug envisaged. From 1975 every worker has the right to unlimited educational leave, though the employer has the right to postpone it for up to six months. In the same year a new system of adult grants was introduced on top of the existing scheme which gives repayable grants to students over 20. The adult grants are of three kinds: for full time study lasting at least a month, for time off work paid on an hourly basis for those in study circles arranged with the help of trade unions in factories and work places, and compensation for short courses. Once again a rationing system operates. There is an annual budget and local education boards decide how to allocate the limited funds. Priority is given to those with low educational qualification or those who live in remote areas or have difficult working hours. A payroll tax was introduced in 1976 to pay for this provision. It began at 0.15 per cent of the payroll and was subsequently raised to 0.25 per cent.

Yugoslavia

Yugoslavia has the longest tradition of recurrent education as we know it today, which dates back to the General Law on Education in 1950 and subsequent statutes and resolutions. Once again Blaug is dismissive of its achievements. There is now, in theory, provision for reduction in daily working hours to attend courses of up to 4 hours a day, with salary at the level of average personal incomes, paid leave for longer periods on full pay, paid leave for taking examinations and much else, including travelling expenses and free books (OECD, 1976). The local works councils decide on who shall be given leave and for what purposes. Courses are almost always work related. My source of information is no different from Blaug's, but again there seems some reason to query his final conclusion: 'Yugoslavian evidence begins to sow seeds of doubt about the magnitude of potential demand for formal study among adult, even when it costs them virtually nothing but leisure time foregone.' This follows the observation that 'about 530,000, or 12 per cent enroll annually for various forms of education and training.' Without wishing to accept Yugoslavian statistics without question a number of points could be made:

First, 12 per cent could be seen as quite a substantial proportion of the workforce to take advantage of education leave in any one year.

Second, the 1972 survey of enterprises claims that on average 27 per cent of the employees of enterprises involved in the schemes enrolled.

Third, it is not up to the individual alone whether he enrolls. He or she must seek the permission of his working colleagues. It would seem quite reasonable for right of absence to be rationed fairly strictly by those who remain at the workbench as it is by academics in Britain and America.

The United Kingdom

The U.K. has not participated in the movements we have described on the Continent. There is no legislation on rights to leave of absence and no financial arrangements except those introduced to provide courses for unemployed young people in recent years. These were both temporary and almost entirely an emergency response to high levels of unemployment amongst young people. But the U.K. does have a long tradition of part time, especially evening, course provision for working people and a fairly comprehensive statutory duty laid on local authorities to provide educational facilities for adults, under the 1944 Education Act (Section 41). Local Education Authorities (LEA's) have a duty to provide for full and part time study for those over 16, and 'organised cultural training and recreation'. Major providers are evening institutes run by LEA's, using existing school premises and part time teachers. Students pay fees that range widely between local areas. Nearly 1.5 million adults attend such classes. They are informally run and are remarkably responsive to local and minority demands – not at all far from Illich's ideals in many ways. They are not vocational and do not lead to formal qualifications.

Further Education colleges are also run by LEA's to provide vocational and professional education for adults, again fees are charged but they are well below cost except in the case of courses run for the Industrial Training Boards (see below). Universities, through their extra-mural departments, provide some evening courses for adults outside the normal range of degree courses. Similarly, and often in conjunction, a voluntary body, the Workers' Educational Association, provides courses especially geared to trade unionists, or other groups of working people. The numbers involved are fairly small, about 400 part time tutors are employed in the whole country. Voluntary organisations have also run a successful adult literacy programme funded by Government.

The Open University, only a decade old, is a major innovation in providing part time education. It is financed directly by the central Department of Education and Science. It provides mainly undergraduate courses by correspondence with the aid of television and radio and has over 60,000 students. Fees again only cover part of the cost. This institution has been remarkably successful in combining technical innovation with high academic standards over most of its courses. It has been less successful in attracting the disadvantaged student, but the technical potential for home based learning in the next 20 years must be enormous.

Full time undergraduates at ordinary British universities are supported in two ways. Under the 1962 and 1975 Education Acts a local authority must provide awards to all those students who are admitted to first degree courses in an approved institution. Their fees are paid whatever the parents' income and their maintenance and living costs are met up to a maximum level depending on whether they are living at home and according to their parents' income. The 'generosity' for this group is in marked contrast to the minimal grants made to low income families who have children staying on at school beyond the age of 16. Most of these in fact leave school and never enter higher education.

Technical courses for those at work are organised through a series of Industrial Training Boards, one for each industry. They levy a rate of up to 1 per cent of the pay roll of firms for this purpose, but only a small minority of young workers gain day release for study.

Despite this wide range of voluntary organisation and statutory bodies responsible for provision, there is no legislation either covering legal rights to educational leave or its finance. Even very modest proposals made by the Russell Committee (1973) to extend Government support have been ignored. In short, Britain has been successful in innovating forms of part time provision, but, perhaps partly for this reason, there has been little attention devoted – notably by the trade unions – to paid leave of absence for education. This is in sharp contrast to their European counterparts who have been the initiators in most instances. Moreover, the financial climate suggests that additional public money for such a venture is now highly unlikely.

Some observations

This brief review of European practice does suggest that primary goal has been the pursuit of labour market mobility. The nature of the courses has been closely controlled though there has been an attempt to channel the available funds to particularly needy groups. A growing element has been the education of worker representatives for various participative arrangements in industry. These developments have not brought an explosion of education spending but on the other hand their impact has been limited. Some links with the social security system have begun to emerge but there has been no real breakthrough that would enable ordinary people to shift their incomes through time for reasons other than unemployment, sickness or old age. No incentives have been introduced for young people to put off entering for their education.

European experience has only conformed to some of the criteria advanced in Section 1 of this paper. What elements would constitute a full realisation?

2. Principles for financing recurrent education in the United Kingdom

2.1 *Remove the perverse incentives for teenagers*

The State gives more financial support to teenagers out of work than to those following courses of full time education. It gives far more generous support to those taking first degree courses than to those on courses that lead to higher education. In response to public expenditure constraints student support has fallen in value compared to alternative earnings. As the opportunity cost of higher education has risen, the already internationally very low rates for students staying on to gain university entrance qualifications have fallen still further. No other form of finance, e.g. loans, has been introduced to compensate. The gap between the proportion of entrants from working class and non-manual homes has widened (Verry, 1977).

Financial assistance for those in study up to the age of twenty should be merged with the income maintenance system. Students not in full time employment would have the right to draw supplementary benefit in their own right either by registering for work or by regular attendance at an approved educational establishment. Students in full time employment would have a right to release from work on full pay for one day a week or for such longer periods as the Training Boards agreed.

2.2 *Relate assistance to previous or alternative earnings levels*

At present a student who has gained a place on a first degree course has the right to a means-tested maintenance grant based on parental means, and free tuition. Only some other courses carry such grants. The size of the grant does not increase with age, until he or she is 26, yet average earnings rise fast during this period. Financial assistance could be extended to a much wider range of courses, part time or full time. The level of assistance could be linked either to some ratio of the average earnings of the age group up to 26, or to the previous earnings of the student after 26. This would avoid the financial penalty students suffer if they postpone entry to higher education and make educational leave feasible for adults. However, in practical terms, such a move would be impossible unless it were accompanied by repayment provisions.

2.3 *A 'graduate' tax*

The debate about loans needs no repeating. In addition to the disincentive problems more recent experience in the United States suggests that practical problems of default may be more difficult than originally envisaged. The 'graduate' tax, levied through the normal income tax system, could recover the cost of financial assistance given to students on any kind of course under 2.2

above. Either the full cost or a portion of it could be recovered as in Sweden, and an interest rate charged. The practical problems have been discussed elsewhere (Glennerster, 1968; Verry, 1977). If Government wished to waive repayments from particular deprived groups or for courses of particular kinds, it would be possible to do so, but it would carry dangers.

2.4 *Rights to leave*

Such provisions for financing leave would have to be combined with legislation to retain one's job on the continental model.

2.5 *Encouraging institutional responsiveness*

Institutions should be presented with greater incentives to adapt to the needs of mature or part time students. Grants could include the cost of fees or could in part consist of a form of education voucher cashed on attendance at approved courses.

In brief

It is thus possible to envisage a major overhaul of student finance which would go some way to make possible the ideals of recurrent education. Progress has been slow but the labour market changes that are in prospect should surely urge some urgency in contemplating some innovations.

ANNEX

Table A1. European schemes of educational leave and its finance

Country	Right to leave				Finance			
	Legal status	Nature of leave	Way in which leave is taken	Major legislation	Legal status	Nature of finance	Who pays	How money is raised
Belgium	National legislation	Vocational, general education for economic, social and cultural mobility	Credit hours: can be during working hours	The Law of Credit Hours (1973)	National legislation	Employers and State contribute. Employee paid by employer during credit hours. Employer reimbursed	50% State, 50% employers	2% of total salary bill from employer and contributions from State
Denmark	None	Vocational training, apprentices and retraining	1) Apprentices: 4 years max. 2) Vocational training: a) 2-3 weeks during the day (semi-skilled), skilled 1-4 weeks b) retraining: 10-30 weeks	None	None	1) Apprentices: employer maintains remuneration and pays the school costs 2) Vocational training: max. remuneration is 125% of unemployment compensation 3) Retraining: support from firm and State	1) Apprentices: employer 2) Retraining: State and employer	
France	National legislation	Vocational and social mobility, training, retraining and personal development	Up to 1 yr. or 1,200 hrs. part time	The Law of 16 July 1971	National legislation	Employers' duty to allocate funds for training as a proportion of the wage bill	Firms and the State for certain priority groups	General funds from State and from wage bill (1.1% on average 1978)

F. R. Germany	Collective agreements and certain legislation recognising the right to educational leave of absence	Vocational: some national and broader coverage in the *Länder*		1) Vocational Training Act 1969 2) Labour Market Promotion Act 1969	Collective agreements	1) In *Länder*, preferred method is for employers to continue paying wages 2) Educational Promotion and Assistance Act – finance out of public funds 3) Labour Market Promotion Act – equal contributions from employers and employees		1) General tax 2) Equal contribution from employer
Italy	National legislation and collective agreements	1) Worker-students have right to education leave 2) Max. credit of 150 hrs. for 3 yrs.		1) Worker-student collective agreements of 69-70 and law 300, May 1970 2) 1973 engineering industry agreements	Legislation and collective agreements for: 1) Worker-students 2) The right to study	**Right of study – paid** leave of absence	**Right of study:** 1) Employer provides wages during leave 2) State provides for cost of training 3) Region may provide materials or subsidies	State – general funds
The Netherlands	None (collective agreements but limited), public employees agreements	Some leave: for young workers and members of Workers' Councils	5-day course for those on Workers' Councils under collective agreements; time off for professional exams; public employees 26 days per year; work related	None	None	Public employees salaries maintained	Government ⅔ and Works Councils ⅓	Works Councils .014% levy on payroll
Norway	None, but 'Basic Agreement' between national unions and employers refers to educational leave	–	–	The Norwegian Adult Education Act passed in May 1976, effective 1 August 1977, provides education for a range of adult needs, *not* leave	–			

Table A1 (continued). European schemes of educational leave and its finance

	Right to leave				Finance			
Country	Legal status	Nature of leave	Way in which leave is taken	Major legislation	Legal status	Nature of finance	Who pays	How money is raised
Sweden	National legislation effective January 1975	General vocational and trade union	Right to leave during working hours	December 1974 law passed on educational leave of absence	National legislation Labour Market Board	1) On-job grants for those facing discharge 2) Training in shortage skills 3) Grants to those unemployed. A bonus on top of unemployment pay	Government	Costs of adult educational programmes paid for by a payroll tax of 0.15% in 1976 which has been raised to 0.25%
Yugoslavia	Legislation	Vocational, general (socio-economic education)	Reduction of working hrs. 1-4 hrs. daily with full salary: self-management bodies decide which individuals should benefit	1) The General Law on education (1950) 2) The Resolution on Vocational Education (1960) 3) Resolutions of the Federal Assembly (1970)	Legislation	Travel expenses, salary, text-books, assistance in taking care of children paid by communities and enterprises	Community pays for pre-school and elementary education	Contribution from everyone who is employed out of his personal income at a rate determined by the assembly of the community
United Kingdom	None	—	—	1944 Education Act	Varied local provision; further and adult education; Open University	Provision subsidised	Central Government grants, local rates, fees. Central Government, fees	

REFERENCES

Blaug, M., and Mace, J. (1977). Recurrent education – the new Jerusalem. *Higher Education* 6: 277-299.

DES. (1978). *Higher education in the 1990s*. London: HMSO.

Glennerster, H., et al. (1968). A graduate tax. *Higher Educational Review* 1(1): 26-38.

Goldthorpe, J. H., et al. (1979). *Social mobility and class structure in modern Britain*. Oxford: Oxford University Press.

Hopper, E., and Osborn, M. (1975). *Adult students: Education selection and social control*. London: F. Pinter.

Kallen, D. P. B. (1975). The economic and financial implications of recurrent education – a critical comment. *Studies in Adult Education* 7(2): 101-116.

Kallen, D. P. B. (1979). Definitions and distinctions. In T. Schuller and J. Megarry (Eds.), *Recurrent education and lifelong learning: World yearbook of education 1979*. London: Kogan.

Levin, H. (1977). Financing recurrent education with post compulsory entitlements. Paris: OECD/CERI.

Maynard, A. (1979). Pricing, insurance and the NHS. *Journal of Social Policy* 8(2): 157-176.

Maclure, S. (1979). Financial support for the 16-18s. *Educational Policy Bulletin* 7(1): 99-124.

Niskanen, W. (1971). *Bureaucracy and representative government*. Chicago: Aldine-Atherton.

OECD/CERI. (1973). *Recurrent education: A strategy for lifelong learning*. Paris.

OECD/CERI. (1976). *Development in educational leave of absence*. Paris.

OECD/CERI. (1977). *Meeting of national delegates on developments in recurrent education*. Paris. (i) Secretariat's synthesis; (ii) Case studies: Belgium, Denmark, France (training, insurance funds and the educational district of Dijon), Netherlands, Norway and Sweden.

OECD/CERI. (1978). *Alternative between work and education: A study of educational leave of absence at enterprise level*. Paris.

OPCS. (1979). *General household survey*. London: HMSO.

Russell Report. (1973). *Adult education*. London: Department of Education/HMSO.

Schwartz, B. (1974). *Permanent education*. The Hague: Martinus Nijhoff.

Schuller, T., and Megarry, J. (Eds.) (1979). *Recurrent education and lifelong learning: World yearbook of education 1979*. London: Kogan.

Stoikov, V. (1975). *The economics of recurrent education and training*. Geneva: ILO.

Tobin, J., and Ross, L. (1969). A national youth endowment. *The New Republic*, May 3, 1969.

UNESCO. (1972). *Lifelong education in a changing world*. Paris.

Verry, D. (1977). Some distributional and equity aspects of the student loans debate. *Education, equity and income distribution*. Open University course E.D. 322, Block 5, Open University Press, Milton Keynes.

Ziderman, A. (1969). Costs and benefits of adult retraining in the U.K. *Economica* xxxvi (144): 363-376.

Comments on M. Peston and H. Glennerster

MARK BLAUG

University of London Institute of Education

Both of these papers seem to me to suffer from inadequate definition of the portmanteau term 'RE', although Peston is more guilty than is Glennerster. For all practical purposes, RE may be defined as any formally organized, post-compulsory system of alternating periods of studying and periods of working – the words are carefully chosen and no qualifications are necessary. RE may be provided full-time or part-time, for long or for short periods, for vocational or for cultural reasons, and by educational institutions, governments, employers, unions, or any other body – none of these features are critical in distinguishing RE from standard educational and training programmes. On the other hand, RE *excludes* apprenticeship schemes and on-the-job (but not off-the-job) training, as well as adult education of the traditional type, either because these are nor formally organized or because they do not involve alternation of learning and earning. It has proved useful to further distinguish two main components of RE, namely (1) *postponement* of post-compulsory schooling and (2) *second-chance* education for adults; in the first case we educate individuals at a later rather than an earlier age, whereas in the second case we educate older individuals who would never have been educated at all under present arrangements.

RE in any one of the senses defined above has had a somewhat chequered career since its inception around 1970, or thereabouts. No country in the world has yet succeeded in *postponing* either secondary or higher education to a later stage in life for anything but an extremely limited number of students. And as for *second-chance* education for adults, the concept of paid educational leave (PEL) that would underwrite second-chance opportunities has been everywhere circumscribed by extremely limited financial aid and by specific directives that confine the leave to vocational updating or retraining.

This defines the question to which Peston and Glennerster's papers are addressed. If fiscal, demographic and labour force trends, as well as a rising concern with the equity implications of educational policies, make RE imperative around the world, as they both claim, why is so little happening on the RE front?

Of all the variations on the RE theme, the one that is easiest to justify on grounds of both economic and educational efficiency is that of postponing full-time higher and possibly upper secondary education by one, two or even three years. Applying conventional cost-benefit analysis to the age-earnings profiles that are generated by the present 'front-end' model of sequential education, Stoikov has shown that a postponement of full-time post-compulsory education of up to three years, although costly, is justifiable in terms of the social and private rate of return on educational investment. But this is not RE proper because it leaves out the element of alternating learning and earning. On the other hand, postponement of formal education simultaneous with its conversion from full-time to part-time (the true RE model) cannot be justified on strict efficiency grounds for periods longer than three years.

Breaking out of the mould of cost-benefit analysis and introducing considerations of the deterioriation and absolescence of knowledge with age does not substantially alter these conclusions. On balance, if the postponed learning in question is at all formal and general, the advantage will always be with those who have had a sound basic education not too long ago; the benefits of RE are greater if it is concentrated on the young who have left formal education recently and who have received sufficient 'preventive' education of a basic kind to benefit from 'curative' RE of the up-dating, retraining type at a later age.

But if there are efficiency arguments for the postponement of post-compulsory education for up to two to three years, the fact remains that mere postponement by a few years will not touch the equity problem of the intrageneration gap in educational provision between social classes, not to mention the intergeneration gap in provision between youths and adults. No doubt, this accounts for the fact that advocates of RE have laid far more emphasis on the *second-chance* version of RE than on the *postponement* version.

The potential for a move towards *postponement* is much greater in America than it is in Europe if only because labour markets in America are more flexibly organized to absorb youngsters in part-time and temporary employment. Besides, the mix of public and private institutions in the American system of higher education makes it easier to break down resistance to a reform of admission policies which would be required to give effect to postponement. All of which is to say that America is likely to lead Europe in introducing the *postponement* version of RE on a significant scale. It is curious that the very opposite statement holds for the *second-chance* version of RE.

This brings us squarely to the second-chance issue or PEL. It is not easy to explain why PEL has caught on in Europe but not in the United States (despite the Manpower Development and Training Act of the 1960s). Perhaps it has something to do with the phenomenon of 'industrial democracy'. In America, workers' participation in the running of business enterprises has been a demand of the radical left, which has so far received little practical implementation and certainly no official endorsement. In Germany and Sweden, on the other hand, there has been a considerable growth of management training courses for workers on leave of absence with full pay as a result of workers' participation both in the faily management of plants and the strategic management of multiplant firms. Similar developments appear to be around the corner in Britain and in general it is clear that industrial democracy and PEL will grow hand-in-hand in Europe in the years to come. Now, why the battle for workers' participation should, so to speak, have been won in Europe, whereas it has not yet been fought in the United States, is a nice question. It is more or less the same question as why European workers are more militant, more class-conscious, and more job-security conscious than American workers, and the answer to that question would take us far afield from our present concerns. Suffice it to say that it has everything to do with the presence of PEL in Europe and the virtual absence of PEL in America.

It could of course be argued that paid educational leave is one of those demands for 'rights' of workers that is more inspired by the class ideology of trade unions than by the felt needs of individual workers. Even in Europe, there has been no massive expansion of adult education as a result of PEL, and in this sense it may be that the lack of PEL in America is simply a reflection of the pragmatic attitudes of American trade union leaders; they are not excited by PEL because there is no demand for it at the grassroots. This raises the central question of demand for RE to which we now turn.

The experience with adult education around the world demonstrates that the demand for adult education is a demand for 'recreation' on the part of the middle classes; there is absolutely no evidence of any burning demand on the part of adult workers for formal education of either the short-cycle or long-cycle variety.

Perhaps this is not surprising since most adult education is either based on or deeply influenced by the single-discipline curriculum and the examination-ridden teaching methods that have been developed in school systems geared to younger age groups. In other words, the character of adult education is more determined by the nature of its supply than by the nature of its demand. After examining six case studies of actual PEL programmes in the United States, Stanley Nollen (1978) concluded that there is indeed a demand for adult education among American workers, but only if (1) there are clear links between the courses taken up and the chances for upward mobility within the firm; if (2) there are substantial quantities of relevant educational inputs; and if (3) both employers and unions play an active role in the creation of the programme. But these ifs begin to suggest what is the problem in assessing the demand for PEL. If PEL is career-oriented, vocational, firm-specific in motivation and short-term, with the workers in question wholly or partly selected by employers, it comes close to being in-service training. Now, it has never been denied that there is a demand for in-service training. The difficulty is that the advocates of RE have had a somewhat different model in mind – namely, PEL for cultural reasons (general training over the longer term amounting to extended full-time study) as the right of all workers without pre-selection by employers. What may be questioned in whether there is much demand for this sort of PEL.

Taking all the arguments together, I see a very slow growth of RE in the decades to come, the postponement version coming faster in the United States than elsewhere, with Europe pointing the way in respect of the second-chance version. The critical factor will be equity rather than efficiency questions and the outstanding equity question will be, not the unequal distribution of formal education between the young and the old, but rather the unequal distribution of formal education between advantaged and disadvantaged groups in the community; there is now deep disillusionment with the notion that a fair start in the race, as embodied in the concept of equality of opportunity in sequential education, serves to equalize the life chances of individuals. Loans, grants, and 'entitlements' will radically transform the time-scale of the coming of RE but even without financial support to individuals to enable them to take up post-compulsory education in recurring phases alternating with periods of work, there will be more and more postponement and more and more drawing of mature students into institutions of higher education.

It is easy to sketch the coming of this 'brave new world' but it is appallingly difficult to specify its outline in concrete terms. RE is an island of aspirations entirely surrounded by a sea of ignorance. It is difficult even now to add much to Selma Mushkin's deeply pessimistic research agenda for RE, penned over five years ago (1974). We know next to nothing about the real demand of workers for education and training. We are equally in the dark about alternative methods of producing different kinds of knowledge and skills that would make less use of expensive plants and expensive educators than do current systems. We fancy that most RE programmes for adults are badly designed, but that is not to say that we know how they ought to be designed, nor even whether they should be located at the work site or in separate classrooms. We are not even sure that RE would solve the equity problem; it is perfectly conceivable that the educationally and socially privileged would take advantage of RE opportunities in adult education as they have taken advantage of practically every other free social service in modern times.

In the circumstances, support for RE must rest largely on faith. In the meanwhile, we need to monitor every experience with the elements of RE wherever they occur, be they postponement, PEL, or manpower training schemes. Community colleges in the United States, colleges of further education in the United Kingdom, PEL in France, and the substitution of work experience for secondary school qualifications in Sweden and Germany are obvious examples. In this way, what has been a faith may gradually become a substantive argument fortified by empirical evidence.

REFERENCES

Nollen, S. S. (1978). Paid educational leave: New element in firm-level manpower policy. Proceedings of the 30th Annual Winter Meeting of the Industrial Relations Research Association. Madison, Wisc.: IRRA.
Mushkin, S. J. (Ed.) (1974). *Recurrent education.* Washington, D.C.: Government Printing Office. 295-319.
Stoikov, V. (1975). *The economics of recurrent education and training.* Geneva: ILO.

Comments on H. Glennerster

E. G. WEST

Carleton University

The organizers of this conference obviously intended to promote discussion on education from a new angle, judging by the Conference's title 'Collective Choice in Education.' Actual discussion tended, however, to wander away from this theme into the English tradition of Benthamite utilitarianism and idealized objectives for government policy to the neglect of institutional structure. One of the best examples of the tension between a public choice approach and an older, 'institutionally innocent' welfare approach may be found in the paper by Howard Glennerster.

Glennerster's paper is tantalizing because institutional reality is first recognized but is then left to one side. He explains that the Department of Education in England shows an enthusiasm for Recurrent Education that is 'entirely consistent with the Niskanen model of bureaucratic and professional self-interest explaining budget strategies.' He also recognizes that adult students are typically middle class. He then argues that (what he calls) the academic self-interest model does not provide a justification for extending State funding of recurrent education; surely all must agree. The purpose of the bureaucratic model is that of positive economics – to predict events in the real world. There is no normative implication here. At the same time, one would expect that any future normative work should be informed by the findings of such positive economic research. Instead, Glennerster, like Peston, proceeds as if he had access to his own benevolent government structure constantly ready to obey his personal wishes. His argument returns to the age-old emphasis on imperfections in the market.

It used to be commonly believed that all one had to do, to make out a case for a new government policy, was to demonstrate market imperfection (in the area of one's interest). To the extent the new public choice discipline has established a new theory of 'government failure', the task is no longer so easy. Public choice discipline has also emphasized that a market cannot exist independently of 'public intervention' in the sense of providing a well-designed set of property rights, legal framework, and policing system. Accordingly, what is often believed to be a *market* imperfection is an imperfection in the design of such property rights and legal frameworks.

It is interesting that the market imperfections listed by Glennerster invariably stem from impediments generated from the *public* sector. Consider, for instance, the second in his list: institutional rigidities. The main rigidity, he argues, is that the present institutions of higher education have had no incentive to promote courses designed to meet the needs of mature students because approved fees have formed only a small percentage of total income of the universities and colleges. 'With no financial incentives there was no reason in the past why institutions should have adapted to these students' different and more costly demands and they have not done so in the main.' Yet the reason for the absence of financial incentives is surely the system of public intervention that prevents it. And, in any case, the logic of this argument is to re-establish fees as a significant percentage of total income in order to provide the incentives required. Yet Glennerster does not draw this conclusion.

Glennerster's third illustration of market imperfections is what he calls barriers to redistributing income streams through time. As an example of this he observes that it is financially advantageous for a young person to leave school and draw supplementary benefit as an unemployed person rather than to stay and receive a much lower, if any, educational maintenance allowance. Again this is surely not a *market* imperfection but a consequence of publicly provided institutions. For, indeed, unemployment assistance and educational maintenance allowances are government provided. Similarly, Glennerster quotes the example of the state forcing individuals to save for retirement through the state retirement scheme which precludes saving for educational or other voluntary leave in mid-career. Once more this is not a *market* imperfection but a government imposed impediment.

Glennerster's fourth 'market imperfection' has to do with what he calls social conventions that discourage individual workers from taking time out in mid-career. Yet if the adult education involved leads to marked improvement in productivity, which is Glennerster's argument, then there would be profits in this practice that would benefit all parties – including the employer. (I am assuming that the employee finances his education where 'general', as distinct from 'specific' training is involved. Such self-financing is much more feasible for a person in mid-career.) The fact that we do not see many instances of voluntary mid-career training of this nature may indicate that it is not as productive as Glennerster imagines. Without relevant evidence his argument cannot, therefore, demonstrate market imperfection.

A remaining area of conflict or tension between Glennerster's conventional economic directives to some obedient government and the realities of political institutions as they exist is his attempt to give priority to the least privileged members of society. No one can quarrel with this objective taken separately. Viewed in the background of real world institutions, however, one could argue that the institutional means selected by Glennerster would actually have perverse results for his target individuals. In his concluding observations he acknowledges that all will have to pay taxes to finance grants for recurrent education. He asks 'why should all employees' wages be lowered or consumer prices be raised ... so that a *few* individuals can benefit from wider educational experience?' (Italics supplied). He answers that the groups chosen are either the illiterate, the unemployed, those in need of vocational training or training for workers' council representatives. Assuming that these groups account for all individuals on the very bottom of the economic ladder, there will be no perverse income distribution so long as every single member of the groups mentioned obtain and benefit from the recurrent education in question. But this is unrealistic. In particular, illiterates will have the most difficulty in obtaining a place in post-secondary education, even if they were so motivated. Those in this group who are excluded, therefore, will be even worse off after paying taxes for those who are included. But the most interesting collective (public) choice observation here is that the policy of reliance on government supplied education for adults is ironically on a system that has had eleven years educational custody over individuals only to turn them out as illiterate! If we were seeking new *constitutional* means of safeguarding against such government failure, one should surely be exploring ways of providing legal avenues leading to malpractice suits against the educational suppliers.

A feature of Glennerster's interesting survey of European experience is the strong influence of trade unions in getting some of the recurrent education established. In the literature of public choice, unions are consistently treated as collectivities of self-interested individuals – in this case pursuing the collective interests of *their members* (the branch of public choice known as 'the theory of economic clubs' is very appropriate here.) The theory does not suggest that the leadership of such collectives are interested in pursuing the interests of *nonmembers*. Since the poorest individuals in society are not likely to enjoy union membership, we face, therefore, the issue of *perverse* income redistribution in systems of recurrent education described in the European experience listed here. Another interested party that emerges is the educational bureau or Department of National Education. Any scheme that expands their budget, as Glennerster points out at the beginning of his article, will be welcomed by them enthusiastically.

Similarly welcome will be any method of finance that contains some element of 'fiscal' or other illusion. Glennerster reports, for instance, that in Belgium costs of vocational training for workers absent from work on full pay is paid for by the State and the employer on a fifty/fifty basis. One illusion here is that the employer is actually covering the cost out of his own resources, an illusion that is fostered because of the descriptive reality of the employer making such payments. In *economic* reality, however, the burden of such costs is usually shifted to the employee. (In the case of a completely inelastic demand curve for labor, the employee pays the whole [nongovernment] amount.) The other illusion is that 'the State' pays 'its' share. The reality here, of course, is that it is the taxpayer who pays and, in view of the multitude of indirect taxes that all persons pay (including the poorest), the likelihood of perverse income redistribution is again obvious.

The widespread existence of the beginnings of a recurrent education system in Europe that Glennerster reports is not in itself a testimony to its efficiency. In fact, one of the crucial details that is missing is evidence of the success of the various vocational schemes in increasing the lifetime incomes of the participants. It is consistent with the economics of bureaucracy that the administrators will discourage such attempts to obtain success rates of output of their institutions.

Meanwhile, even if the long-term results are not productive (and Glennerster himself observes that the teaching is often very formal or directed to vague social objectives), there are reasons that one could expect, from a public choice standpoint, that recurrent education programs would be *politically* attractive. The main reason is that if vocational schools can absorb large numbers of unemployed then the figures of statistically reported unemployment drop and political advantages are gained. It is in this context that Glennerster's report on Denmark is of special interest. In that country those attending vocational training schemes are paid out of government funds at a rate of something more than that of the unemployment benefit. Our hypothesis is that this is a relatively cheap way for politicians to purchase short-run reductions in statistically reported unemployment.

PART IV

'Clubs', negotiations, and decision processes

The university department as a non-profit labor cooperative

ESTELLE JAMES and EGON NEUBERGER

State University of New York at Stony Brook

1. Introduction

In this paper, the academic department at a university is viewed as a non-profit labor cooperative. We shall draw on two theoretical strands to analyze its behavior: the growing literature on non-profit organizations (NPO's) and the literature on collective decision-making. Where appropriate, we shall compare the academic department with other NPO's and collectives, such as the Yugoslav enterprise and the Israeli kibbutz.[1]

It is important to note, first, that not all NPO's are cooperatives or collectives: in the 'bureaucratic' NPO, decision-makers may be individual managers or a few members of the technostructure, rather than a large group of workers or consumers. Similarly, all collectives are not NPO's. Indeed, the prototype collective heretofore analyzed is a (per capita) income maximizing unit, aiming primarily to accumulate a monetary residual which is then distributed to its members for private consumption. In the pure NPO, this option is ruled out, and all its resources must be used internally, so that utility depends on organizational rather than individual expenditures.

Section 2 of this paper presents a model of the multi-product NPO. Central to our approach is the thesis that a multi-product NPO is typically engaged in some mixture of production and consumption (both termed 'activities') so the theory of the firm and the household are both relevant. It carries out profitable production activities which do not yield utility per se, in order to derive the income it can then spend on the consumption of loss-making utility-maximizing activities. The former, in effect, subsidize the latter; organizational consumption activities provide the only raison d'être for production, and production activities in turn provide the financial wherewithal for consumption. This distinction is important because, as will be demonstrated below, NPO's will 'underproduce' or 'overproduce,' will react differently to changes in revenues and costs, and may generate a backward bending supply curve, depending on which of these activities is involved.

Section 3 applies this theory to the university department, under the assumption that it is an NPO, run by its workers or faculty members, all of

207

whom agree on a single utility function which they proceed to maximize in choosing its product and factor mix. The reader interested primarily in higher education may wish to move directly to this section. A proposed objective function is used to generate hypotheses which seem consistent with observations of department behavior. The fact that the department is labor-managed rather than consumer or capitalist-managed, influences this objective function and means that the resulting activities will include opportunities for on-the-job consumption, even if these do not minimize costs or price. Basically, faculty members at a university are seen to carry out profitable activities that society is willing to pay for, e.g., the teaching of lower division undergraduates in large classes, in order to obtain the resources for costly utility-maximizing activities that society will not fully and directly subsidize, i.e., research and the teaching of small advanced classes. (Of course, we claim that the activities we prefer are also in the best interest of society at large, even if society does not recognize this.)

A collective NPO, however, faces the various difficulties associated with group decision-making – intransitivities and free rider problems – which are not encountered by the bureaucratic NPO (where a single person's utility function reigns) or by the income-maximizing collective (where the objective function is assumed to be single-peaked and uniform for all). Section 4 describes these problems, involving the relationship between the department and its members, and the mechanisms used to handle them in academia, drawing some comparisons with the Yugoslav (Illyrian) enterprise and the Israeli kibbutz.

We shall demonstrate that the academic NPO collective, where many benefits are shared rather than parcelled out, does not have the tendency to restrict size in order to maximize average income, which is characteristic of the prototype collective. If we compare the output of the NPO and profit maximizing organizations (PMO), we find that the NPO will 'underproduce' some goods and 'overproduce' others, but, overall there will virtually always be a pressure for the organization to expand its resources and activities.

We also demonstrate that, like the Illyrian firm but unlike the PMO, some activities of the academic department will have backward-bending supply curves, and this may be generalized to all multi-product NPO's.

2. A model of the multi-product NPO

Consider an NPO which produces and sells two sets of goods, Q_i, $i = 1, \ldots, n$ and Q_j, $j = 1, \ldots, m$, at total costs C_i, C_j and parametric prices P_i, P_j. The enterprise managers wish to maximize their utility function $U\left(Q_i, Q_j, \dfrac{Q_j}{C_j}\right)$

subject to the zero profit constraint $\sum C_i(Q_i) + \sum C_j - \sum P_i Q_i - \sum P_j Q_j$
$- FR = 0$, where $\dfrac{\partial U}{\partial Q_i}$ and $\dfrac{\partial U}{\partial Q_j} \gtreqless 0$, $\dfrac{\partial U}{\partial Q_j/C_j} < 0$. FR represents lump sum
revenues (from government, private philanthropists or endowment income)
that accrue in fixed amounts regardless of current decisions about Q. Later, we
explain why FR, which does not appear in the theory of the PMO, may play an
important role in the theory of the NPO.

Unlike the situation in the Israeli kibbutz or the Yugoslav enterprise, we
assume that private salaries are determined in competitive markets or by
some other exogenous force (such as trustees or legislators) so that NPO
managers cannot simply distribute to themselves a monetary residual in the
form of wages. However, they can spend potential profits in non-pecuniary
on-the-job consumption, which yield them utility directly and are not so
readily monitored. This process is a central concern of the present paper and
to facilitate our analysis we assume that organizational and private consumption are separable.

Another important feature of our model is a technological (or quality)
preference. In the case of goods designated by i, the enterprise has no technological preference so C_i simply appears, as usual, in the constraint, as a
function of Q_i. In the case of goods designated by j, the NPO does have a
technological (or quality) preference that enters into the objective function
and causes it to operate at a higher cost than the minimal $C(Q)$ frontier. This
preference may arise because expensive modes of production are considered
more prestigious than others; it may be justified by a (correct or mistaken)
belief that higher cost functions produce a higher quality product. Denied the
option of a monetary residual, an NPO is more likely to indulge its technological preference than is a PMO. For such goods, a rising output does not
necessarily imply rising real inputs or dollar costs, but if Q_j increases with C_j
constant, this implies a technological (or quality) deterioration, hence a loss of
utility and a subjective cost; technological preference, rather than simply
dollar cost, serves to limit the expansion of Q_j.

Output and costs of all goods (and bads) are determined simultaneously by
the NPO, such that:

$$\frac{\partial U}{\partial Q_i} - \lambda\left(\frac{\partial C_i}{\partial Q_i} - P_i\right) = 0 \qquad i = 1,\ldots,n \tag{1}$$

$$\frac{\partial U}{\partial Q_j} + \frac{\partial U}{\partial (Q_j/C_j)} \frac{1}{C_j} + \lambda P_j = 0 \qquad j = 1,\ldots,m \tag{2}$$

$$\frac{\partial U}{\partial (Q_j/C_j)}\left(-\frac{Q_j}{C_j^2}\right) - \lambda = 0 \qquad j = 1,\ldots,m \tag{3}$$

$$\frac{\partial U}{\partial (Q_j/C_j)} \frac{1}{C_j} = \frac{-\lambda C_j}{Q_j} \tag{4}$$

and, by substituting from (4) into (2)

$$\frac{\partial U}{\partial Q_j} = \lambda \left(\frac{C_j}{Q_j} - P_j \right) \tag{5}$$

Expansion continues so long as the positive (price plus utility) effects outweigh the negative (cost plus disutility), with the equilibrium output mix occurring where relative net utility equals relative net costs:

$$\frac{\partial U/\partial Q_{i1}}{\partial U/\partial Q_{i2}} = \frac{(\partial C_{i1}/\partial Q_{i1}) - P_{i1}}{(\partial C_{i2}/\partial Q_{i2}) - P_{i2}} \tag{6}$$

$$\frac{\dfrac{\partial U}{\partial Q_{j1}} + \dfrac{\partial U}{\partial (Q_{j1}/C_{j1})} \dfrac{1}{C_{j1}}}{\dfrac{\partial U}{\partial Q_{j2}} + \dfrac{\partial U}{\partial (Q_{j2}/C_{j2})} \dfrac{1}{C_{j2}}} = \frac{P_{j1}}{P_{j2}} \tag{7}$$

and, by substituting from (3) into (2)

$$\frac{\partial U/\partial Q_{j1}}{\partial U/\partial Q_{j2}} = \frac{C_{j1}/Q_{j1} - P_{j1}}{C_{j2}/Q_{j2} - P_{j2}} \tag{8}$$

Now, if $\frac{\partial U}{\partial Q_i} = 0$, we have the case commonly dealt with by production theory where Q does not enter into the utility function, either directly or indirectly. Such an activity will be carried out in the long run if and only if it is revenue-yielding, i.e., if $P_i \geq \frac{C_i}{Q_i}$, and output optimization occurs where $\frac{\partial C_i}{\partial Q_i} = P_i$. We call this 'pure production.' (Goods denoted by j are automatically excluded from this category since Q enters into the utility function via Q/C.)

If $P_i < \frac{\partial C_i}{\partial Q_i}$, we have the case commonly dealt with by consumption theory. Such an activity will be carried out only if it is utility-yielding, both marginally and globally. We call this 'pure consumption.' $\Big($ This category may also include goods denoted by j if $P_j < \frac{C_j}{Q_j}$. $\Big)$

Pure production, then, does not result in utility or disutility per se, but provides the income which the organization may then spend to derive satisfaction. Pure consumption, on the other hand, consists of spending this income in a costly manner which directly maximizes utility. If all activities fell into these two categories, we could decompose the decision-making process of the NPO into two distinct steps: First, maximize profits from pure production, and second, use up these profits as well as FR for pure consumption.

This sequential process breaks down, however, for those Q's that enter into the utility function and also generate positive profits; these are joint production-consumption activities. Particularly important is the case where $P_i > \dfrac{\partial C_i}{\partial Q_i}$ or $P_j > \dfrac{C_j}{Q_j}$ but $\dfrac{\partial U}{\partial Q} < 0$. Such activities will be carried out with the implied technology if and only if the revenue thereby raised is sufficient to offset the resulting disutility, and their production quantities must be determined simultaneously with the consumption activities of the enterprise.

The following points are suggested by this discussion: (1) Although we usually think of firms as producers and households as consumers, the multi-product NPO is a hybrid, engaging in profitable production activities in order to generate resources which are then spent on costly utility-enhancing consumption.

(2) Consequently, interdependence among activities exists for the NPO, even if production and demand functions are completely separable; output levels and technologies for each product cannot be determined or analyzed in isolation from each other.

(3) Corresponding to the simultaneous presence of profitable and loss-making goods, some groups of NPO consumers will be subsidizing others; the NPO thus serves as a mechanism for redistributing real income in our society.

(4) Equation (1) makes it clear that, for those Q_i whose $\dfrac{\partial U}{\partial Q_i} > 0$, an NPO will supply more than a PMO and for those whose $\dfrac{\partial U}{\partial Q_i} = 0$, it will behave precisely like a PMO. However, for those whose $\dfrac{\partial U}{\partial Q_i} < 0$, a multi-product NPO will stop producing at a point where $P_i > \dfrac{\partial C_i}{\partial Q_i}$ and hence will produce less than its counterpart PMO. By comparing equations (1) and (2), we see that a strong preference for an expensive technology has a similar negative output effect. Contrary to the usual expectations of NPO behavior, such products will be 'underproduced' relative to the profit-maximizing competitive norm.

(5) In general, we would hypothesize that most NPO's will scarcely break even, will generate a constant desire to grow and undertake new ventures and will face a perpetual shortage of funds with which to do so. The root of this situation is not, as has been suggested previously, that these are labor-intensive service industries with a chronic productivity lag.[2] More fundamentally, as we have seen, NPO's should be regarded as a producer-consumer hybrid, and consumers never have 'enough' income. So long as the (selfish or altruistic) marginal utility of any good exceeds zero there is always a 'need' for more, a pressure for the organization to expand its activities and its resources.

3. Choice of product mix and technology in the academic department

3.1 *The department's objective function*

In this subsection, the theory of NPO behavior is applied to the academic department, which is viewed as a key decision-making unit at the university. The department is a multi-product NPO, engaged in undergraduate teaching, graduate training and research, and is managed by its workers, or faculty members. We start by assuming that all faculty members have the same objective function regarding (their outputs from and time expenditures on) these activities, which is separable from the utility derived from their private salaries, and which therefore becomes the 'team' objective function of the group. In the following subsection, this crucial uniformity assumption is dropped.

Let us postulate a simple linear departmental objective function:

$$W = \alpha U + gG + aQL(U) + bQL(G) + cR(F, TL) + \frac{k(G + AU)}{GC + AUC}$$

where

U = # undergraduates = LU (lower division) + AU (upper division)

G = # graduate students

$QL(U)$ = quality of undergraduates; $\dfrac{\partial QL(U)}{\partial U} < 0,$

$QL(G)$ = quality of graduate students; $\dfrac{\partial QL(G)}{\partial G} < 0,$

$R(F, TL)$ = research, a function of F and TL

F = # faculty

TL = average teaching load = $\dfrac{UC + GC}{F}$

$\dfrac{G + AU}{GC + AUC}$ = # of graduate and advanced undergraduate students ÷ number of G and AU classes = average class size at advanced levels

$\alpha, a, b, c, g > 0; k < 0.$

In other words, the department's utility depends positively on the quantity of its students, possibly because faculty enjoy 'proselytizing' their subject matter, proving that their area of study is indeed worthwhile. (In a non-linear model we could show more realistically that a small number of students are appreciated while a large number may constitute an unwelcome diversion of faculty time from other preferred activities.)

Departmental welfare depends on student quality as well as quantity, and there is a trade-off between the two. The department may feel that its marginal product will be maximized if combined with superior raw material and may regard the process of screening for intellectual ability as one of its major social tasks. Or, the faculty may simply consider brighter students more fun and less effort to teach; the final product and the prestige of the department will be greater with a brighter class, even if the value added by the professor is less. The student quality argument means that, after a point,

$$\left(\frac{\partial W}{\partial U} + \frac{\partial W}{\partial QL(U)} \frac{\partial QL(U)}{\partial U} \right) = \left(\alpha + a \frac{\partial QL(U)}{\partial U} \right) < 0,$$

even if α is always positive; the same argument holds true for G.

We assume that research enters directly into the department's objective function. Faculty may enjoy spending their time on research and, furthermore, may regard themselves as morally responsible for expanding society's stock of knowledge. Alternatively, we may view the department as responding to the reward structure of the national discipine, in which case R may be considered a proxy for visibility, status and prestige.[3]

Since R will play a central role in our paper, several important qualifications might be mentioned here:

1) Each faculty member may care, in particular, about his own R; that is R^j and $R^{i \neq j}$ may enter into the objective function of person j with different weights. We shall discuss in Section 4 the possible conflict between the individual and the group that this situation may create.

2) For example, j may feel that his promotion prospects, access to grants and future earnings depend strongly on his own research productivity. By this interpretation, although an individual's current wage is exogenously given, his lifetime salary is endogenous. It is influenced by his university activities, enabling the department to engage in a kind of disguised pecuniary profit distribution which is difficult for outsiders to monitor.

3) Relatedly, faculty may care about the research productivity of their colleagues because this, too, enhances their own opportunities for grants and lucrative consultantships, and, thus, constitutes an avenue to future pecuniary returns.

4) Following this line of inquiry we might, in a more complex model, capture differences in research productivity by making R a function of $F^i, i = 1 \ldots F$ where $\frac{\partial R}{\partial F^i}$ signifies the quality of the ith professor. This model would help explain the department's elaborate concern with personnel recruitment and retention, discussed in Section 4. For the present, however, we proceed with our more elementary version.[4]

Finally, technology, in the form of average class size, also enters directly into the preference function, with respect to AU and G, but not LU. That is, LU is an i good while AU and G are j goods. This disparity may stem from the faculty's selfish interest in teaching small advanced classes or from an altruistic belief that the educational production function requires this technology at the higher (but not the lower) levels. The decision about class size may also be viewed as a choice about product quality.[5] The existence of a quality or technological preference has a major impact on optimal quantity and instructional subsidy across levels and also influences the desired teaching load (TL) and research/teaching (R/T) mix of the department, as we shall see below.

There is a danger in writing about something we are all familiar with: the simplifications inherent in an abstract model are harder to accept. In reality, the departmental objective function is considerably more complex, as we all know. The simplified model we use in the text is justified mainly by the fact that it yields results which are both interesting and empirically verifiable.

3.2 *The choice variables*

What then must the department decide? It must choose its optimal *product mix*, i.e., the amount of research (R) versus teaching (T) and the distribution of its instructional activities among LU, AU and G. (We are here abstracting from the significant administrative loads the department must carry, which may be viewed as an intermediate input into R and T.) The R/T product mix depends on the teaching load (TL) required in relation to that TL which would use up a professor's full time and energy. Specifically, we define a 4-course per semester TL (which is required at many 2- and 4-year colleges) as a 'full employment' situation in which a professor will have no time left over for R. Then, a 2-course TL implies that $1/2$ of all faculty resources are devoted to R and the R/T input mix is $1/1$.

In addition to choosing its product mix, the department must also choose its *teaching technology*. That is, it must determine the number of courses and hence the average class size or student/faculty ratio at each level, which in turn determines its 'cost' per student. Note that teaching is here considered a type j activity with technology and average costs a choice variable rather than an exogenously determined function. Since average class size overall $= \dfrac{U + G}{TL \cdot F}$ and $R/T = \dfrac{4 - TL}{TL}$, the choice of product mix (R versus T) and factor mix (teaching technology) are seen to be interdependent via the key role played by TL. In the optimization condition below we (arbitrarily) choose an index for R such that a one-course reduction in TL yields 100 units of R for each professor, 100F units for the entire department and, consequently, $\dfrac{\partial R}{\partial F} = 100(4 - TL)$.

Finally, the department must choose the *quantity* and corresponding *quality* of G and U. Decisions about quantity of G are made directly by the department, which draws from the national or regional student pool. With respect to U, the department can draw only on the university pool, so $LU \le \overline{LU} \cdot AU \le \overline{AU}$. It may, however, increase or decrease its share of total university enrollment indirectly by manipulating the non-pecuniary price of its courses (e.g., homework, grading and prerequisite policies) and directly by restricting entry to specified numbers.[6]

3.3 *The incentive structure: costs, revenues and profits in the department*

The feasible options facing the department depend on the incentive structure, i.e., the costs and revenues associated with alternative strategies. We assume that faculty and students are the only resources used for teaching and research. Fixed resources $= 0$ and there are no extra-university sources of funds, such as grants or contracts. Teaching is the only activity remunerated by the university and it is rewarded instantaneously in faculty resources. Specifically,

Table 1. Costs, revenues and profits from instructional activities

Class level and size	Faculty revenue per student/per course		Faculty cost per student/per course		Profit per student/per course		Profit available for T, per course		
							$TL=1$	2	3
LU									
33	$\frac{1}{99}$	$\frac{1}{3}$	$\frac{1}{132}$	$\frac{1}{4}$	$\frac{1}{396}$	$\frac{1}{12}$	$-\frac{2}{3}$	$-\frac{1}{6}$	0
50	$\frac{1}{100}$	$\frac{1}{2}$	$\frac{1}{200}$	$\frac{1}{4}$	$\frac{1}{200}$	$\frac{1}{4}$	$-\frac{1}{2}$	0	$\frac{1}{6}$
100	$\frac{1}{100}$	1	$\frac{1}{400}$	$\frac{1}{4}$	$\frac{3}{400}$	$\frac{3}{4}$	0	$\frac{1}{2}$	$\frac{2}{3}$
AU									
27	$\frac{1}{81}$	$\frac{1}{3}$	$\frac{1}{108}$	$\frac{1}{4}$	$\frac{1}{324}$	$\frac{1}{12}$	$-\frac{2}{3}$	$-\frac{1}{6}$	0
40	$\frac{1}{80}$	$\frac{1}{2}$	$\frac{1}{160}$	$\frac{1}{4}$	$\frac{1}{160}$	$\frac{1}{4}$	$-\frac{1}{2}$	0	$\frac{1}{6}$
80	$\frac{1}{80}$	1	$\frac{1}{320}$	$\frac{1}{4}$	$\frac{3}{320}$	$\frac{3}{4}$	0	$\frac{1}{2}$	$\frac{2}{3}$
G									
17	$\frac{1}{51}$	$\frac{1}{3}$	$\frac{1}{68}$	$\frac{1}{4}$	$\frac{1}{204}$	$\frac{1}{12}$	$-\frac{2}{3}$	$-\frac{1}{6}$	0
25	$\frac{1}{50}$	$\frac{1}{2}$	$\frac{1}{100}$	$\frac{1}{4}$	$\frac{1}{100}$	$\frac{1}{4}$	$-\frac{1}{2}$	0	$\frac{1}{6}$
50	$\frac{1}{50}$	1	$\frac{1}{200}$	$\frac{1}{4}$	$\frac{3}{200}$	$\frac{3}{4}$	0	$\frac{1}{2}$	$\frac{2}{3}$

The columns are derived as follows:

Class sizes are taken as illustrative examples.

Faculty revenue per student $= \frac{1}{100}, \frac{1}{80}$ and $\frac{1}{50}$ for LU, AU and G, respectively, as assumed in the text.

Faculty revenue per course = revenue per student $\times$ class size.

Faculty cost per course $= \frac{1}{4}$, based on a full employment definition of $TL = 4$.

Faculty cost per student = cost per course $\div$ class size.

Profit per student (course) = revenue minus cost per student (course).

Profit used for R, per course, is $\left(\dfrac{4 - TL}{4} \right) \dfrac{1}{TL} = \frac{3}{4}, \frac{1}{4}$ and $\frac{1}{12}$ for $TL = 1, 2$ and 3, respectively.

Profit available for T = profit per course minus profit used for R, per course.

one faculty line is granted for enrollment, of 100 LU, 80 AU or 50 G each semester. Comparable numbers have been in use at many large universities over the past decade, although students are sometimes not weighted by level, and rates of remuneration typically vary by department.

We now calculate the revenue, cost and profit per student and per course for various possible decisions. The (faculty) reward per student received by the department is given by the above ratios; for per course rewards we simply multiply by class size. The cost to the department of teaching a course = 1/4 by our definition of a full-employment TL; for per student costs we further divide by class size. The resulting profit per student or per course can be used by the department to subsidize its loss-making utility-yielding activities. That is, if a large class size is chosen at one level, this will permit either a small class size at another level or a low TL, hence a high R, overall.

Table 1 presents these costs and revenues under differing assumptions about level of student, class size and teaching loads. The 'break even' class size (where profit available for other instructional purposes = 0) decreases with level due to price differentials. Since it also decreases as TL increases, the department is seen to face a trade-off between a small-class technology and a high R/T product mix. Table 1 may also be used to construct a set of feasible options regarding enrollments, class size and TL, from which the department may choose its most preferred point [e.g., the TL may be set at 1 (or 3), with class sizes of 100, 80 and 50 (33, 27, 17) respectively, or the TL may be set at 2, with 1 LU class of 100, offsetting 3 G classes of 17].

3.4 Optimizing behavior

Since price does not adjust for quality in this model, we would predict a tendency to downgrade the product, unless quality is constrained or enters directly into the objective function. This is a familiar problem in models of centralized planning. In the case of the academic department collective, under the postulated set of tastes and incentives, we would expect to find a small number of very large lower division courses. In fact, unless there is some university rule to the contrary (or some fixed constraint such as room size), the department, in our model, will choose to teach all LU in one large class so that $LUC = 1$, average class size of $LUC = LU$, and, consequently, $AUC + GC$ $= TL \cdot F - 1 \sim TL \cdot F$ for large F, so that $\dfrac{\partial(AUC + GC)}{\partial TL} = F$ and $\dfrac{\partial(AUC + GC)}{\partial F} = TL$, as assumed below. Bearing in mind this simplifying assumption and recalling also that $\dfrac{\partial R}{\partial TL} = -100F$, $\dfrac{\partial R}{\partial F} = 100(4 - TL)$, we obtain the following conditions for optimizing LU, AU, G, TL (and hence R/T) subject to the constraint that

$$UC + GC = TL \cdot F = TL\left(\frac{LU}{100} + \frac{AU}{80} + \frac{G}{50}\right):$$

$$\frac{\partial W}{\partial LU} = \alpha + \frac{a\partial QL(U)}{\partial U} + c(4 - TL) - \frac{k\left(\dfrac{G + AU}{100}\right)}{TL \cdot F^2} = 0 \qquad \text{(LU)}$$

$$\frac{\partial W}{\partial AU} = \alpha + \frac{a\partial QL(U)}{\partial U} + \frac{5c(4 - TL)}{4} + \frac{k\left(F - \dfrac{G + AU}{80}\right)}{TL \cdot F^2} = 0 \qquad \text{(AU)}$$

$$\frac{\partial W}{\partial G} = g + \frac{b\partial QL(G)}{\partial G} + 2c(4 - TL) + \frac{k\left(F - \dfrac{G + AU}{50}\right)}{TL \cdot F^2} = 0 \qquad \text{(G)}$$

$$\frac{\partial W}{\partial TL} = c\frac{\partial R}{\partial TL} - \frac{k(G + AU)}{F \cdot TL^2} = -100\,cF - \frac{k(G + AU)}{F \cdot TL^2} = 0 \qquad \text{(TL)}$$

Note that because of the low-cost technology used, LU is a profitable activity for every possible quantity. We may now consider two cases. In case 1, the LU enrollment constraint, $\overline{LU}$, is reached while $\alpha + \dfrac{a\partial QL(U)}{\partial U} \geq 0$. Then, the supply of LU places goes to $\overline{LU}$, just as it would for pure production where LU did not enter into the utility function at all. The profits from LU can be viewed as fixed revenue, to be spent on loss-making, utility-maximizing activities such as small advanced classes and research, and a sequential decision process, in which decisions about LU precede decisions about TL, G and AU, can be used. In the second case, which we shall take to be the more typical one, $\alpha + \dfrac{a\partial QL(U)}{\partial U}$ becomes negative before the enrollment constraint is reached, because of the dominance of the student quality argument in the objective function. Then, at the margin, LU yields disutility and is enrolled only because of the profit it yields for research and small advanced classes. LU enrollment may be viewed as a hybrid of production and negative consumption, and its optimal size must be determined simultaneously with that of the other variables in the model.

As for AU and G, they are clearly competitive, both consuming the scarce faculty resources needed for small classes. In contrast to LU, their expansion is inhibited by the technological preference: if the additional faculty generated by incremental AU and G is less than the average used for them (as is often the case), enrollment increases necessitate either an increase in class size or a decrease in R once LU is given. This trade-off obviously limits the willingness of the department to enroll AU or G, which will consequently face enrollment restrictions even without the student quality argument needed to explain this phenomenon for LU. The student quality argument, however, plays a central role in explaining why an equilibrium occurs with a mixture of AU and G rather than with a specialization in G, which yields a higher faculty revenue per student. In particular, the quality argument helps explain why we often find enrollments of $G < AU$, implying either that $b > a$ or that $\frac{\partial QL(G)}{\partial G} < \frac{\partial QL(U)}{\partial U}$. (The division of $TL \cdot F$ between AUC and GC and hence the average class size of these two levels is indeterminate in this simple model.)

Finally, the department must choose its optimum TL, realizing that a reduction will increase R but will also increase average class size, *ceteris paribus*. According to the above equation, TL is optimized where $100cF + \frac{k(AU + G)}{F \cdot TL^2} = 0$, $k < 0$. The first term which is positive and constant may dominate and lead to decreases when TL is large, but as TL declines, the second term (which is negative) grows in absolute value and eventually brings these decreases to a halt. Rearranging, we find that equilibrium occurs where

$$TL^2 = \frac{-k(AU + G)}{c100F^2} \text{ so that } TL = \frac{\sqrt{(-k/c)(AU + G)}}{10F}.$$

In this model, faculty resources are 'produced' by T and 'consumed' by R. Relatedly, the faculty resource is viewed as a benefit rather than a cost and (undergraduate) students are viewed as inputs used to produce faculty, rather than vice-versa. The fact that TL has not $\to 0$ suggests that teaching technology does indeed enter into the department's utility function and serves to check the rise in R/T that would otherwise take place, if departments are free to choose TL.

3.5 *Empirical observations and comparative statics of departmental behavior*

Based on the objective function and incentive system described above, we would make the following empirical predictions about departmental behavior:

1. We would predict, and the data confirm, that the faculty engages in both teaching and research activities at a university. Although, in our model, departments receive resources primarily for the former, teaching loads are kept low enough to produce substantial R. An empirical study indicates that over one-third of faculty time and other resources are devoted to R, a major loss-making activity.[7] As discussed above, the diversion of resources to R may be interpreted as a form of non-pecuniary utility – maximizing on-the-job consumption or, alternatively, as a mechanism for distributing pecuniary profits in a way which cannot be readily monitored.

2. Every increase in U or G yields an increase in F and therefore R which, in turn, increases W at a constant rate, c. The R of one faculty member, in this sense, serves as a collective good to all other faculty members of the depart-

ment. The fact that $\dfrac{\partial W}{\partial R} > 0$ and is not subject to diminishing returns, constitutes a positive influence on optimal U, G and F and helps explain the pressure for departmental expansion that we frequently observe.

3. We would predict and the data confirm, that large classes predominate for lower division undergraduates, while small classes are found at the upper division and graduate levels. Thus, in addition to the fact that much faculty time and effort is devoted to R, a profit for T is also created by LU and used up by AU and G. In this sense, lower division students are subsidizing all the other teaching and research activities at the university.[8]

4. We would therefore predict that G and (basic) R would generally not be found without U, while the opposite is not true. While it has sometimes been argued that the rationale for combining U and G at one institution is to use the large supplies of cheap G to teach LU, this analysis suggests that the causation may actually run the other way: Departments wish to teach a large number of small GC, and the heavy resources burden thereby incurred can only be covered by earning and diverting an implicit profit from their production of LU.[9]

5. Moreover, if G and R were excluded as feasible products, U would be carried out in a more costly way, in order to meet the zero profit constraint, when other more preferred goods were not available. This corresponds to the fact that U instruction is more expensive at colleges than at universities and LU is most expensive of all at the community college.

6. We would predict large variations in average costs and student/faculty ratios across institutions for the same discipline and level of instruction, due partially to different objective functions and constraints. The data do indeed confirm that cost variations in higher education are greater than in many other sectors of the economy.[10]

7. We would expect from the above model and do indeed observe that departments practice non-price rationing, especially at advanced levels where technology as well as student quality matters. Entry is restricted and preference is given to the brighter, more motivated students by direct control over admissions of G and by manipulating the grading and homework 'price' or prerequisite structure for AU.

8. The theory of equalizing wage differentials would predict, and the data confirm, that universities would pay their faculty and, in general, NPO's would pay their managers lower salaries than those received by people with comparable training in PMO's, because of the superior opportunities for on-the-job consumption through the activities of the enterprise. For the same reason, wealthy universities with large endowments will, in general, not be at the top of the faculty salary scale. This wage reduction partially offsets the more expensive technology which faculty may choose, in the determination of total university cost.[11]

9. Although there are no fixed resources (FR) in this simple model of the academic department, they may exist and play an important role in some cases. As FR increases for the NPO, this has the same effect as an exogenous increase in income for the consumer: consumption of different goods will grow at different rates and some bads (or inferior goods) will even contract. The fact that universities and other NPO's will respond to changes in FR while PMO's will not, helps explain why people make voluntary non-earmarked contributions to the former but not to the latter.

Specifically, suppose that additional (public or private) donations are made to the university department. The traditional theory of the firm would predict a zero reaction to lump sum donations which change neither marginal revenue nor marginal cost. In contrast, we would predict a rise in G and/or AU, GC and/or AUC, as well as R. Some of the FR may also be spent on a reduced TL and smaller class size at advanced levels. On the other hand, profitable lower division enrollments may be unchanged if $\left[\alpha + \dfrac{a\partial QL(U)}{\partial U}\right] \geq 0$, and may actually decline if $\left[\alpha + \dfrac{a\partial QL(U)}{\partial U}\right] < 0$. Thus, we would predict that universities with large endowments would be characterized by a higher R/T and G/U mix and a costlier technology in AU and/or G than universities with little or no endowments. This pattern is also consistent with empirical observations of changes in university budgets during periods of affluence (as in the 1960s); we would expect the same pattern but in the reverse direction as austerity takes over (in the 1970s and 1980s).

10. The income effect results in non-zero cross-elasticities of supply among the various university activities, even when their production functions are completely separable. It also means that backward-bending supply curves are possible for some production activities – just as they are in the Illyrian firm, but unlike the classical PMO.[12]

Specifically, suppose the university's 'central planner' wishes to induce more attention to lower level undergraduates and therefore raises the faculty 'price' paid to the department for each LU. The traditional theory of the firm would predict an unambiguous increase in LU. In our model, however, LU may actually decrease if $\left[\alpha + \dfrac{a\partial QL(U)}{\partial U}\right] < 0$ and the income effect outweighs the substitution effect; in that case, we have a backward-bending supply curve of LU places. As above, R, AU and G, AUC and GC will rise while TL and average class size at the advanced levels will fall: the cross-elasticities of supply are non-zero, due to the income effect.

On the other hand, if the faculty price per G rises, both the income and substitution effects will induce an expansion of G (a positive own-elasticity of supply) but these two forces will lead in opposite directions with respect to AU, with the net outcome uncertain. The production of LU is unchanged if

$$\left[\alpha+\frac{a\partial QL(U)}{\partial U}\right]>0 \text{ but falls if } \left[\alpha+\frac{a\partial QL(U)}{\partial U}\right]<0 \text{ (negative cross-elasticity}$$

of supply). The increased F, of course, exerts a positive impact on the consumption of R. While this modification of the reward structure is sometimes recommended on grounds that the real cost per G to the department is higher than the price normally paid, it should be clear that the subsidy from U to G and R will in no way be terminated by such a move.

These hypotheses about own- and cross-elasticities of supply obviously have important public policy implications, since they speak to the limited feasibility of influencing university behavior by manipulation of relative prices.

4. Group decisions and intransitivity

Unlike the bureaucratic NPO, with a single head, or the capitalist firm or labor-managed cooperative, both of which are assumed to have a single objective (maximizing total or per capita profits, respectively), the non-profit collective faces the need to aggregate over many preference functions, each having several arguments. Until this point in our discussion of the academic department we have ignored this problem by assuming a team objective function, common to all faculty members. This section considers some types of differences that may arise and the mechanisms the department uses for reaching and enforcing group decisions.

It is well known that, when differences in preferences are found, there may not exist a method of aggregation that yields a transitive ordering with a unique 'first best' point. Moreover, even after the group has reached a decision, monitoring and enforcing it is difficult; each faculty member retains substantial control over how he spends his own time and may become a 'free rider.' How does the academic department handle this situation? In answering this question, we compare the department with other labor cooperatives, the Israeli kibbutz and the Yugoslav enterprise.

4.1 Majority voting

The method most commonly used is direct democracy with majority voting. As in the Israeli kibbutz, direct democracy is facilitated by the small size of the group, the high level of their education, and the spreading of information that results from job rotation and informal communication. We know that if all members' preferences are single-peaked, direct democracy with majority voting will avoid the cycling problem. However, double-peaked preferences are likely to arise in two types of situations: where there are increasing returns to a particular activity causing specialization to be preferred to diversification, and where a single decision has two or more attributes, each of which is weighted differently by the various participants.

To illustrate the first source of double-peakedness: Suppose a 3-member department with a fixed resource endowment chooses its optimum U/G mix. Three choices are possible – concentrate on U, concentrate on G, or do some of each, M. Member 1, who has an objective function characterized by decreasing returns, e.g., $W_1 = a\sqrt{U} + b\sqrt{G}$, $a > b$, ranks the alternatives MUG. Member 2, who has a linear objective function characterized by constant returns, e.g., $W_2 = cU + dG$, $d > c$ ranks them GMU. Both of these, it should be noted, have a single-peaked preference on a scale moving from lower to higher U/G ratios. Member 3, however, experiences increasing returns, e.g., $W_3 = eU^2 + fG^2$, $e > f$. This may stem from his belief that if students are concentrated at a given level, the department can do a better job with that group. In any event, he will rank the alternatives UGM, yielding a double peak. As a result, majority voting entails the familiar intransitivity problem: MPU, GPM, but UPG.

A similar situation arises if the department is considering the choice between hiring person A or B or hiring no person at all (N), where A and B combine a variety of different attributes that are weighted differentially by each member.[13] It may be impossible to secure a majority for A, B or N that cannot immediately be overturned by one of the other alternatives. In other words, this department may be unable to agree on its recruitment strategy – a not unfamiliar situation to many of us who have spent a few years in academia.

4.2 Log-rolling in a sequence of votes

When a whole sequence of choices are to be made, members may trade votes in accordance with their intensity of preference and thereby resolve the intransitivity problem. For example, member 3 may agree to vote for B rather than N in the example given in note 13, with the understanding that member 2 will vote for his choice in the next round of recruitment. This allows the department to move ahead with the appointment of person B, now.

4.3 Weighted decision-making

Another frequently used device for resolving intransitivity problems is to vest considerable power in a department chairman who, in effect, becomes a dictator when the rest of the department cannot agree on a unique choice. The chairman, who on the one hand is a representative of the faculty and on the other a representative of the administration, occupies the same ambivalent position as the Director of a Yugoslav enterprise did during the 1950s and 1960s. The resolution of this ambivalence varies from institutions where the chairmanship rotates and he is likely to rule by consensus, versus those institutions where the chairman is a long-term 'head' who exerts strong decision-making power of his own.[14] In a less extreme version of weighted decision-making, a small group of influential faculty may 'count' more than others and if they have similar preferences, indecisiveness may be avoided. While the 'one man – one vote' rule holds in the formal organizational structure of the kibbutz, informal differences in status and power undoubtedly exist, weighting the decision-making there, too.

4.4 *Segmented decision-making*

Closely related is segmented decision-making, which occurs when the set of issues is divided up so that particular subsets of members have exclusive power over corresponding subsets of decisions. Often, people with similar preferences or access to relevant information are grouped together and have prime influence over specified inputs or outputs. For example, an undergraduate and graduate committee may be formed to oversee these two programs, respectively. In many fields (e.g., mathematics and psychology) theorists and applied faculty constitute two completely separate departments, thereby avoiding conflicts between them. The allocation of certain resources, such as computer usage, is sometimes handled completely apart from other inputs, with the user group exerting strong influence over the final outcome.

Segmented decision-making is found, too, on the Israeli kibbutz, where certain decisions are decentralized to committees or branches, and in the Yugoslav enterprise where each of the basic organizations (BOALs) makes certain decisions for themselves. While this system may involve an efficiency loss, since trade-offs and spillovers are not taken into account, it may also reduce the cost and indeterminacy of the decision process itself, as an offsetting gain.

4.5 *Tenure and firing decisions: The concept of membership classes*

A particularly important example of segmented decision-making involves firing and tenure. It has been noted that self-managed enterprises generally have a hard time firing people; close personal relationships and mutually protective coalitions may well develop. On the Israeli kibbutz members cannot be fired for economic reasons and in the Yugoslav enterprise firing is possible but very difficult. Yet, sometimes workers turn out to be incompetent or a job no longer needs to be done. How does the academic department handle this type of decision?

Basically, the faculty are divided into two mutually exclusive classes of members: those without tenure, who can be fired and those with tenure, who make the decisions about firing. The former are comparable to probationary members of a kibbutz; the latter have already acquired lifetime membership rights. This is obviously not a first-best solution, in the sense that some people who are fired may be better than some with tenure. Nevertheless, it is a

224

structure which avoids the danger that no one will be fired at all, and may constitute one plausible raison d'être for the tenure system.[15]

Firing is also facilitated by the 'up or out' rule, which decrees that any faculty member retained for more than 7 years must be given tenure. This rule substantially and discontinuously increases the cost to the department of an eighth year of employment, and therefore makes it less likely. A faculty member can be kept with relative ease for 7 years, but released at that point with a statement that he is good but not quite good enough for a lifetime job guarantee. This action is somewhat less destructive of social relationships than an ordinary firing would be. Passage through the 'up or out' point often requires additional approval from college-wide review bodies and administrators, a more impersonal decision-making group. Thus, for this crucial decision, self-management in the academic department is partially replaced by a system of centralized control.

4.6 Uniform teaching loads

While the tenure system may help the department to fire faculty members who are still in their probationary period, it does so at some expense: making it more difficult for the group to enforce its collective will upon the individual who already has tenure. Tenure constitutes a kind of employment insurance with a corresponding moral hazard and free-rider problem, leading some faculty to shirk those job responsibilities which the group has already determined should be carried out. This problem is further exacerbated by the traditional egalitarian ethos in academia and the more recent elimination of 'merit pay' in union contracts.

To illustrate the possible conflict between the individual and the group, let us consider a department with n members, each having an identical objective function $W^i = aGC^i + bR^i + cR(F)$. That is, each member derives utility from his own graduate classes (GC^i) and Research (R^i) and from the total departmental research (R), which in turn depends upon F, but derives no positive or negative utility from teaching undergraduate courses. $F = gUC + hGC$, $g > h$ because of the much larger undergraduate class size. TL is assumed to be fixed.

Then, if individual i shifts one of his courses from GC to UC his utility changes by $c(g - h) - a, (g - h) > 0$. (1)
If $a > c(g - h)$ this expression will be negative and the individual will not willingly make this shift.

If however, some other individual j shifts from GC to UC, i's utility changes by $c(g - h)$ and this, we know, is positive. Therefore, each member of the department wishes that others would teach some UC, and may vote for a high UC/GC ratio, but each is unwilling to do so himself and the group decision is difficult to enforce on tenured faculty.

Now, suppose all members get together and each agrees to do one unit of UC. The welfare of a typical member now changes by $nc\,(g - h) - a$.   (2)
Where n is large, we may well find that (2) is positive, while (1) is negative: All members are better off if they jointly agree to do some UC even though, acting atomistically, none will do so on his own. While a uniform teaching load, including a share of UC, may be inefficient in the sense that it does not take comparative advantage into account, it may be viewed as a second-best mechanism for resolving the free-rider problem under tenure. This is similar to the concept that everyone should pitch in and do some of the less desirable tasks on the Israeli kibbutz.

4.7 Indoctrination, screening and self-selection

Perhaps the most important mechanisms for handling the group decision and free-rider problems have to do with the formation of individual preferences before tenure and the selection of people whose preferences will cause them to vote and act as others in the group want, after tenure. In this sense, the academic department is similar to the Israeli kibbutz, which also engages in a careful indoctrination and selection of its members. In both cases, members consider themselves as belonging to a small special group set apart from the rest of society; a positive work ethic, a feeling of solidarity and a sharing of common values are encouraged; and free-riders pay the price of social pressure and social isolation. These factors are particularly strong on the kibbutz, whose members live together 24 hours a day.

Most kibbutz members share a common socialization from childhood, having been brought up together on the kibbutz or joined a youth movement which early directed them toward a kibbutz life and ideology. In academia, the indoctrination process begins in graduate school, where student protégés absorb the values of their faculty mentors. It has been noted that groups such as minorities and women who were excluded from this protégé-mentor system were thereafter at a disadvantage in the job market. This indoctrination continues during the probationary pre-tenure period, so that people who get tenure are likely to have had their preferences shaped by the group.

At the same time, the initial members of the department (and the kibbutz) are likely to take into account the expected values of the candidate in hiring new members and in granting tenure. Thus, if future voting patterns could be accurately predicted, a majority could easily perpetuate itself. Change comes from the unpredictability of future preferences or from the fact that other characteristics, such as research ability and prestige, may count more than voting behavior.

The majority may also choose people whose utility functions include arguments that will circumvent the free-rider problem, i.e., people who derive direct utility from the type of work the department desires. It follows that academic jobs, which cannot be readily monitored, are likely to be awarded to and held by people for whom their work is a source of positive rather than negative utility, just as is true for members of the Israeli kibbutz.

Finally, we know that different types of higher educational institutions emphasize different activities – G and R at universities, U at colleges, etc. Therefore, young faculty will tend to self-select themselves into those institutions where others have similar preferences, where they will be more satisfied with the group decisions about input and output mix. Self-selection, then, lends credibility to the concept of a 'team' objective function, where intransitivity disappears, and combines with indoctrination and screening to preserve homogeneous departmental groupings over time. The same is true of potential kibbutz members who join kibbutzim belonging to the Federation whose ideology corresponds most closely to their own preferences. People with non-compatible preferences may leave academia, or the kibbutz life, completely.[16]

5. Conclusion

In summary, we have characterized the academic department at a university as a non-profit faculty collective that engages in the 'production' of large profitable introductory classes in order to finance its 'consumption' of bright advanced students in small classes, as well as research. The implications of this model help to answer a number of questions regarding institutional behavior in higher education, including the following:

1. Why do people make donations of discretionary resources to universities, despite the economist's expectation that fixed costs or revenues (i.e., costs and revenues that are not tied to specific activities) will not influence behavior?

2. Why are faculty members paid less than people with comparable training in government or private industry?

3. Why is a large proportion of faculty time devoted to research, even where this is not separately funded?

4. Why do we observe huge cost variations across institutions, even when level and discipline are held constant?

5. Why is undergraduate education carried out in a more cost-intensive way at colleges than at universities?

6. Why are graduate training and research (G and R) (almost) always found in conjunction with undergraduate education (U), while U is often found without G and R?

7. Why is non-price rationing used extensively by academic institutions?

8. Why do universities typically face a pressure for departmental expansion, a perpetual need for 'more' resources?

9. Why do elaborate recruitment mechanisms, probationary periods with

value indoctrination, segmented and committee decision-making prevail in academia?

10. How can the theory of the labor-managed firm help explain the prevalence of tenure and uniform teaching loads at universities?

This has been primarily an exercise in positive analysis; in a more normative approach to the subject we would have to specify the criteria for evaluation and the viewpoint we were adopting – that of students, faculty, university administrators and taxpayers. As we have seen above, there may well be conflicts among all of these interests so the assignment of decision-making power also implies an assignment of property rights and real income which, therefore, influences resource allocation. Potential sources of divergent interests between the department and the broader university of which it is one component, are explored in the Appendix.

In comparing the output levels of the non-profit collective such as an academic department, with that in the competitive PMO or the Illyrian firm, we have found that some goods (e.g., graduate education and research) will be 'overproduced' by the NPO, way beyond the point where total or per capita profits are maximized, because of the positive utility which they yield, often on a 'collective goods' basis, to the NPO managers. On the other hand, profitable products that yield negative utility will be 'underproduced' relative to the PMO and (as in the Illyrian firm but for a different reason) may have a backward-bending supply curve and an unstable equilibrium. This may be the case for undergraduate instruction. Attempts to increase the quantity of such products by increasing lump sum revenues or price may actually have a contrary effect.

We have also found that input-output relationships or total and marginal costs of each product, may be treated as choice variables, entering into the objective function, rather than as exogenously determined technological constraints. Moreover, interdependencies among activities exist for a multi-product NPO such as an academic department, even if production and demand functions are completely separable.

In general, since the choice of product mix and factor mix depends on subjective utility functions of the faculty-managers, these may vary from one department to another and the response to parametric changes may also vary. This means that the central administration at the university or the state planner overseeing it is clearly limited in his ability to influence resource allocation when decisions about product and factor mix are in the hands of the departmental non-profit collective. If the planner wishes to achieve his ends by manipulating the incentive structure facing the department, rather than by direct controls, he must first understand which activities are regarded by the faculty-managers as production, which are utility-yielding consumption, and which are a mixture of production and negative consumption. The group decision process, cycling possibilities, and monitoring and enforcement impediments further complicate the situation. Unless he is aware of these difficulties, he may find income effects, backward-bending supply curves, non-zero cross elasticities, intransitivities and free-rider problems that were not predicted by the traditional theory of the firm and that may yield an input-output mix which differs from his expectations or intent.

Appendix: The department versus the university

Until now, we have assumed that the department is an autonomous decision-making unit and have ignored the fact that it is but one unit within the broader university. It is beyond the scope of this paper to examine the decision-making structure of the university as a whole, but in this Appendix we discuss briefly three potential sources of divergent interests: differing objective functions and constraints between the department and the university, spillover effects across departments, and the bargaining relationships that develop in determining the appropriate student faculty ratio and other reward rates, which vary from one department to another.

Differing objective functions and constraints

The decision-makers for the university may have different goals and face different constraints from those of the departmental faculty-managers. One particularly important case in point concerns the nature of the student demand functions. In the model presented in Part 3, student demand was independent of teaching technology. This may be substantially true for the department, which faces an undergraduate enrollment constraint based on numbers of students registered in the institution. It is probably less true of the entire university, which may be able to attract more and better students by offering a small class technology overall. That is, $QL(U)$ may be a function of both U and $\dfrac{U}{UC}$, and in the university's objective/constraint function the latter may exert a stronger effect than it does for the individual department. In that case, the department's optimizing behavior may not be consistent with optimization for the university as a whole.

This inconsistency may come to the fore in the 1980s, as the potential pool of students diminishes. With undergraduates becoming scarce, the university faces a potential decline in student quantity and/or quality, unless its teaching technology improves enough to raise its market share. Under these circumstances, the university may urge the departments to invest more of their resources in LU, while each department in isolation will want to maintain its customary mode of behavior, leaving it to other departments to adjust.

Thus, we would predict increasing pressures and controls by the university's central administration on departments, urging and, at times, requiring them to compete in the diminishing market for undergraduates by using a more attractive teaching (and advising) technology. This pressure stems from the dual fact that *LU* enrollments are profitable, and that quality as well as quantity of *LU* matter. However, to the extent that the pressure is successful, competition for (bright) *LU*'s will raise the proportion of resources devoted to them and make them less profitable. This, in turn, will leave fewer resources to subsidize *G* and *R*. We would expect, in the competitive atmosphere of the 1980s, to find a diminishing (albeit still positive) profit from *U*, a diminishing (albeit positive) subsidy to *G*, a move toward convergence in their two technologies, and less departmental autonomy within the university as a whole.

Spillover effects

In other respects, too, departments may be affected by each other's activities; yet, the decision process often does not take these spillovers into account. In this sense, the academic department is unlike the branches in Israeli kibbutzim, whose production functions are generally separable, and is more similar to the BOALs in Yugoslavia, whose activities interact in the enterprise's production process.

We have already noted that a desirable teaching technology in other departments may attract more and better students to the university, constituting a superior pool from which all departments then draw. In addition, undergraduates may wish to take a diversity of subjects and are more likely to enroll in an institution which offers them greater variety; this is probably the reason why many departments are grouped together in a single university instead of becoming completely separate entities. Other spillover effects occur in connection with specific courses: mathematics is a prerequisite to many economics courses, so economists care about how mathematics is taught, and the same is true for chemistry as an input into biology. Also, departments may be concerned about the (nonmonetary) price charged by other departments – e.g., the ease of grading, amount of homework assignments – since this may affect the relative demand among students for their products and hence the resource allocation across departments. Interdisciplinary programs, in particular, may care about what is being taught in the disciplines. Faculty members whose interests cross disciplinary lines may find that only part of the benefits they are generating will be taken into account by the departmental unit which controls rewards.

As evidence of these externalities and as one mechanism for dealing with them, we observe a variety of university-wide committees which deal with promotion and tenure decisions, undergraduate teaching and grading policy, etc. These committees evaluate faculty from the university's point of view, rule out certain forms of competition as 'unfair' and 'illegal,' and resolve jurisdictional battles among departments and schools. In this sense, the academic department has less autonomy than the kibbutz. Nevertheless, decision-making over curriculum and personnel remains substantially vested in the individual department and, as with the Yugoslav BOALs, the incentive system does not systematically induce them to take account of those external effects which do exist.

230

Bargaining over reward functions

It is well known that the reward per student, in terms of faculty and other resources, differs across departments. This is partly because of the tenure system, which prevents downward adjustments in size of faculty as enrollments shift. These variations also arise because technological requirements differ across departments.

Each department tries to convince the central administration that its programs inherently require a higher rate of funding, that it will use the additional resources to further the interests of the university, and that severe quality deterioration and enrollment decline will ensue if the resources are not forthcoming. The administration, on the other hand, must make its own assessment of the technological needs of each department as well as the quality impact of differing reward ratios; it must also decide which departments will be subsidized from general revenues and which will be expected to earn a profit, based on the tuition and/or state payments it generates. The difficulty with this negotiation is that very little is known objectively about educational production functions and the department has more information than the university about the technological requirements of its own discipline as well as its projected use of any incremental resources. Manipulation of information is therefore one important ingredient in the negotiation, just as it is for Soviet plant managers negotiating with the Central Planning Board regarding input and output targets. The reward rate that is finally agreed upon is thus the result of a complex bargaining process, with the outcome depending on the preference functions and bargaining ability of university administrators and department chairmen, in a context of asymmetrically imperfect information; hence, it may well not be in the best interests of the university as a whole.

It is useful to contrast this situation with that of the Yugoslav BOALs. The BOALs may sell their wares to (or buy their intermediate products from) BOALs in another enterprise. Hence, a market develops in each good, limiting the scope for bargaining. (Bargaining over terms of trade may still occur, to a limited extent, if transactions costs and informational imperfections are reduced for exchanges within the same enterprise or if each BOAL has a stake in the success of the entire enterprise.) An academic department, however, may not unilaterally sell its courses to (students from) another institution, nor may the university send its students to an alien department, except in special cases. Since the department is tied to a single buyer and the university to a single seller, the area for bargaining and indeterminacy expands. University and department administrators, then, have a wider latitude for discretion than managers in either a profit-maximizing firm or a Yugoslav enterprise.

NOTES

1. The model of the multi-product NPO used here is developed more fully in James (1979).

2. For a discussion of the chronic impoverishment of NPO's, which they attribute to a productivity lag, see Baumol and Bowen (1966).

3. Thus, the model of the department as a prestige-maximizer, which has been convincingly presented in the literature, is consistent with our model and shows up here as operating through both the student quality and research variables. The best presentation of the prestige-maximizing model may be found in Breneman (1971), who uses this to explain departmental behavior with respect to graduate enrollments, attrition and length of time required for the Ph.D.

4. The above points emerged in comments by conference participants, who convinced us that they merited more attention than we gave them in an earlier version of this paper.

5. There is no clear evidence that more is learned in small classes, but many believe this is so. For a discussion of the controversial studies on this topic, see O'Donoghue (1971: 158 ff.). (In addition, surveys indicate that students prefer small classes, so subjective consumer valuations place the quality of large classes as lower than that of small ones.)

6. Two important simplifying assumptions are inherent in our formulation. First, we assume that departments can determine their AU enrollments independently of their past or present LU enrollments, either because their preferred AU is less than last year's LU or because of large numbers of transfer students. In a dynamic model, the connection between present AU and past LU would have to be considered explicitly. Secondly, we assume that student demand for a department's offerings does not depend upon the teaching technology chosen by that department, i.e., other factors dominate in a student's choice of courses to take. However, teaching technology may play a greater role in determining a student's choice of universities, initially, setting up a potential conflict between the department's and the university's incentive-constraint structure.

7. For a discussion of this data set, as well as that noted in points 3, 4 and 5, see James (1978). We have tested several other objective functions that are often cited by the conventional wisdom as an approximation of reality, and found these to be inconsistent with one or more of these empirical observations, leading us to have greater confidence in the objective function used in this paper. The utility functions tested were: $W = R(F, \overline{TL})$, with class size and TL fixed; $W = R(F, TL)$, with class size and TL variable; $W = U + G$; $W = U + gG + aQL(U) + bQL(G) + cR(F, TL)$. The inconsistent results yielded by the latter formulation serves to emphasize the important role played by the technological (or quality) preference argument in the faculty's objective function.

8. This subsidy would be even greater if we had shown the revenue per student as equal across levels – as would be true at many universities. Thus, our presentation probably underestimates the actual subsidy. For a complementary view of the same issue from a more macro point of view, see James (1978).

9. A study conducted by one of the authors indicates that, contrary to popular impression, graduate teaching assistants are paid more than equivalent part-time services would cost on the market and more than they could earn elsewhere, while continuing their studies. Thus, graduate TA's are used not because they are a source of cheap labor, but because the university wishes to enroll them and to do so must subsidize their foregone earnings as well as their instructional costs.

10. See Balderston (1974: 155, 172-176) for the United States and O'Donoghue (1971: 154) for some other countries.

11. A further comment is needed to explain why workers in a labor-managed NPO do not simply vote themselves a wage increase, as they are able to do in a conventional labor cooperative. We assume that there exists some external authority, such as a board of trustees or legislature,

that determines the wage offer or prevents NPO workers from paying themselves more than the competitive price. Given this constraint, worker managers can only increase their utility (or their future market earnings) through their choice of product mix and factor mix. As organizational consumption increases, the pecuniary wage necessary to attract workers to NPOs declines in accordance with the theory of compensating wage differentials.

If an increase in on-the-job consumption causes decreases in private consumption why should faculty try to maximize the former, as they do in our model? There are at least four possible justifications for such behavior:

1) faculty may be myopic and not aware of the theory of compensating wage differentials;

2) informational deficiencies on the part of workers would cause market clearing wage differentials to depend on expected on-the-job consumption in the NPO sector as a whole. In this case, if individual organizations perform better than average their workers can benefit from organizational consumption without a corresponding drop in monetary wages;

3) the market clearing monetary wage will depend on the preferences of the worker at the margin of choice between the NPO and PMO sectors. If workers with a taste for on-the-job consumption self-select themselves into labor-managed NPOs, the compensating wage differential will be less than the value of the organizational consumption to infra-marginal workers;

4) the monitoring agent may not be aware of the full cost or value of on-the-job consumption and may therefore permit wages to locate somewhere between the PMO and the market-clearing (compensating) levels.

The above arguments indicate that a labor-managed NPO may undertake on-the-job consumption activities because a fully compensating wage differential is not expected. On the other hand, a PMO will undertake such activities if and only if the expected wage reductions (usually assumed equal to the marginal benefit) exceed the direct cost. Therefore, if we consider on-the-job consumption activities as another set of outputs, NPOs will choose a different product mix from PMOs, as a disguised method for distributing potential profits to its managers.

We are grateful to Sherwin Rosen for his suggestion that we explore more fully the significance of compensating wage differentials for our analysis of the non-profit labor cooperative.

12. The backward-bending supply curve has been shown to exist for the single-product Illyrian firm (Ward), but probably not for the multi-product firm (Domar). In contrast, it probably does not exist for the single-product NPO but does for the multi-product NPO, which may produce 'bads' as well as 'goods.'

13. Suppose A does research R_A on topic A and does primarily undergraduate teaching while B does research R_B on topic B and teaches G. The utility function of the typical member, with respect to these four arguments is $W = aR_A + bT_U + cT_G + dR_B$. Member 1, for whom $a > b > c > 0$, $d < 0$, $|d| > |c|$ ranks these choices ANB. Member 2, for whom $d > c > b > a > 0$ ranks them BAN. Member 3, for whom $c > b > 0$, $a < d < 0$, $|d| > |c|$ ranks them NBA. Again, because of the different values placed on the jointly supplied attributes by each participant, we find by majority, BPA, APN, but NPB.

14. This mechanism allows the department to function, but it also introduces a certain amount of game play into the voting process. For instance, suppose that member 1 is the chairman in the example cited above in note 13, and if cycling continues he will impose his preference – for hiring A. If member 3 knows the rules of the game and also knows the chairman's preference, he may vote for B rather than N, in order to avoid the cycling problem and the A outcome, which is least desirable to him. The very possibility, then, of a dictatorial decision, may cause the group to make its own unique choice. We have all experienced the pressures for a department to present a 'united front' to the university administration, in order to avoid the rationale for a third-best imposed solution of type A when B is viewed as a first- or second-best alternative by the majority.

15. For a fuller analysis of the tenure system, see James (1980).
16. Sometimes, of course, none of these mechanisms work and the department simply ceases to function. We are all aware of examples of sick or paralyzed departments that cannot reach group decisions or, if such decisions are made, cannot enforce them. This situation may be self-correcting, as the psychic costs involved induce some members to leave and others to find some decision-making system that works. If the situation does not correct itself, the faculty collective may be replaced by bureaucratic or centralized planning, and commands from above replace group control from below.

For example, the university administrators may exert dictatorial power, rejecting the department's recommendations for hiring or tenure. The group in question may be merged with another departmental unit, which will dominate it. New professors may be recruited or a new chairman imposed, with weighted voting, to change the balance of power. In other words, when group decision-making breaks down, there is a procedure for extablishing a new group or a new decision-making structure, to carry on the work of the university.

REFERENCES

Alchian, A., and Demsetz, H. (1972). Production, information costs, and economic organization. *American Economic Review* 62: 777-795.
Alchian, A., and Kessel, R. (1962). Competition, monopoly and the pursuit of pecuniary gain. In *Aspects of labor economics*. Princeton: NBER.
Balderston, F. (1974). *Managing today's university*. San Francisco: Jossey-Bass.
Baumol, W. J. (1959). *Business behavior, value and growth*. New York: Macmillan.
Baumol, W., and Bowen, W. (1966). *Performing arts – The economic dilemma*. New York: Twentieth Century Fund.
Ben Ner, A., and Neuberger, E. (1979). On the economics of self-management: The Israeli kibbutz and the Yugoslav enterprise. *Economic Analysis and Workers' Management* 13: 47-71.
Breneman, D. W. (1971). *An economic theory of Ph.D. production*. Berkeley: Ford Foundation Program for Research in University Administration, Report P-8.
Clarkson, K. (1972). Some implications of property rights in hospital management. *Journal of Law and Economics* 15: 363-385.
Domar, E. (1966). The Soviet collective farm. *American Economic Review* 56: 734-757.
Freeman, R. (1973). Demand for labor in a nonprofit market. University Faculty. Discussion Paper 300, Harvard Institute of Economic Research.
Furubotn, E. (1976). The long-run analysis of the labor-managed firm: An alternative interpretation. *American Economic Review* 66: 104-123.
Ginzberg, E., Hiestand, D. L., and Reubens, B. J. (1965). *The pluralist economy*. New York: McGraw-Hill.
Graaf, J. de V. (1950-51). Income effects and the theory of the firm. *Review of Economic Studies* 18: 54-86.
James, E. (1978). Product mix and cost disaggregation: A reinterpretation of the economics of higher education. *Journal of Human Resources* 13: 157-186.
James, E. (1979). A contribution to the theory of the non-profit organization. Presented at the Conference on Institutional Choice, Madison, Wisconsin.
James, E. (1980). Job-based lending and insurance: Wage structure in tenurian labor markets. Discussion Paper No. 12-80 Pinkas Sapir Center for Development, Tel-Aviv University.
Layard, R., and Jackman, K. (1973). University efficiency and university finance. In M. Paskin (Ed.), *Essays in modern economics*. London: Longman.
Leibenstein, H. (1979). 'The missing link' – micro-micro theory? *Journal of Economic Literature* 17: 477-503.

Neuberger, E., and Duffy, W. J. (1976). *Comparative economic systems: A decision-making approach*. Boston: Allyn and Bacon.

Neuberger, E., and James, E. (1973). The Yugoslav self-managed enterprise. In M. Bornstein (Ed.), *Plan and market: Economic reform in eastern Europe*. New Haven: Yale University Press. 245-284.

Newhouse, J. P. (1970). Toward a theory of nonprofit institutions: An economic model of a hospital. *American Economic Review* 60: 64-75.

O'Donoghue, M. (1971). *Economic dimensions in education*. Chicago: Aldine.

Pauly, M., and Redisch, M. (1973). The not-for-profit hospital as a physician's cooperative. *American Economic Review* 63: 87-100.

Scitovsky, T. (1943). A note on profit maximization and its implications. *Review of Economic Studies* 11: 57-60.

Vanek, J. (1970). *The general theory of labor-managed market economies*. Ithaca: Cornell University Press.

Ward, B. (1958). The firm in Illyria: Market syndicalism. *American Economic Review* 48: 566-589.

Weisbrod, B. (1975). Toward a theory of the voluntary non-profit sector in a three-sector economy. In E. Phelps (Ed.), *Altruism, morality, and economic theory*. N.Y.: Russel Sage Foundation. 171-195.

Weisbrod, B. (1977). *The voluntary non-profit sector*. Lexington, Mass.: Heath and Co.

Williamson, O. (1967). *The economics of discretionary behavior*. Chicago: Markham.

Comments on E. James and E. Neuberger

LAURIE HUNTER

University of Glasgow

Section 1

This I found to be a rewarding and well-constructed paper which was convincing in its basic analysis. It draws on the theory of non-profit organisations and on the theory of self-managed firms to illuminate the behaviour of the university department. In so doing it answers a number of questions about departmental behaviour that may appear puzzling on a preliminary analysis. It also might provide useful insights for a university administrator anxious to know how best to modify departmental actions in desired directions.

Its basic approach may be defined in a simplified form in terms of three propositions:

(i) The department is a key decision-making unit in a university;
(ii) the department is a producer/consumer hybrid; that is to say, production in the form of undergraduate courses is undertaken for reasons unconnected with its utility to producers. Undergraduate teaching is viewed as yielding a surplus which in the context of a non-profit organisation must be fully consumed or deployed to maximise utility. That utility is to be found primarily in research and in graduate teaching which are the main positive elements in the utility function;
(iii) collective utility is separable from individual utility where the latter might be defined principally in terms of salaries. Salaries are assumed exogenous and determined by market forces.

The analogy with the analyses of Williamson and Marris is clear. Such discretionary theories of management behaviour give rise to the assumption that profits are given up in order to maximise arguments in the utility function of the coalition (defined as the *key* decision group in the organisation). So in this case the loss making but high utility activities, such as research and graduate teaching, are able to be developed by the department acting as a coalition on the basis of profit made on the production of undergraduate courses.

Section 2

Within the context of a comparative conference, it seemed worthwhile considering how this model and its predictions would stand up in a different environment, such as that of the U.K. From that standpoint, these three propositions call for some comment. First, how far is the department really a key decision group in the university, at least in the fairly autonomous or free standing sense implied in the paper? While I can see this applying readily in many situations in the U.S., the U.K. may be rather different, influenced as it is by a different system of university finance and a different system of student funding. In the U.K., the department still acts as a planning unit but is probably subject to stronger controls from the administration and Faculty boards. Arguably, U.K. departments are more constrained in their decisions – more reactive and less pro-active.

Secondly, how far is collective utility really separate from individual utility and how far do the arguments in the postulated utility function really act as a proxy for salary or pay? My first reason for questioning this comes from the U.K. salary system of fixed scales which are less responsive to market forces and essentially represent an administered price system. Admittedly, market forces even here play some role, for example in terms of grade drift through the salary structure or in the shape of opportunities for external earnings, but, arguably, market forces play a more limited role than in the U.S. Once this is admitted, the determination of pay cannot be relegated to external market factors, but must be brought within the model, and the interplay of individual and collective utility functions is strengthened. More importantly perhaps the dominance of collective utility is less clear-cut if we allow that the benefits of research in particular may have important individual advantages. It seems certain that in our own individual utility functions the quality of the department in which we work is an important factor. This includes not only the quality of students and the quality of our colleagues, but also the quality of research in the department as a whole from which we may derive a spin-off benefit. These factors could of course simply reflect non-pecuniary benefits from our work, perhaps giving rise to a negative compensating differential, cf. observation 8, p. 597, but these factors also confer on the individual status by association which may be related to enhanced promotion prospects or opportunities for consultancy, both of which yield additional pay and hence individual benefits. Thus the collective utility function arguments may reflect in part sources of individual utility and the implied interdependence raises a doubt about the sharp cut-off in the model between individual and collective utility functions.

Thirdly, how far is the Department truly a collective? One very interesting section of the paper is concerned with problems of majority voting, voting sequences and log-rolling, but this is based on equality of participation in decisions, one person – one vote. The discussion allows, however, for weighted decision-taking and segmented decision-taking, and this seems to be more relevant in a U.K. setting. The U.K. Department, though still in some respects a collective, is typically rather hierarchical. There is something of a paradox here, for in the U.K. the tenure even of junior staff is more secure: appointment to tenured positions is generally subject only to a probationary period of 3 or 4 years (and there are difficulties in removing probationers even then), as compared with the usual 7 year period in the U.S., which appears to be more strictly applied. In these circumstances we might predict more intensive screening of applicants before appointment in the U.K., but the evidence suggests that it is actually less intensive, with less faculty time allocated to it and more administrative involvement and procedures. For example, the department may not know the full list of applicants, or even the 'short list': or if they do, they may have no opportunity to exercise a collective preference. Thus in the matter of hiring new recruits to the decision group – obviously a key area of decisions for the collective, the U.K. department acts differently from its U.S. counterpart, and not altogether as we would expect of a true collective. A *general* theory of the department would have to account for these anomalies between the two systems.

My personal feeling is that the U.K. situation may be rather more akin to an industrial relations situation in which the Department chairman (or caucus) *bargains* with administrators for departmental benefits, such as extra staff, staff/student ratios, accommodation improvements etc., subject to the need to satisfy the collective and individual utility functions of the rank and file members. In that case the department would seem less a collective than a collective bargaining agent such as that envisaged in the Ross model. Here bargaining is a triangular process involving union leadership, rank and file membership, and the employer, and the political sensitivity of the leadership is important in sustaining its credibility. The implied hypothesis that the department may operate as a labour union would need much more thorough investigation, even for the U.K., but it may be worth consideration. Even in the U.S., one wonders if at least some departments might not conform to such a model, particularly those in which a hierarchical system is in evidence, and the participation of non-tenured faculty in some areas of decision-making is reduced.

Section 3

What these points suggest is the possibility that institutional and conventional factors play a significant role in determining departmental behaviour. It is interesting then to look at James and Neuberger's empirical observations (pp. 596-599) to see how far they hold up in a U.K. context.

On the whole they do, and this may be taken to be generally encouraging for the model, but a couple of minor points need to be made. First, observation 2 is that every increase in undergraduate or graduate teaching yields an increase in Faculty and therefore Research. Apart from wondering if this is altogether true even in the U.S., I have to say that such a relation is far from clear in the U.K., where increases in student numbers and student/staff ratios are much more a matter of centralised regulation and university budgets are provided from central government funds and are based on implied commitment to the continuation or expansion of specified activities. At least in certain ranges there are discontinuities which may have the effect of actually reducing Research as student numbers and student/staff ratios are geared up. Secondly, observation 6 notes that large variations will be predicted in average costs and student/staff ratios across institutions but in the same disciplines. This may be so, but I suspect the variance is less in the U.K. than in the U.S. where 300-400 per cent variations are observed for graduate work. Such a degree of variation might indeed be suggestive of what Williamson has termed 'control loss' within organisations subject to discretionary management decision-taking. The U.S. system might then be closer to the unitary model of the decision unit, as compared with the U.K. system characterised by greater financial and strategic control at the centre.

More generally, one area which, for me, carried less than complete conviction, was the role of technology, though perhaps this is partly a matter of definition. It is arguable that if, as the model indicates, no utility attaches to undergraduate teaching except as a means to graduate teaching and research, one would expect greater attention to have been paid to technological innovation at the lower level, typified by the large class. If this hasn't happened, why not? Admittedly, *some* substitutions and adaptation have occurred to this end, as for example in the use of graduate students for some undergraduate teaching duties, and the acceptance of large lecture class formats at the lower undergraduate level. It occurs to me that intensive screening of student intake may contribute to the same purpose of freeing faculty time from undergraduate chores. But university departments have been slow to develop programmed and mechanised learning, and self-instruction aids which would surely be effective in freeing more time for graduate teaching and research. This might suggest that undergraduate teaching has intrinsic positive utility – perhaps lower than that of G or R. This, added to a slight unease about the general handling of the technology aspect of the paper, at least indicates that it might reward further consideration.

Section 4

In summary, I find that the non-profit organisation aspects of the model are particularly convincing, but I am less sure of the generality of the labour managed collective postulate which seems to be more affected by institutional and conventional factors.

As indicated, my own view is that there is greater inter-dependence between the individual and collective utility functions than the model allows. It also seems that salary, through accelerated promotion or prestige attaching to research, is at least as important in explaining the prominence of Research in these functions, as compared with Research in its own intrinsic right.

This comment should not close without reference to James and Neuberger's interesting Appendix, which sets the department in a university context. Maybe because I view the U.K. as having a more centralised system, I see university constraints and effects of other general environmental features on departments as having a prominent role in determining departmental behaviour. This Appendix rings very true, especially in its comments about the tightening of competition as the pool of students reduces in size, about efforts to economise in teaching resources, and about the problems of information manipulation and bargaining between administrators and departments. But given the validity of these comments, might one venture the hope that further work will be done to integrate the department as conceived in this paper into its wider context?

Despite these caveats, this paper appears to present a fruitful method of analysing departmental behaviour, and the authors have provided us with some useful insights into an area that we are perhaps too close to, and that consequently has not been given the attention it deserves, especially in these days of financial stringency and declining student populations.

Extra-governmental powers in public schooling: The unions and the courts

E. G. WEST   and   R. J. STAAF*

Carleton University   *Virginia Polytechnic Institute*

Introduction

Up to quite recently welfare economic analysis of public schooling confined itself to a review of normative arguments why education should be a major concern of government. The reasons were customarily classified under two heads: (a) external benefits, (b) the need for the special protection of infants. Such an approach is no longer adequate. The comprehensive analyst is ·obliged, at least, to complement it with some theory of government. Many economists today are accordingly scrutinizing the very institution that previously was assumed to be the unquestioned resolver of all 'market failures.'

In America the economists' new investigation of 'government failures' has found some focus in the controversy triggered off by Proposition 13. But others believe that there are deeper problems not addressed by the balanced budget and tax limitation amendments. These relate to those less conspicuous political powers that lay beyond formal government itself and reside in independent agencies and the courts. In the field of education, for instance, many believe that the busing program has largely been the outcome of independent and executive branch activity supported by a policy-involved judiciary.

Clearly, if economists continue to wish to hand over some educational responsibility to a 'democratic government' they need to know what that agency really means in practice if their analysis is to be complete and to be free from the charge of being institutionally sterile.

Our paper will investigate the non-trivial extra-governmental powers in education now employed by the new regulatory-judicial complex in America. Our task involves some discussion of constitutional and labor law, some economics of politics, as well as some conventional micro-economic theory of markets. The subject selected for special attention here is the emerging regulatory obligation to employ teacher union services via agency shops in the negotiation of the terms of employment together with the current judicial

241

support for the idea. The discussion, which will focus upon one recent Supreme Court Case, demonstrates how the resort to government authority might face citizens with educational costs for higher than otherwise and so bring into question the older normative presumptions.

The legal setting

Agency shops are distinguished from union shops in that, while they compel employees to pay a service charge as their contribution to the union's collective bargaining expenses, they do not require membership in the union. In recent years non-union employees have challenged the expenditure of their compulsory dues to finance, via unions, political and ideological causes that they do not support. They have argued that their obligatory service charges amount to compulsory financial support of unions. This being the case, their First Amendment rights are violated.

Although the Supreme Court has ruled that agency shop assessments required of non-union members cannot be used for political purposes which those employees oppose,[1] it has, nevertheless, found that agreements which condition employment on agency or union shop membership do not, on their face, impinge upon constitutionally protected rights of association.[2]

In 1977, The Supreme Court in *Abood v. Detroit Board of Education* examined the constitutionality of agency shop clauses in the *public* employment sector.[3] It held that public employees may be compelled to pay union service charges for legitimate collective bargaining activities. The Court ruled, additionally, nevertheless, that unions could not use these funds for political causes to which non-union employees objected.

We present below a critical analysis of the central argument underlying the Court's judgement in *Abood*. We shall initially focus upon that part of its deliberation that reflected previous reasoning of Congress. The latter stems largely from the Labor Management Relations Act of 1947, an act whose language suffered from reliance on undefined or imprecise terms. These included 'the benefits of collective bargaining,' the need for 'industrial peace,' the essentiality of 'stability,' the need to avoid 'confusion' in labor markets, the disadvantages of 'inter-union rivalry,' and the need to discipline potential 'free-riders' who want to benefit from union bargaining without contributing to the costs.

Section 1 scrutinizes the current arguments for collective bargaining agents in public employment. Section 2 examines 'labor stability' and 'union rivalry' in terms of a competitive economic model. The concept of 'free-riders' is examined in Section 3. Section 4 applies the labor monopoly model. Section 5 examines the more recent concept of 'forced-riders.' The Legislature's reasons why bargaining should be done through an exclusive agent, are explored in

Section 6. Section 7 will assess the 'countervailing power' argument. Section 8 examines the final bearings of the real world regulatory-judicial complex on the economists' hitherto cloistered arguments for the role of the 'public sector' in education.

1. Arguments for collective bargaining

Among the more important precedents recognized by the *Abood* Court in the area of labor relations, was the Labor Management Relations Act of 1947. Acknowledging problems in restrictions to 'free employment' that the closed shop created, Congress, nevertheless, decided that non-union members would legitimately be obliged to defray the 'substantial expense' involved in union bargaining activities. The act set out to 'remedy the most serious abuses of compulsory union membership' and yet promote stability by eliminating free-riders (REP. No. 105, 80th Cong., First Sess. 7, 1947).

In the words of the *Abood* Court in 1977:

Designation of a single representative avoids the confusion that would result from attempting to enforce two or more agreements containing different terms and conditions of employment and prevents inter-union rivalries from creating dissent within the work force and also frees the employer from the possibility of facing conflicting demands from different unions and permits the employer and a union to reach agreements on settlements that are not subject to attack from rival organizations (*Abood*, page 1783).

This reasoning seems to amount to the argument, simply, that costs of negotiation, when channelled through an exclusive agent, are lower than otherwise. In addition, the use of compulsion in obliging all workers to contribute to negotiation costs is necessary in order to resolve the 'free-rider' problem. The latter, it was emphasized, was not confined to the private sector.[4] In the precise terms of the Court's deliberation both 'labor stability' and 'labor peace' could only be effectively served by a system of exclusive representation.

Since the Court acknowledged that unions provide a wide variety of services, including political lobbying, it was important to be clear on the types of services that should be paid by all employees whether union members or not. These were summarized under the heading of 'negotiation costs.' In turn these were described as including: 'Collective bargaining, contract administration, and grievance adjustment' (*Abood*, p. 1798).

2. An economic model: The comparative market case

We now proceed to a presentation of the items in the legal discussion, so far, that uses conventional economic tools. Our first simple model starts with the

244

assumption of a private and competitive market in education. The argument will later be modified to accommodate the facts that (a) the most labor is employed in the *public* sector, (b) obvious and important imperfections in competition prevail.

In economic terms 'negotiation costs of employment' are embraced in the wider term 'search costs.' In any market buyers 'seek out' sellers and vice versa. This process involves the expenditure of time, and time is of economic value. Objective resources in transport, communication, and advertising are also expended. Once buyers and sellers are in touch with each other, they then have to search for mutually acceptable terms of employment. This too takes time and involves further costs such as the cost of legal documentation, and setting up and conducting interviews.

It is important to notice that both buyers and sellers share in the search costs. A seller of labor, for instance, will undergo costs of transport, time costs of consulting job-opportunity columns, and costs of mailing and following up applications. Once in touch with a prospective buyer of his labor, the potential worker will undergo costs of negotiating terms and conditions. Likewise the employer will be involved in costs of search which involve expenses in advertising, transport, and preliminary screening of suitable types of candidates for the vacancies in question. Once the educational employer is in touch with prospective candidates he will then contribute his further share of

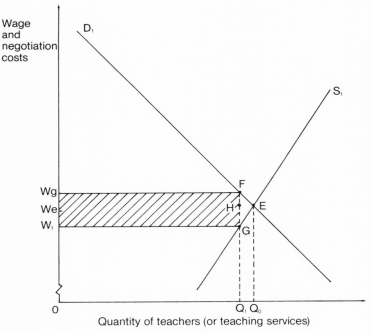

Quantity of teachers (or teaching services)

Figure 1.

the search costs, for instance, by meeting the cost of interviews, by more specific screening operations, and by covering the costs of legal documentation.

These points can be illustrated diagrammatically. Refer to Figure 1. The curve D_1 is the employer's demand curve for teaching services per time period. The curve S_1 is the supply curve for teaching services. In the absence of any search costs, and assuming a competitive market with homogeneous workers, the wage will be determined at the industry level where the demand curve intersects the supply curve at point E. The resulting wage will be We and the quantity of labor employed will be Q_0.

The presence of search and negotiation costs results in an unavoidable restriction of the quantity of labor employed to Q_1. At this quantity the cost of search and negotiation per unit of labor is shown as FG. The determination of Q_1 can be viewed as a decrease in the supply curve causing it to shift to the left and a new intersect at F; or a decrease in the demand curve causing a parallel shift to the left causing a new intersection with the original supply curve at G; or a combination of both when costs are borne by both.

Compared with the zero negotiation cost equilibrium at E and a corresponding wage of We, the employer now is faced with an equilibrium at F with a corresponding higher gross wage Wg (the gross wage includes the search costs). The employer's share of the costs of negotiation is here the difference between We and Wg (= HF). The employee, meanwhile, faces a new *net* wage (net of search and negotiation costs) of W_1, determined by the equilibrium at G. His share of the search and negotiation cost are the difference between We and W_1 (= HG). The total search and negotiation costs are the costs per worker (FG) times the number employed. This is shown as the shaded area of the diagram or $WgFGW_1$. These costs, as illustrated, are shared approximately equally between the buyers and sellers of labor.

We shall next consider five available institutional methods of handling the negotiation costs. First, employers may make individual contracts with each separate employee. One way of doing this would be for the employer to advertise one fixed wage, qualification, and employment condition. The employees in this case are price-takers. Although all the costs of negotiations would be handled directly by the employer, this is not to say that a share of these costs would not be borne by the employee. Some will undoubtedly be reflected in his (lower) net wage.

The second institutional method would be for groups of workers to employ competing collective agents. These would negotiate on behalf of the workers directly with the employer.

Third, employees could employ the services of competing unions. Unions, of course, do not typically confine themselves simply to negotiating contracts. They supply other services, many of them political, as *Abood* acknowledges. But in our case employees could select the package of political-plus-

246

negotiation services that they preferred. For there would be a list of competing unions from which to choose.

The fourth method is the institution of the closed shop. In this case all employers would agree to negotiate through one union exclusively. All employees, meanwhile, would be obliged to be members of that same union.

A fifth method, the one favored by the *Abood* Court, is that of the *agency* shop. All employees are obliged to pay agency fees limited to the costs of negotiation. In the terminology of *Abood*, these include the cost of collective bargaining, administering the contract, and grievance procedure. No nonunion employee would be obliged to pay for any other costs, such as union political lobbying costs.

The reasoning behind the National Labor Relations Act of 1947 was that *exclusive* representation through one agent, methods four and five, keeps negotiation costs at their lowest. In Figure 1 this smallest possible negotiation cost is the shaded area. The presumption is that methods one, two, and three would result in larger shaded cost areas. Figure 2 compares the costs of method one whereby each employer negotiates a separate contract for each employee at a given, higher, average, cost. This cost is shown here in Figure 2 as JI. Such higher costs would result in a lower total employment of Q_2. The new shaded cost area would be Wg_2IJW_2. The result of a change from the exclusive agent to individual negotiation would evidently have two disadvan-

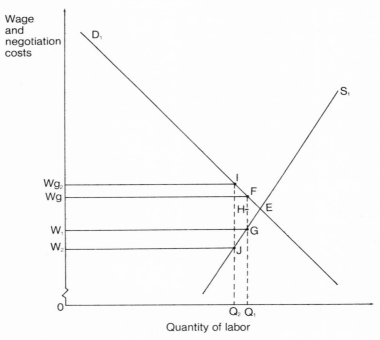

Figure 2.

tages. The first is a reduction of employment of Q_1 to Q_2. The second is an increase in search and negotiation cost, shared by both sides, when Q_2 labor is employed.[5]

Suppose we start at this equilibrium, at Q_2 employment. Believing that negotiation costs can be reduced by resort to institutional method number two (competing unions), some workers may attempt to join unions, or other collective agents, to perform their negotiation for them. It may soon become apparent to them, however, that other workers will 'free-ride' and therefore enjoy the largest reduction in costs of search and negotiation. Because of the manifestation of 'free-riders,' the potential numbers of collective negotiation agents would eventually hold back or withdraw from them unless all other workers were obliged to pay their share of the costs.

It is this scenario that the Court has in mind when it refers to 'free-riders' and the 'labor instability' they cause. It should be noticed, however, that it is only when attempts are being made by some workers to obtain the services of collective agents, while other workers stand back, that any possible chance occurs of what the Court calls worker 'dissension,' or disturbances of 'industrial peace,' or an interference with 'labor stability.' When potential members of collective agents eventually give up the attempt to join, because of the lack of cooperation of the free-riders, the situation falls back to the first institutional alternative: individual negotiation. This is represented in Figure 2 with employment of Q_2 and search and negotiation costs of JI. At this equilibrium there *is* labor stability; for there is no further incentive to change from this position.

Another reason for concluding 'labor dissension' will not occur, at least in the long run, is that, at this equilibrium, all workers will contribute the same amount in negotiation costs. For, in the competitive situation here assumed, if any one employer attempts to impose a higher negotiation cost on one employee than another, employers elsewhere in the system will bid for the services of the 'exploited' worker at a lower cost of negotiation. A succession of such costs will bring all negotiation costs to equality.

Such an outcome also rules out another of the fears of the legislature and the Court: the fear that 'confusion' will prevail in the absence of an agency shop. (See the quotation of *Abood* p. 621.) Clearly there can be no confusion if uniformity of gross and net wages prevails.

3. Free-riders

In terms of Figure 2, the *Abood* judgement is that the negotiation costs, shown as IJ in the individual contracting equilibrium (with Q_2 employment), can only be reduced (to FG) through compulsory agency shop legislation, because free-riding prevents any 'free market' alternative.

While compulsion, necessarily generates funding for the provision of the 'public good' of collective negotiation, by definition, we shall show later that it does not necessarily solve the preference revelation problem. Prior to this we need to explore a serious ambiguity of the public good that the agency shop is argued to bring.

4. Labor monopoly case

The public good component in the *Abood* decision is the reduction in costs that can be obtained from the agency shop compared with the alternative bargaining methods. Recall that without a collective agent, the transactions costs of individual bargaining are shown in Figure 2 by the area Wg_2–I–J–W_2. These are shared between employer and employee. The introduction of a bargaining agent reduces these costs to Wg–F–G–W_1. The public good, reduction in transactions cost is equal to $[Wg_2$–I–J–$W_2] - [Wg$–F–G–$W_1]$ $= [Wg_2$–I–F–$Wg] + [W_1$–G–J–$W_2]$.

Note that everyone gains. Taxpayers pay a reduced wage rate, Wg_2 to Wg and thereby increase their demand for teachers, while employees receive a higher net wage W_1 instead of W_2 inducing more teachers to enter the market. Thus, the external benefits accrue to taxpayers and employees alike.

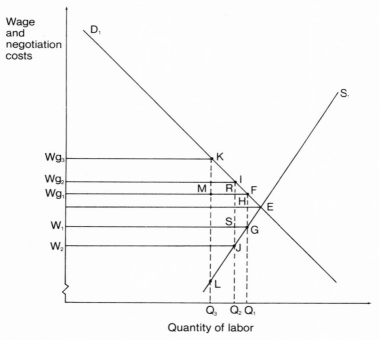

Figure 3.

The free-rider problem involved here is that, if there is no coercion, once a collective bargaining agreement has been reached and cost savings are realized, one member may refuse to pay his union dues W_1 up to the limit of W_2 and thereby increase his net wage from W_1 to Wg. If one individual has such an incentive, so do all employees. Eventually, therefore, the voluntary collective union will collapse with no members. The situation will revert to individual bargaining and higher transaction cost where both taxpayers and employees are worse off. Further analysis, however, suggests that even if compulsory agency shops reduce transaction costs, other educational costs to taxpayers may be seriously increased in a more than offsetting manner.

Refer to Figure 3. Assume that we have initially reached the equilibrium with Q_1 labor and negotiation costs of FG. Since the legislature, supported by the Court, has given *exclusive* negotiation rights to the one selected agent, a monopoly has been created that enjoys the full backing of the authorities. There is no reason to suppose that this monopoly is any different from others in that it will attempt, in time, to exploit its monopoly position and charge a price for its services that is higher than its marginal costs. In other words, although the negotiation costs are priced initially at FG there is no reason to suppose that the price charged will stay at this level for long. Ultimately the price charged for exclusive bargaining rights may be pushed higher than the individual contracting equilibrium shown in Figure 3 at employment of Q_2.

In terms of Figure 3 the initial benefits in contracting cost reduction is $Wg_2IJW_2 - Wg_1FGW_1$. Since the exclusive agent has a monopoly of bargaining, it is possible, at one extreme, for all these benefits to be appropriated entirely by *him*. This being so, the contracting costs will be pushed back to IJ. The final monopoly rents earned by the agent will then be $Wg_2IJW_2 - Wg_1RSW_1$ since demand will contract to Q_2. Society as a whole will certainly benefit from reduced costs. But the benefits will be distributed almost entirely to the monopoly agent instead of mainly to its clients.

If the legislature and the Court wish to avoid this outcome they should have at least made provision for the periodic competitive tender of the services of agency contracting. That is, although a single agent may enjoy the right to provide services in one particular year or a period, say, of three years, it should do so in the knowledge, that after its period of tender has expired it will have to compete with other agency bidders for future business. This competition for collective agents would result in a competitive price charge of FG. There is no evidence in the political and legal debates of the recognition of the need for this provision. Indeed, *Abood* speaks of the social value of *reducing* competition between unions, a situation it condemns as 'union rivalry' (*Abood*, p. 1783). It may however be true that, at least implicitly, the Court is assuming that a periodic tendering scheme can be simulated through the democratic process. That is, such a process can bring pressure to bear upon any one school board to change, periodically, the union that is selected as the agency shop. But even if this is the case, we shall show subsequently that there are further costs involved in substituting such a process for the ordinary market tendering.

We next consider the encouragement to monopoly of a more severe kind. We shall analyze in a later section the precise details of this encouragement. Suffice it here to say that, in coercing all teachers to negotiate through one agency, that agency is presented with powers of discipline that are normally more difficult to exert in a competitive system. The agency, in other words, can undertake bargaining that is 'aggressive,' or that leads to wages *above the normally competitive level of Wg_2* in Figure 3. Suppose, for instance, such aggressive bargaining leads to the wage of Wg_3. This new monopoly wage will enlarge the total wage bill. For, as drawn, Wg_3 times $Q_3 > Wg_2$ times Q_2.[6]

These changes may be viewed as induced *negative* externalities. They are of two kinds. First, there is the injury to a minority of teachers who lose their jobs. This minority will be the difference between Q_2 en Q_3 labor units. (Or the difference between Q_1 and Q_3 if we start from the beginning with the agency shop legislation.) The second negative externality is the increased bill to taxpayers. This is the difference between the areas OWg_3KQ_3 and OWg_2IQ_2 (or OWg_1FQ_1 if agency shops are authorized).

The second induced externality raises a particularly serious constitutional issue. It focusses on the action of a government in delegating, in effect, its powers of taxation to some non-elected group. For, indeed, the increased wage bill that is caused by the monopolizing union has the equivalent effect of an extra tax on citizens. It is interesting that the appellees in *Abood*, themselves advanced the analogy of agency-fees to 'taxes.' Their argument was that:

When Congress in the [National Labor Relations and Railway Labor Acts] adopted employee self-government in labor relations, and approved pro-rata taxation for its costs, it was replicating the principle long operative of every level of our government systems. A citizen, so long as he remains a member of the community must pay his share of its governance costs, local state and federal. His personal agreement with the expenditures of taxes is not a condition of his duty to pay.

This argument assumes 'governments within governments' where there are special jurisdictions covering subgroups in society. Its validity will be questioned later on in our analysis. Whatever its justification, in its own terms, however, the argument of 'democracy under majority voting' within groups is different from one where a given group in society is allowed to tax another group outside its jurisdiction. And that is what the monopoly price increase from Wg_1 to Wg_3 in Figure 3 amounts to – the taxation of individuals, as citizens, who are outside the labor union.

It is in *this* sense that Robert S. Summers (1976: 1) could be justified in his conclusion that:

Public employee collective bargaining is a law-making process to which a public employer is a party. By this process the parties adopt (and administer) laws and legally *authorize policies* that shape public benefit conferral. A collective bargaining agreement is law for the parties, for affected public beneficiaries, and for taxpayers. ... The threshold enquiry must therefore be: Is public employee collective bargaining democratic? Or does it conflict with democracy?

Where labor monopoly is demonstrated as an outcome of the agency shop legislation, the argument that such a negotiation system is necessary on the grounds of a compelling interest becomes ambiguous. While it may be in the interest to take advantage of *lower* costs through economies of scale in negotiation (a contention that we are challenging in any case), this maybe more than offset by the *increased* costs of monopoly, as explained. The only possible way to meet the above quoted objection of Summers, that monopoly pricing is, in fact, 'taxation without representation,' is to argue that the legislature finds, simultaneously, *two* compelling interests: One, to obtain the negotiation cost decreases through the agency shop; two, to redistribute from the rest of society to teachers as a class, or to those of them who will still be employed after the monopolization via agency shop legislation has taken place.

5. Forced riders

We shall now return to the *pre-legislation* equilibrium that is denoted in Figure 3 by the gross wage Wg_2 and labor quantity Q_2. Our focus will switch to the empirical problem of 'proving' that potential free-riders do compel this position. It is important to notice that, even if the economies of scale of collective negotiation through a single agency shop are available, the problem of excluding free-riders becomes costly primarily *after* the creation of the collective good by voluntary (private) agreement. Prior to a contract within the community to produce the collective good, there will be no such good for any member, and exclusion will apply to all by definition. Since exclusion is the factor that elicits demand, intermediaries might suggest terms demanding an offer from an individual provided it is matched by some assurance that the remainder of the community would make a similar offer. If other members of the community do *not* eventually pay, our particular individual will have, in effect, a 'money-back' guarantee. At this *ex-ante* stage the dominant motive thus switches away from the desire to ride free at the expense of the group, to the wish to be assured that the others will make an appropriate contribution. Similarly, the individual's offer becomes not only his actual payment but also a commitment to others that he will participate (Brubaker, 1975).

On this reasoning individuals will behave, not according to the clever, or 'cheating,' free-rider who calculatingly fails to reveal his preferences, but instead, according to what Brubaker calls 'a golden rule of revelation of demand for collective goods.' According to *this* rule, under pre-contract group excludability the dominant tendency will be for each individual to reveal accurately his preference for a collective good, provided that he has some assurance that others will match his offer in appropriate amounts.

The 'golden rule of revelation' hypothesis is thus a rival to that of the 'free-rider.' The only scientific method of choosing between them is the empirical test. And what empirical tests have so far been made fail, in fact, to give unambiguous support to the free-rider hypothesis (see especially Bohm, 1973: 111-130).

The proposition that people do *not* reveal their preferences seems to have prevailed, nevertheless, even though it amounts only to an assertion. The assertion, moreover, has typically been followed by another one: That the coercive police power of government is required to induce full expression of demand. But the difficulty with this argument is that it is not obvious that police power, alone, can generate the necessary missing information.

The resort to blunt coercion in the face of unverified information may lead to unintended detrimental side effects. There could result 'forced-riding' by individuals who are coerced into expressing non-existent 'demands' for collective goods. Worse still, and especially in the case of *Abood*, some people may regard the 'good' as in fact a *bad*.

In the absence of clear information as to demands, it is arguable that the American Constitution places a higher rank on unanimous decision-making among individuals rather than the resort to simple *majority* voting rules expressed through government. Indeed, when the Court strikes down legislation as being unconstitutional, it may be argued that it is indirectly appealing to what we have referred to as a rule of unanimity.

6. Individual versus collective agencies

As a preliminary to the argument in this section it is important to emphasize that our discussion initially started with a competitive model. It is difficult to conceptualize public education today as a competitive market. Single school districts that encompass the state of Hawaii or the District of Columbia are clear examples of education monopolies. An earlier era of little red school houses therefore might have been a better example of our scenario.

Nevertheless, it will be helpful to dwell a little further with the competitive model. In a competitive market, transactions costs can be lowered by the use of agents, but there will be competing agents in the market and an absence of collective bargaining agents reflecting the interests of a *collectivity* of buyers and sellers. We observe many institutional arrangements that emerge from the market voluntarily that reduce the costs of doing business. Real estate agents, employment agencies, stock brokers, department stores, retail stores, catalogue stores, for instance, all serve to reduce transaction costs in this way.

Correspondingly we can picture a world in which each separate teacher hires a separate agent for himself or herself, just as he or she employs an agent to purchase a house. Imagine for instance, a world where there are five teachers of varying qualifications. The first teacher has a marginal productivity worth $5000 per year, the second $10,000, the third $15,000, the fourth $20,000 and the fifth $25,000 per annum. In a world of private and separate contracting there would be five separate transactions using at most five separate agents. Suppose that each contract has a negotiation cost of $100. The total transaction costs would be $500.

Next, suppose that an agent approaches all the teachers with the proposition that he could reduce the total transaction costs from $500 to something just above $100 provided he could be given permission to negotiate one uniform wage which is the average of the presently earned wages which equals $15,000 per annum. Each teacher would then have to face negotiation (contracting) costs of just over $20 instead of $100.

Such a proposition would clearly produce the 'public good' of reduced negotiation costs. It would, nevertheless, be rejected. This is because two of the teachers, namely those already earning $20,000 and $25,000, would be worse off. In other words, what this common transaction would do, besides reducing negotiation costs, would be to compress differentials or reduce the dispersion of wages. Only coercion of some kind could achieve this result.

To overcome this barrier, a private agent may next offer to conduct a single transaction to obtain a uniform wage of $26,000 a year. This is just above the highest wage already being earned. He could do this by attempting to offer two services: (1) the service of reduced transaction costs, (2) the service of producing a labor monopoly for his clients.

In all probability this arrangement too would fail because the change to a monopoly wage is a move upwards along the demand curve for teachers such that at the margin some teachers lose their jobs.

In the third scenario our single agent, realizing that private coercion is insufficient, and that the government power of legislation alone will provide him with the labor control that he seeks, he may successfully lobby his government to provide legislation that results eventually in a new wage of $26,000 and *prevents the employer from employing anybody at less than this wage*. It is this last provision that gives the power of coercion that is necessary to make the monopoly viable. Moreover, his chances of obtaining lobby support will be increased if, as is likely, he can get a majority of the five teachers to support him. Indeed, it is not necessary to obtain a new monopoly wage of $26,000. A wage of $16,000, for instance, would suffice, for three teachers out of five would support it, those previously earning under this amount. This majority of teachers will be presented with a 'tie in sale' by the agent. In order to obtain their increased income net of (lower) negotiation costs, they will have to 'buy' also a reduced dispersion of incomes.

The negotiator will lobby the government primarily with the argument that the chief benefit from the new arrangement, an arrangement that can be effected through the agency shop, is the reduction of transaction costs. These will be reduced from $ 500 to something just above $ 100. This will be the 'public good' aspect of his argument to the legislature. He will also argue that he is unable to achieve this cost saving because individuals will not operate voluntarily to achieve the same result because there is a tendency to 'free-ride.' The agent will not, of course, make conspicuous the other and more important cost of his proposal, the cost of monopoly pricing, a cost that to taxpayers more than offsets the reduction in negotiation costs.

There is at least *prime facie* evidence to suggest that this last piece of reasoning fits the facts of agency shop legislation in America. Thus a testable hypothesis is that collective bargaining via legislative union and agency shops will be followed by a compression of wage differentials, or a reduction in the dispersion of teacher's salaries. Econometric evidence is now available (Freeman, 1978) that, in effect, clearly supports our hypothesis.

Of course it is not necessary for the monopoly 'benefits' of the new arrangement to be taken out entirely in the form of monetary income increases. There is a variety of ways, all of them non-pecuniary, of obtaining equal benefits. For instance, teachers may bargain for preferred curricula, increased vacations or a reduction in hours. One case of bargaining for reduced hours, for example, was reported in the New York Times (quoted by Summers, 1976: 37) as follows:

In some places, bargaining has resulted in a significant shortening of the school day. New York City now provides one example in which many children are affected. During the 1975 bargaining round after a brief strike, the New York City Teacher's Union and the city school board agreed to a school day that for some junior high school students lasts less than five hours on certain days each week.

The argument, in this case, would have been that the reduction in hours was necessary for the welfare of the *children*. Nevertheless, as Summers (1976: 37) argues, it is the *teachers'* welfare that enjoys unambiguous increase: 'Hours are like money. Reduced work is like a raise. Thus, employees put high value on it and frequently seek it, in various forms, at the bargaining table.' Indeed, it is to be expected that as higher incomes are negotiated there will be *increasing* pressure to take out benefits in reduced hours. This is because leisure is not taxed whereas increasing marginal increments to income are, and at increasing rates.

7. Countervailing power: The monopsony case

The impression is frequently given when reading the *Abood* decision, that the *main* 'public good' that the agency shop allegedly brings is not the reductions

of transactions costs in bargaining but a simple use of countervailing collective power to confront a strong and potentially exploiting employer. The
extreme case of such exploitation, is known in economics, as 'monopsony,' the
situation where employees have no alternative employer than the present one.
If this is, indeed, the reasoning of the Court it calls for the following five
observations:

First, there is the possibility (already mentioned) that the extra gains from
bargaining on the union's side be appropriated largely by the agent itself
instead of its clients. Second, the conventional monopsony argument predicts
that after collective bargaining employment will not fall but may even expand.
As far as we know there has been no systematic evidence collected to test the
hypothesis in this way. Third, if monopsony exists it is likely to stem from the
supersession of a private by a public school system. It is certainly true that, in
the real world, the number of alternative employers has been reduced considerably in most public systems of education. And, indeed, with the recent
development of 'consolidation' among school districts, the number has
shrunk dramatically. Fourth, a fundamental objection to erecting a monopoly union with the aim of correcting or countervailing the power of a
monopsonist employer, is that the employer in this case is the government. As
Summers (1976: 11) argues: 'It is one thing for private groups to countervail a
big profit-seeking corporation and quite another for them to countervail the
government. A system of *political* checks and balances already exists. The
public employer is financed by the taxpayer and is supposed to be subject to
the control of and answerable to the citizenry.'

A fifth point is that even where monopsony prevails, the policy implications
are obscure. It would only be by coincidence that the 'bargaining powers' of
both sides exactly offset each other. A newly authorized agency shop may, as
we have argued, discover monopoly powers stronger than those of the employer. The resulting monopoly wage will burden taxpayers and cause some
disemployment of teachers. The agent, meanwhile, need only satisfy a *majority*
of its constituent electorate and membership. If workers were assumed to be
self-interested with no regard for fellow employees at the pre-compulsory
stage, there is no reason to assume that they will suddenly, under compulsory
agreement, be benevolent to their fellow employees. The only constraint they
face is that their self-interest coincides with a majority coalition. Those who
form a majority coalition to elect their agent who has the exclusive right of
bargaining will now take a 'free-ride,' not by avoiding a share of the cost of
collective bargaining, but by forming a majority to extract all the collective
gains from exclusive collective bargaining while forcing the minority, who
receive no gains, to contribute to the costs. This if 'free-riding' in reverse.

At the extreme is the situation, discussed previously, of increasing the wage
rates above the competitive level such that unemployment results. Here, the
majority is taking a 'free-ride' on those who were formerly employed and who

now become unemployed. This type of 'free-riding,' induced by compulsion, has a much more malevolent character. Under voluntary arrangements, a 'free-ride' resulted in a cost that was shared by a large number of fellow employees. Under compulsion, free-riding behavior imposes costs that are concentrated among a few. This would hardly be termed a more 'equitable' solution.

In summary, the popular view, implicit in Court decisions, that collectives act in the public interest and individuals act in their own interest, involves a 'bifurcated man' assumption.[7] But there is no reason to assume that man will necessarily act selfishly in a private store and suddenly act benevolently with regard to his fellow man when he enters a voting booth or a quasi public office. In fact, the 'free-rider' argument is an explicit rejection of the 'bifurcated man' assumption. The rejection being complete, it seems irrelevant for the Court to stress that 'The designation of the union as exclusive agent carries with it great responsibilities,' and that, in carrying out its duties, 'the union is obliged "fairly and equitably to represent all employees, ... union and nonunion..."' (*Abood*, p. 1792). If men are predominantly self-interested, those in the union will be responsible to nobody but themselves, or to their majority voting supporters. And if we can entrust such men to make 'fair and equitable representation' we can trust all men not to 'free-ride' in the first place.

8. Public education and participatory democracy

All collectives and associations are ultimately attempts to influence government in a more significant way than the sum of their individual influences through the ballot box. Associations are a way of reducing transactions costs in a manner similar to our previous discussion of union bargaining. But exclusivity and compulsory fees are not the result of a *voluntary* agreement such as the Golden Rule Revelation model. Exclusivity and compulsory dues rest on *state action* – the creation of a legal monopoly or a legally imposed association. This is not simply a case of freedom of contract. Rather it is the denial of the freedom to contract out of the state-created monopoly. It is a denial of the freedom to disassociate. Whatever justification exclusivity and compulsory dues may have in the area of the production of goods and services in the private sector, that same justification does not seem appropriate in the public sector. This would seem to be especially true in the field of public education that rests on principles of competition of ideas rather than a monopolization of ideas.

Justice Powell, in responding to the majority opinion that justified the elimination of confusion and conflict (i.e., competition) of rival (competing) teacher unions, said:

I would have thought the 'conflict' in ideas about the way in which government should operate was among the most fundamental values protected by the First Amendment. See *New York Times*

v. Sullivan, 376 U.S. 254 (1904) ... [A] State or municipality may [not] agree to set public policy
on an unlimited range of issues in closed negotiations with one category of interested individuals'
Madison School District 97 S. Ct. at 426. Such a commitment by a governmental body to exclude
minority viewpoints from the councils of government would violate directly the principle that
'government must afford all points of view an equal opportunity to be heard' *Police Department of
Chicago v. Mosley* 408 U.S. 92 (1972) – (*Abood* at 1813).

Justice Stewart, speaking for the majority, countered this argument by
contending that the dissenting employee still has his right to influence public
policy through the ballot box.

But suppose that there are no dissenting employees such as D. Louis
Abood. Assume that a rule of unanimity, rather than majority rule, is required
to form and maintain a union. Under this assumption, there are no dissenting
employees and therefore no disenfranchisement of public employees. How
does the labor monopoly affect the ordinary taxpayer-voter? The taxpayer-
voter, unlike his consumer counterpart in the private sector, has no alternatives to choose among. For example, a union in a system of 'purely private
education' is not exclusive in the same sense as it is in the public sector. A
consumer of private education can turn to alternative suppliers (schools) if he
does not agree with the policy of the union. Moreover, the consumer can
withdraw his support from the firm that provides services he does not desire.
In a 'public system' the alternative of private education is certainly still open to
the voter-taxpayer who becomes disenchanted with the policies of the public
school and its monopoly union. However, the taxpayer-voter is still required
to contribute taxes to a policy he does not support.

This line of reasoning suggests that Justice Stewart has not gone far enough
in terms of the implications of a governmentally imposed labor monopoly. Of
course, the issue before the Court was the First Amendment rights of D. Louis
Abood and others who were public employees. However, these same individuals have two sets of rights, as Justice Stewart recognized; as public employees and as voter-taxpayers. It is the latter that are compromised significantly. It is not sufficient to say that D. Louis Abood has rights that can be
exercised through the ballot box, when these rights are diminished by a
monopoly that restricts his freedom of choice as a voter. A public agency shop
is in a sense a *redistricting* that gives a majority of workers a significant
influence in public policy matters that does not exist in the absence of
exclusive representation. While exclusive representation in the private sector
may lead to a redistribution of goods, services, and income, it does not lead to
a redistricting of political power in a democracy.

The scope-of-bargaining in teacher negotiation is expanding daily. Class
size, student discipline, and curricular reform are three subjects with major
policy implications that have already found their way into the bargaining
process. The New Haven contract, for instance, provides that no class shall
have more than 34 pupils. Similar contracts prevail in New York City and in

Chicago. The point is that:

... if there are many more important factors in education, all of which compete with class size for too few dollars, then one can legitimately be anxious about the distortion, built into educational policy decisions, that may result from determining class size through collective bargaining (Wellington and Winter, Jr., 1974: 138).

Unions are not likely to reflect more than what its own members believe is good educational policy, consistent with their own self-interest. Wellington and Winter cite one case where the contract entitles a teacher to refer a student to a psychologist without the approval of his principal. They also document the way in which joint control over curricular matters has been taking hold in such places as Chicago, New York City, Washington, Philadelphia and Detroit (the location of the Abood controversy) (Wellington and Winter, Jr., 1974: 139-141).

Conclusion

While economists traditionally argue for 'a government role' for education, the precise institutional implications are not usually specified. From our article it is apparent that governments have been delegating policy-making to independent agencies and the courts. This tendency raises the question of what kind of democracy is envisaged by those who continue to urge that education should remain firmly in the 'public sector?' Economists who argue from efficiency grounds must, in future, accommodate the fact that the law allows greater encouragement to labor monopoly in the public than in the private sector. The implicit increases in costs to citizens is additional to the large extra expenses of the public bureaucracy (a subject we have not addressed here).

All these issues, meanwhile, have a direct bearing on the 'orthodox' reasoning based on 'externalities.' Without public intervention, citizens will buy education privately at a given cost (as they did before intervention). After intervention they purchase it at another cost via taxes of *most* kinds (and everybody pays taxes). Externalities are only important when they are 'Pareto relevant,' that is, when some individuals purchase 'insufficient' quantities at the margin. But the purchases are related to price. In those circumstances where the price in the public sector rises appreciably (because of labor monopoly and bureaucracy), it is possible that *less* education will be purchased than in entirely private provision. The logic of externalities would then call for the contraction of 'public provision,' a term that should be understood to encompass all those extra-government powers now bestowed on the judicial and regulatory bodies that have been examined above.

NOTES

1. See *Brotherhood of Ry. Clerks v. Allen*, 373 U.S. 113 (1963); *International Ass'n of Machinists v. Street*, 367 U.S. 740 (1961); *Railway Employees' Dep't v. Hanson*, 351 U.S. 225 (1956).
2. See, e.g., *International Ass'n of Machinists*, 367 U.S. at 749.
3. 431 U.S. 209 (1977).
4. 'The desirability of labor peace is no less important in the public sector, nor is the risk of "free-riders" any smaller' (Abood, p. 1794).
5. The sharing of costs is based on the assumption of competition among educators and competition among schools. We shall consider asymmetry in cost-sharing in other market structures in a later section.
6. A debate exists over what union leaders attempt to maximize. A monopoly by definition is a price (wage) searcher constrained by the demand curve. If Wg_3 is the bargained wage, then the union is attempting to maximize the total wage bill as Figure 3 has shown. This outcome has the smallest effect on employment. On the other hand, the union may change to a higher wage rate than Wg_3 which has the effect of higher wage rates for those still employed but a larger unemployment effect. Plausible union goals derived from union membership are the highest wage rates for members and the smallest effects on employment. The downward sloping demand curve ensures that these are conflicting goals. Because a union only operates under a majority rule, it is able to sacrifice a minority of employees to the unemployment ranks for the benefit of a majority who are able to obtain higher wage rates. A decision rule of unanimity would result in the same employment level as a competitive market and a monopoly union could only gain by price discrimination.
7. The 'bifurcated man' is one who has one set of ethics for behavior in the market place, and an opposite one in the political process' (Buchanan, 1962).

REFERENCES

Bohm, P. (1973). An approach to the problem of estimating demand for public goods. *Swedish Journal of Economics* 55: 111-130.

Brubaker (1975). Free ride, free revelation; or golden rule? *Journal of Law and Economics* 28: 147-161.

Buchanan, J. M. (1962). Politics, policy, and the Pigovian margins. *Economica* 29: 22-36.

Freeman, R. B. (1978). *Unionism and the dispersion of wages.* Harvard: Harvard Institute of Economic Research.

Summers, R. S. L. (1976). *Collective bargaining and public benefit conferral: A jurisprudential critique.* New York: Institute of Public Employment. 65 pp.

Wellington, H. H., and Winter, Jr., R. K. (1974). *The union and the cities.* Washington, D.C.: The Brookings Institution.

Comments on E. G. West and R. J. Staaf

WILLIAM L. BOYD

The Pennsylvania State University

In critiquing the effects of public employee unions, West and Staaf's paper goes far beyond the concerns of the Supreme Court in the *Abood* case, the case which provides the point of departure for their paper. Along with many other observers, I agree with their view that public employee unions possess extensive powers that may be used against the public interest. Indeed, it has been said with justification that the public employee unions are the 'new political machines' in this country, the successors to the old ethnic and patronage-based political machines.

Public employee unions have been able to gain this kind of power largely because of *qualitative differences* between public and private sector collective bargaining. Among the most important of these differences are:

1) that the behavior of both employees and employers is less constrained in public than in private sector collective bargaining by the behavior of consumers in the marketplace;
2) that whereas a strike in the *private* sector places economic pressure on both management and the union, a strike in the *public* sector, by contrast, tends to put pressures on consumers by interrupting the delivery of services they can't easily get elsewhere;
3) that public employee unions may be able to shape, through collective bargaining, public policy issues that reach well beyond simply matters of salary and working conditions and, perhaps most disconcerting;
4) that public sector unions, by engaging in political campaign activities, can elect both sides of the bargaining table.

Despite these problematic differences between collective bargaining in the public and the private sectors, public employees may have a *right* to form unions on the basis of their right as citizens to free association. (Some lower courts have held that this is the case.) Moreover, public employees, as union members, do not forfeit their *right* as citizens to engage in political activity.

Therefore, the courts are in a difficult position to try to constrain the activities of public employee unions. What seems needed is action by legislatures to modify the ground rules governing public sector bargaining in order to provide some counterbalances against the tendencies now built into the process.

I think that it might help to clarify the argument in West and Staaf's paper to note that it is not the 'agency shop' provision that creates the basis for a labor monopoly, but rather the granting of the right of 'exclusive representation' to a union, a matter that was not at issue in the *Abood* case. In this regard, it is interesting that in New York state, where until recently the agency shop – not to mention the union or closed shops – was illegal, public employee unions possessing exclusive representation flourished despite the 'free-rider' problem.

West and Staaf suggest that the legislatures and courts should have 'made provision for the periodic competitive tender of the services of agency contracting.' In fact, this already has been done. In most states both employers and employees have the right to try to bring about the decertification of unions that have won the right of exclusive representation. This fact presumably affects the behavior of the unions in power. Their leaders know that they do not possess a permanent monopoly, that unless they perform well for their membership they may be challenged by other unions, or that their members may even opt for no union at all. The fact that unions enjoying the right of exclusive representation do not possess a permanent monopoly over this right would seem to require a modification of the analysis that West and Staaf present.

In conclusion, I'd like to emphasize what I only touched on earlier, namely that contrary to West and Staaf's concerns about the 'new regulatory-judicial complex' in America and its 'extra-governmental powers' and abuses, in the case of the troublesome powers of the public employee unions it appears to me that the main culprit in the creation of these new political machines is our legislatures rather than our courts and executive agencies. This, doubtless, is no accident, for it is precisely in our legislatures that our public employee unions can have the most influence. Our dilemma, then, if we desire to curb excessive power on the part of public employee unions, is how to counterbalance the formidable lobbying power in legislatures of large, well organized unions with bulging campaign chests. Temporarily, at least, 'Proposition 13 fever' has provided a partial answer. How long this will last remains to be seen.

Comments on E. G. West and R. J. Staaf

RONALD G. EHRENBERG

Cornell University

E. G. West and R. J. Staaf's provocative paper argues that agency shop provisions in state public sector collective bargaining legislation, provisions that have recently been found to be constitutional by the Supreme Court in the Abood case (*Abood v. Detroit Board of Education*, 97 S.Ct. 1782 (1977)), may increase the costs of public education. Their underlying analytical framework is that of a state which confers monopoly power on a public sector union and a union whose sole concern is to win monopoly wage gains for its members. West and Staaf claim that the costs of these wage gains may far exceed the benefits of the legislation, the resulting reduction in negotiation costs, that are perceived by legislatures and the judiciary. In sum, *they* conclude that agency shop provisions in public education are undesirable because the provisions aid and encourage unions and the latter have primarily negative effects on the educational process.

I must confess to being unsympathetic to their conclusions and less than totally satisfied with their paper, for it presents little empirical support for the propositions they set forth. Allow me to offer four examples here.

First, one might get the impression from their paper that agency shop provisions in the public sector are fairly prevalent in the U.S. and are uniform across states. In fact, nothing could be further from the truth. As of January 1978, only 16 states explicitly provided for *any* form of union security clause, other than voluntary dues check-off, in their public sector collective bargaining legislation and not all of these contained agency shop provisions. Moreover, 31 states explicitly prohibited union security clauses for public school teachers (see Hanslowe et al., 1978).

The variation in legislative provisions across states provides one with the means to test one of their fundamental propositions, namely that union power is abetted by union security clauses. Presumably this could be done by modifying the models used in previous studies of public sector wage determination to allow the effect of unions to vary with the form of union security clause present in the state and then estimating the modified models (for example, see Ehrenberg and Goldstein, 1975). Of course in doing so, an econometric methodology that allows for the form of the legislation to be endogenously determined should be used (see, for example, Heckman, 1978).

Second, their paper at least implicitly asserts that public sector collective bargaining *per se* is unambiguously undesirable; the main effect of public sector unions that they discuss is the unions' welfare distorting effect due to the increases in their members' wages that they achieve. Nowhere do they consider the positive effects that unions may have on productivity; a point long recognized by institutional economists. In recent years Richard Freeman, James Medoff and their colleagues at Harvard, have resurrected interest in this subject, traced the routes by which unions may increase productivity (these include reducing turnover, increasing morale and motivation, and increasing informal on-the-job training) and presented empirical evidence on the effects of unions on job turnover and productivity (for a good nontechnical treatment of their views see Freeman and Medoff, 1979). Indeed, several of their recent studies suggest that union/nonunion productivity differentials may be substantial in U.S. manufacturing.[1] Furthermore, nowhere do West and Staaf consider the possibility that part of any observed union/nonunion wage differential in the public sector may be merely a compensating differential for the relatively unfavorable working conditions that unionized workers may face. Greg Duncan and Frank Stafford (1979) have presented some evidence on this point for private sector blue-collar workers in the United States; they estimate that over one-third of the observed union/nonunion differential is really a compensating differential.

West and Staaf's argument would be strengthened if one could demonstrate that observed union/nonunion wage differentials in public education were not primarily compensating differentials for inferior working conditions (some evidence on this point is presented in Antos and Rosen, 1974). It would also be strengthened if one could document that unions do not affect 'productivity' in public education. To my knowledge, however, no studies of the determinants of students' test scores or estimates of educational production functions have considered the role of unions. These are clearly important areas for future research.

Third, in the main, West and Staaf work with a purely competitive model in which an increase in teachers' wages necessarily leads to reduced teacher employment. If in fact the market for public school teachers is a monopsonistic one, then the possibility that a union-induced increase in wages would lead to increased employment and, to the extent that output is related to employment, to increased educational services exists. Thus, the alleged evils of union power that they discuss would be less obvious in this case. Indeed, as they note in Section 7, a justification for the agency shop presented in the Abood case is that it aids unions in confronting 'a strong and potentially exploiting employer...' (p. 633).

A number of studies have documented that the wages of public school teachers do tend to be lower in areas where school districts have monopsony power.[2] Presumably monopsony power arises because public school teachers are relatively immobile; the relevant labor market is local rather than regional or national. Since an overwhelming majority of public elementary school teachers are female (83.5 percent in 1970) and most female teachers are married (69 percent in 1970), mobility in the occupation is much lower than otherwise would be the case.[3]

To the extent that public school teachers' labor markets are not competitive, unions may, as noted above, actually increase employment levels. Again, their argument about the evils of union power would be strengthened if one could show that unions do reduce employment levels in the public sector. The evidence on this question, however, is not unambiguous; this is another area where more research is needed.[4]

Fourth, in discussing how collective negotiation agencies may arise under agency shop provisions (Section 6), West and Staaf derive the implication that collective bargaining will lead to 'a compression of wage differentials or a reduction in the dispersion of teachers' salaries' (p. 632). They cite a study by Freeman that they claim supports this hypothesis. My impression was that this study referred to the private sector; they only study of the effect of unions on public school teachers' wage differentials that I know of is by Alan Gustman and Martin Segal (1978). In their study of 93 central city school districts, Gustman and Segal found that collective bargaining reduces the number of years it takes to reach maximum salary, increases the differential between the minimum and maximum steps on the M.A. salary schedule *and* has no effect on starting salaries. It is not clear from these results whether collective bargaining does reduce the dispersion of teachers' salaries; this is another empirical proposition that needs further study.

While the last empirical issue I discussed is not essential to their overall conclusion, the first three are. Before one can accept the alleged evils of union shop provisions and, at least implicitly, also collective bargaining in the public sector that West and Staaf set forth, it is clear that a considerable amount of empirical research is required. At this point in time, their conclusions are simply not justified.

Allow me to conclude my discussion by turning to an argument they set forth, which I confess I have never fully understood. Building upon the work of my colleague, Robert Summers from the Cornell Law School, they argue that even if monopsony power was present in local school districts, since the employer is the government, erecting a monopoly union with countervailing power is inappropriate. For, to quote them quoting Summers (1976): 'The public employer is financed by the taxpayer and is supposed to be subject to the control of and answerable to the citizenry.' The implication is that not only is public sector collective bargaining detrimental to society, it also is inconsistent with taxpayer control of local government.

I believe this argument is incorrect. Although collective bargaining takes the decision out of the hands of the public in the short run, the settlement must be approved by the elected school board. If voters are unhappy with a settlement, the school board can be denied reelection and different negotiators employed the next time around. As long as the statutes permitting collective bargaining were adopted by the voters, I see no conflict between collective bargaining and taxpayer control.

NOTES

1. See, for example, Brown and Medoff (1978). Lest one concludes that unions always increase productivity, the evidence available for coal mining in the U.S. suggests the opposite (see Connerton, Freeman and Medoff, 1979).
2. For example, see Landon and Baird (1971), Schmenner (1973), and Lipsky and Drotning (1973). Monopsony power is often measured in these studies by variables like the inverse number of school districts in the area or the proportion of teachers in an area employed by the school district.
3. U.S. Bureau of Census (1973: Tables 1 and 31). Note that the percentage of female teachers in secondary education was only 48 percent in 1970; this may imply that school districts have less monopsony power with respect to secondary teachers and explain why in some districts secondary school teachers are paid more than elementary school teachers. For a discussion of migration in the context of a family decision model and how wives' mobility is reduced, see Mincer (1978).
4. My own attempt to test for the effect of unions on the demand curves for noneducational municipal employees proved inconclusive (see Ehrenberg, 1973). Hall and Carroll (1973) present suggestive evidence that in their sample of 100 Chicago area school districts, unions reduced the demand for teachers.

REFERENCES

Antos, J., and Rosen, S. (1974). Discrimination in the market for public school teachers. BLS Working Paper No. 24.

Brown, C., and Medoff, J. (1978). Trade unions in the production process. *Journal of Political Economy*, June: 355-379.

Connerton, M., Freeman, R., and Medoff, J. (1979). Productivity and Industrial relations: The case of U.S. Bituminous coal. Mimeo.

Duncan, G., and Stafford, F. (1979). Do union members receive compensating wage differentials? Mimeo.

Ehrenberg, R. (1973). *An economic analysis of local government employment and wages*. Final report submitted to the U.S. Department of Labor, December.

Ehrenberg, R. G., and Goldstein, G. S. (1975). A model of public sector wage negotiations. *Journal of Urban Economics*, July: 223-245.

Freeman, R., and Medoff, J. (1979). The two faces of unionism. *Public Interest*, Fall: 69-93.

Gustman, A., and Segal, M. (1978). Teachers' salary structures: Some analytical and empirical aspects of the impact of collective bargaining. In *Proceedings of the Thirtieth Annual Winter Meeting of the IRRA*, Madison, Wisc. 437-446.

Hall, W. C., and Carroll, N. (1973). The effects of teacher organizations on salaries and class size. *Industrial and Labor Relations Review*, January: 834-841.

Hanslowe, K., et al. (1978). *Union security in public employment: Of free-riding and free association.* New York State School of Industrial and Labor Relations, Ithaca, N.Y.

Heckman, J. (1978). Dummy endogenous variables in a simultaneous equation system. *Econometrica*, July: 931-961.

Landon, J., and Baird, R. (1971). Monopsony in the market for public school teachers. *American Economic Review*, December: 966-971

Lipsky, D., and Drotning, J. (1973). The influence of collective bargaining on teachers' salaries in New York. *Industrial and Labor Relations Review*, October: 18-35.

Mincer, J. (1978). Family migration decisions. *Journal of Political Economy*, October: 749-774.

Schmenner, R. (1973). The determinants of municipal employees' wages. *Review of Economics and Statistics*, February: 83-90.

Summers, R. (1976). *Collective bargaining and public benefit conferral: A jurisprudential critique.* New York State School of Industrial and Labor Relations, Ithaca, N.Y.

U.S. Bureau of Census. (1973). *1970 Census of population: Occupational characteristics*, Vol. PC(2)-7a. Washington, D.C.

Rejoinder

E. G. WEST   and   R. J. STAAF

Carleton University   *Virginia Polytechnic Institute*

We welcome this opportunity presented by Ronald Ehrenberg to attempt to connect our argument with the empirical literature.

Empirical discussion must certainly be taken seriously. Indeed much of our article consists in the presentation of new hypotheses that require testing. It should not be overlooked, however, that our *primary* endeavor was an essay in 'law and economics,' and in particular, an attempt to model the reasoning of the law courts in terms of the language of the economist. Without this, very little progress can be expected in the influence of economics upon educational policy. This task alone was surely sufficient justification for our paper.

Consider next the four examples of empirical criticism that Ehrenberg makes of our paper as it stands. First, he has the impression that we intended to convey that agency shops were very prevalent in the U.S. This is not so. In any case we treated the agency shop question as it relates to education exclusively. Even here we did not suggest that the institution is already widespread throughout most states. All we argued was that the Supreme Court has now removed any uncertainty that might previously have been an impediment to the growth of agency shops in education. An important question, therefore, is the potential impact of the agency shop institution in the U.S. The question is of most immediate significance, of course, in those states, such as Michigan, that have already adopted the agency shop. We thoroughly agree, in the meantime, that the variation in legislative provisions across states provides the means to test our propositions.

With respect to Ehrenberg's second example, he interprets us as arguing that 'public sector collective bargaining *per se* is unambiguously undesirable.' Again he reveals a misunderstanding, for a close inspection of our paper will reveal no such proposition. We are not objecting to collective bargaining as such. Indeed, we see the workers' free access to unions of their choice as consistent with the ordinary rights of freedom of association. But where there is relatively free entry in the 'union business,' one can normally expect several unions operating in different school districts and sometimes simultaneously in the same district. This situation gives workers some positive choice. This

269

can be exercised by moving to an adjacent neighborhood and sometimes by changing one's union membership at the place of existing employment.

The situation that we are addressing, however, is not one of competition in the 'union business,' but one of *monopoly* therein. This features both the union shop and the agency shop. With competitive unions, the agents (the union organizers) can earn no more than normal profits for the services rendered. With the agency shop, only one union is selected and the spur of competition is removed. One should certainly predict from this that agency shop areas will experience higher wages than ordinary unionized areas. This has, of course, not been tested yet, and this, no doubt, because the agency shop is typically a very recent phenomenon. We would, of course, welcome any empirical test when there are enough observations to work with.

But supposing that ultimate evidence produces the same kind of findings as those already available for the effects of ordinary unions. We must consider their relevance to the costs of education facing the taxpayer, for this is the question that we are primarily addressing. First, as Ehrenberg concedes, the present findings are mixed. Those unions in manufacturing, for instance, appear to increase productivity, while those in the coal industry do the opposite. But second, the apparently favorable findings on the manufacturing sector have yet to be qualified by answers to some important questions. The primary example is that referred to in the work of Weiss (1966) who suggests that unionized firms are (on average) more productive, not because they are unionized, but simply because unions organize the most productive firms. Also, union restriction on entry forces employers up their labor demand curves to points of higher marginal productivity. But this still leads to a lower social product because excluded workers move to *lower* points on non-unionized labor demand curves.

Ehrenberg argues that our argument would be strengthened if we could demonstrate that observed union/non-union wage differentials in public education are not compensating differential 'productivity' in public education. We fail to see how this is possible. Teacher renumeration is not a conventional wage rate since wages have no relationship to output. Wage differentials are based simply on teachers' education and experience. If there is any incentive for the teacher it is simply to get more education *for himself*. The evidence shows there is no unambiguous connection between this and the education of the children under his care.

Suppose, nevertheless, that the productivity increase of unionized workers is 'genuine' so that their labor demand curves shift upwards. And consider Ehrenberg's cited article by Brown and Medoff (1978) which concludes that unionized and non-unionized can compete in the same product market since unionized workers are paid more. The differential roughly offsets the difference in productivity. But if we apply this finding to education, it means simply that the taxpayer will not reduce the costs of education by encouraging or discouraging unionized employment. He will simply pay more for higher productivity.

Taking into consideration therefore the mixed nature of the evidence, and the fact that our concern is not with the unions *per se* but with agency shops, the total uncertainty involved should tip the scales against any hasty adoption of the latter institution on behalf of citizen voters.

Ehrenberg argues that we work mainly with the purely competitive model. Yet the whole of our Section 7 is devoted to the non-competitive model and is entitled 'The Monopsony Case.' Our argument, to repeat, was an attempt to model the reasoning of the Supreme Court. Our discussant apparently agrees with us in our translation of its deliberation into the economic terms of monopsony. But what of his conclusion that the evidence on monopsony 'is not unambiguous' and that there is a need for more research? In view of this the Court and the Legislature cannot confidently act on the assumption that monopsony is the universal model.

Ehrenberg seems to be pointing out, independently, that the monopsony argument predicts that after collective bargaining employment will not fall but may even expand. In fact, these are the actual words that we use in Section 7. We are, of course, interested in any appeals to evidence that will test this model. But we must confess to some difficulties with Ehrenberg's reasoning. Arguing that monopsony power is a function of immobility, he is impressed that most teachers are female and most of them are married, circumstances that reduce mobility. But the alternative model of the competitive (non-monopsonist) labor market does not require that 100 percent of the workers be mobile. All that is needed to make the market effective is a *margin* of mobile individuals. In Ehrenberg's case the potentially 'mobile margin' is quite substantial if it comprises (as he appears to intend) single teachers (male or female). For on his figures, it consists of over 42 percent of the total teaching population.

In other discussion Ehrenberg refers to findings of lower teaching salaries in monopsony areas where monopsony power is measured as the inverse of the number of school districts in the area. But these findings are contradicted by Robert Staaf (1977: 144) whose evidence shows that the costs of education, including the salaries of teachers *and administrators*, are a function of district size. These findings are consistent with the predictions of the economics of bureaucracy.

The setting of a kind of official 'seal of approval' (after *Abood*) on the agency shop has obviously been based on a view of the world that is not *universally* supported by the evidence. Suppose we accept Ehrenberg's quoted evidence that monopsony exists in consolidated districts, but not in others. This situation does not invite one *universal* response but a mix of policies according to the circumstances of each locality.

Monopsony, in any case, is a short-run phenomenon. In the long run, it disappears because potential employees are *all* mobile. This is because they can choose to be trained initially for a non-teaching profession. The establishment of long-term social institutions to meet short-term problems, therefore, is unwise.

The argued need to countervail the power of monopsony is also a second-best solution. The first best would be to remove the monopsony conditions directly. This is feasible since, according to most accounts, these conditions stem themselves from the public policy of consolidation. Even if one employs the second-best policy, its reliance on the countervailing power of a union will not guarantee an *exactly* offsetting bargaining power. For there is no insurance that a trade union will not go beyond this power and negotiate a monopoly wage. Indeed, the ordinary model of unions as organizations containing maximizing individuals, would lead one to expect that they will act in the immediate interests of their members rather than in the public interest. Although Ehrenberg seems reluctant to discuss the model of the union, attention to it, as well as to empirical work, is surely equally necessary.

We believe that Ehrenberg has misunderstood Robert Summers's argument against the use of union countervailing power on the grounds that the public employer is financed by the taxpayer and is supposed to be subject to the control of and answerable to the citizenry. Ehrenberg argues that if voters are unhappy with the (collectively bargained) settlement the re-election of the School Board can be challenged. But the same avenues are open to teachers. If they, as voters, are unhappy with their wage settlement, they too can press for a re-election. There is no call for a separate institutional avenue of redress for the citizen *suppliers* of education any more than there is for citizen *consumers* of education.

Ehrenberg does not dispute our observations that unions conduct their collective contracting in ways that involve their special influence on such things as educational curriculum, discipline and class size. To argue for an agency shop as a check to monopsony power is presumably to be reconciled to all these aspects of union bargaining. This is surely a very questionable position. The consequence of gaining increasing control over the political agenda is a relative decline in the influence of other citizens. It is in this context that Abood's claim for protection under the First Amendment seems the strongest of all.

REFERENCES

Brown, C., and Medoff, J. (1978). Trade unions in the productive process. *Journal of Political Economy* 86(3): 355-379.

Staaf, R. J. (1977). The public school system in transition: Consolidation and parental choice. In T. Borcherding (Ed.), *Budgets and bureaucrats*. Durham, N.C.: Duke University Press. 130-148.

Weiss, L. (1966). Concentration and labor earnings. *American Economic Review* 56(1): 32-42.